THE BEST SHORT PLAYS 1984

THE BEST SHORT PLAYS *1984*

edited and with an introduction by
RAMON DELGADO

Best Short Plays Series

Chilton Book Company
Radnor, Pennsylvania

Copyright © 1984 by Ramon Delgado
All Rights Reserved
Published in Radnor, Pennsylvania 19089, by Chilton Book Company
Library of Congress Catalog Card No. 38–8006
ISBN 0-8019-7411-9
ISSN 0067–6284
Manufactured in the United States of America

PN6111
B47
1984

1 2 3 4 5 6 7 8 9 0   3 2 1 0 9 8 7 6 5 4

for Jon Jory,
    Julie Beckett Crutcher,
        and
    Actors Theatre of Louisville

BOOKS AND PLAYS BY RAMON DELGADO

The Best Short Plays 1981 (*with Stanley Richards*)
The Best Short Plays 1982
The Best Short Plays 1983

The Youngest Child of Pablo Peco
Waiting for the Bus
The Little Toy Dog
Once Below A Lighthouse
Sparrows of the Field
The Knight-Mare's Nest
Omega's Ninth
Listen, My Children
A Little Holy Water
The Fabulous Jeromes
The Jerusalem Thorn
Stones

CONTENTS

INTRODUCTION

The artistic climate for the writing and production of the short play has rarely been better. The 1982–83 theatre season in New York, concluded at the time of this writing, hosted productions of one-act plays by Arthur Miller, Jean-Claude van Itallie, Samuel Beckett, and Murray Schisgal (whose *A Need for Brussels Sprouts* appeared in the 1983 edition of *Best Short Plays* prior to its Broadway outing). The Antoinette Perry (Tony) award went to Harvey Fierstein for his three one-acts presented under the title *Torch Song Trilogy,* and the Pulitzer Prize was awarded to Marsha Norman's *'night, Mother,* a ninety-minute one-act play. Off-Broadway and Off-Off-Broadway scores of groups featured at least one program of short plays as part of their season, and the Studio Ensemble Theatre promoted its annual "Marathon Series" of short plays, which drew critical responses as favorable as those given to full-length works.

Not only in New York but also throughout American regional theatre—in San Francisco, Boston, Philadelphia, Louisville, and other havens of culture—the short play attracts enthusiastic performers and audiences. A group of recent graduates from our B.F.A. program at Montclair State College in New Jersey have started a new theatre (the Ironbound Theatre) in Newark, and their first three programs have been sell-out evenings of one-act plays (several published first in this series, I'm pleased to report).

The dedication page of this year's collection is a recognition of the tremendous boost given to the short play by the industrious staff of the Actors Theatre of Louisville. Under the inspiring guidance of artistic director Jon Jory and through the attentive reading of literary manager Julie Crutcher and her tireless co-workers, scores of new playwrights have been given the opportunity to see their work produced under the finest of production conditions in the annual SHORTS Festival, made possible through the generous support of the Bingham Enterprises Foundation. Four plays in this volume (*Nice People Dancing to Good Country Music, Partners, Bartok as Dog,* and *Chug*) premiered at *Shorts* Festivals.

The excitement and importance of the short play is described by Actors Theatre of Louisville director Jon Jory:

"I love the one-act. It is too often regarded as a seedling rather than a separate and distinct form. We speak of it as we might of a talented child that may with nurturing grow out of its current incarnation and into a respectable full-length play. It is not only a separate form but, for our age, very possibly a better form. It leaves no room for the interminable literary fill with which longer work tends to pad itself. It enforces clarity. It highlights theme. It demands at least one fully dimensionally written character. And, most importantly, American writers do it well, even superbly. In this century there are at least as many fully conceived and executed masterpieces in the short form as there are in the long . . . and probably a good many more."

Finally, on a more personal note, I express my thanks to my dear friend Ellen Kauffman for keeping me showered with review clippings of new plays and for trekking with me into Manhattan to scout the season's productions. And again, thanks to the agents and playwrights who sent me many pages of interesting reading. I extend my appreciation for their patience while my teaching and directing responsibilities often prevented prompt responses to their submissions. All of these playwrights have my respect for their efforts, whether selected for this series or not, for they are indeed the "abstracts and brief chronicles of the time."

RAMON DELGADO
Montclair, New Jersey

Lee Blessing

NICE PEOPLE DANCING TO GOOD COUNTRY MUSIC

Lee Blessing

Nice People Dancing to Good Country Music was one of the top audience pleasers in the Actors Theatre of Louisville's 1982 SHORTS Festival. Playwright Lee Blessing has written a delightful character comedy in which a young novice, dismissed from her religious order for uncontrollable, offensive language, attempts to start a richer life through a visit to her liberated aunt, who operates a rowdy bar in Texas. As Dudley Saunders of the *Louisville Times* observes, "*Nice People* . . . looks at the world with a cautious optimism that suggests if we aren't happy with what life has given us, then we'd damn well better go out and find something else."

Mr. Blessing, who won the 1979 American College Theatre Festival's National Playwriting Award for *The Authentic Life of Billy the Kid,* has received widespread recognition for his plays. His one-act *Pushups* was presented at the Illusion Theatre in January 1982. *Oldtimers Game,* which was presented at the 1981 Midwest Playwrights' Program in Minneapolis and in 1982 at the Actors Theatre of Louisville Humana Festival of New American Plays, is currently under option for commercial production in New York. Mr. Blessing served as a Resident Playwright at the Playwrights' Center in Minneapolis and has received a Schubert Playwriting Fellowship, a Wurlitzer Foundation Fellowship, and a 1982 McKnight Fellowship.

His latest play, *Independence,* was selected for the 1983 O'Neill Writers Conference in Waterford, Connecticut, and presented in the 1984 Humana Festival at Actors Theatre of Louisville.

Characters:

CATHERINE EMPANGER, 22, a novice
EVE (EVA JUNE) WILFONG, 38, Catherine's aunt
JASON (JAY BOB) WILFONG, 15, Eve's son
JIM STOOLS, 40, the man Eve lives with
ROY MANUAL, 30, a suitor

Place:

An outside deck, above a bar in Houston.

Time:

The present, late afternoon in September.

Scene:

The scene is an outdoor deck, on the third floor of an old house, the bottom floor of which is a bar. Behind the deck is the peaked roof of the house and a small door, converted from an attic window. A street light is visible stage right, and the top of a telephone pole is stage left. On the deck, which is surrounded by a simple railing, are a couple of cheap but comfortable pieces of furniture—chaise, chair, etc. Also on the deck is a sizable flower pot, with soil but no flower, and a hibachi. Just below the deck, upstage, is the back of a sign that runs down the building out of sight.

Catherine Empanger is on the deck. She's dressed very simply in dark, casual clothes. She sits on the chaise reading. She closes the book, looks around restlessly. She stands, slowly moves into an amateurish try at a two-step while singing quietly to herself the first line of "Deep in the Heart of Texas." We suddenly hear Hank Williams singing, "Your Cheatin' Heart." She turns, walks upstage, and looks down over the railing. Over the song offstage a male voice shouts from below.

VOICE: (Off) Now that is music! Ain't it? That is no damn shit. (Another voice laughs derisively) That's none of your mule-puke Kenny Rogers Muppet Show horse crap! That is Hank Williams—the king of music!

(*A moment passes, as Catherine listens. She starts to sway to the music, a little awkwardly. Eve enters from the house. She's wearing a cowboy shirt, jeans, and loafers. She carries a hammer and nails. She is smiling, robust, and speaks in a broad Texas accent*)

EVE: There you are. There you are. We got you treed, don't we? I'm sorry, honey. Didn't mean to drive you way up here. That's what happened, isn't it? You were looking for a quiet place in this madhouse and you just kept on rising till you found one. (*Looking over the railing*) Not too quiet even up here. That jukebox sure carries, don't it? Well, hold on— I got a little project to take care of, then we'll get that door shut and it'll be quiet as you please. (*Shouting down*) Hey! Hey, down there! Hey! I'm shouting!

CATHERINE: Eve, you don't have to . . .

EVE: Don't worry. They always hear me eventually. (*Shouting*) Come on you boys! I'm shouting up here! Jim! Roy! T.R.!

VOICE: (*Off*) Who's that?

EVE: Up here, Roy! Look up! That's right!

ROY: (*Off*) Oh, howdy, Eva June!

EVE: Do me a favor, Roy . . . toss up that rock down there. The one with the rope around it?

ROY: (*Off*) What? Oh, sure! Here goes!

EVE: Watch out, Honey. (*A rock with a line tied to it lands on the roof*) Thanks, Roy. Now could you shut that door down there? My little niece and me are drowning in Hank Williams.

ROY: (*Off*) Your niece up there with you? Let me say hello to her and I'll shut the door.

EVE: Come on now, Roy . . .

ROY: (*Off*) Just want to say hi.

EVE: (*To Catherine*) Want to say hello to that Roy fella, honey? You saw him in the bar this morning, I think.

(*Catherine pauses, goes to the railing*)

ROY: (*Off*) Evening, Miss Empanger! (*Catherine waves, almost imperceptibly*) Will you be coming down later? I'd like you to dance with me is all.

CATHERINE: I don't know . . .

ROY: (*Off*) What? You'd *like* to dance with me!?

CATHERINE: (*Louder*) I don't know.

EVE: Shut that door, Roy, or I'll come down there and dance *on* you! (*The door closes, cutting off the music*) There. That's better. Almost livable out here now, ain't it? Imagine that Roy Manual holding us hostage that way just to get a dance with you. (*Starting to pull up the rope attached to the rock*) The men in this bar sure take some getting used to. I got half a mind to tell him all about you. That'd shut him up.

CATHERINE: No—I'd rather you didn't.

EVE: Why not? Nothing's wrong with being a nun.

CATHERINE: I'm not a nun, though. I'm . . .

EVE: Nothing wrong with being a novice, then. Hell, I'm not ashamed of you. You should let me tell Roy. He'd leave you alone for sure.

CATHERINE: No. People . . . get nervous when they hear that about me. Jim, for instance.

EVE: Jim just hates Catholics, that's all. (*Stops pulling*) He's treated you all right today, hasn't he?

CATHERINE: Oh, sure—pretty much. Once this afternoon he sort of . . . came up and stared at me.

EVE: Did he say anything?

CATHERINE: He just said, "A nun," shook his head and went back down. I haven't seen him since. I've been up here all day. Trying not to be any trouble.

EVE: How could you be any trouble?

CATHERINE: (*As Eve begins pulling again*) Showing up unannounced, for one thing. I'm sure you weren't too happy about that. What is that you're doing?

EVE: Pulling up a banner for the Labor Day weekend. Says, "WORK HARD DRINK HARD." Made it myself. Brings in business. (*Starting to nail it to the rail*) I'll tell you something, honey. You got an open invitation here. Couldn't be any trouble if you tried. It's so good to see my sister's little girl again. When I got your call last night, I was dancing around in a little circle, I was so happy. You should've seen me. So talk to me—how's your life going?

CATHERINE: Oh . . . fine. (*She moves away, kneels down by the hibachi*) Do you use this much?

EVE: That? Not since last spring. Too hot out here in the summer. You're lucky it's September. Houston in July is inhuman. (*Finishing the banner*) There.

CATHERINE: It looks a little grimy.

EVE: What? Houston?

CATHERINE: No—the grill.

EVE: There's probably birds nesting in it, for all I know. Why are you . . . ?

CATHERINE: I thought I could cook something.

EVE: Cook? Honey, I'm taking you out for dinner. Sweet Jesus, you think you got to do for yourself up here on the roof?

CATHERINE: I was only . . .

EVE: I'm taking you somewhere nice. We'll leave in about a half-hour, OK?

CATHERINE: OK.

EVE: (*Smiling*) Eating alone. Hell, I thought it was your mother that was mad at me, not you.

CATHERINE: Oh, I'm not mad at you. Really, I'm not. And Mom isn't either, really. Not really.

EVE: Sure. That's why I haven't heard from her in six months, huh? (*Pause*) Well, I don't blame her. It's a hard thing for her to accept. One minute I seem to be a happily married mother of one, the next minute I'm divorced, leaving my kid behind, and trotting down to southeast Texas with some shit-kicker I met in an airport. That was a lot to throw her way all at once. Especially when I keep telling her it's all for the best. (*Pauses*) It is, though. I'm a new person. Hell, I'm not a *new* person, I'm not a person at all. That's the difference. It's like where I was all day today. Going to business meetings. *Business* meetings. Me. How about that? Never happened when I was with Robert.

CATHERINE: But Robert was your husband. You had a marriage with Robert.

EVE: I had something with him, all right. Maybe that was marriage, who knows? (*A pause. Eve shudders*) Robert. I can't believe it sometimes when I think of the things he used to make me do.

CATHERINE: Uncle Robert? (*As Eve nods solemnly*) What things?

EVE: Deadly things.

CATHERINE: Uncle *Robert*?

EVE: Honey, your "Uncle Robert" is a deadly human being. Deadly dull.

CATHERINE: (*Sighing with relief, then reproachfully*) Eve! You had me really scared there for a minute.

EVE: You should have been. Honey, Robert is a terminally

boring man. That's nothing to laugh about. In fact, he's the most boring man possible: he's a professor of Latvian.

CATHERINE: Well, I know, but . . .

EVE: And when you're a professor of Latvian, there's only eight other people in the whole world who care. I discovered I wasn't one of 'em, and I knew I was in trouble right then. 'Cause he kept trying to make me one, you see? Kept demanding that I care who the kings—or whatever they were—of ancient Latvia were. And the more I said, "No baby, I am not interested to learn about the Hanseatic League," the angrier he'd get. And you know, the angrier he got, the cooler and more logical he'd be. That's when it really got dangerous. 'Cause then he'd prove to me, literally prove, beyond the shadow of a doubt, that I could not go through another day without becoming a dedicated scholar of Baltic Studies. So, after a few hours of listening to him, I would numbly nod my head, pick up some learned paper by a colleague of his—one of the eight—and study it like a little schoolgirl with her homework assignment before bed. And he would just sit there beaming at me. The next morning I always woke up knowing the coordinates of Riga and wondering how to kill my husband. (*Pauses*) Well I knew that wasn't a healthy situation. And about that time I met Jim, while changing planes—the luckiest connection of my life—and he took one look at me and knew just what to say.

CATHERINE: What was that?

EVE: He said, "I got a bar in Houston. Interested?" I was. Well, look at that.

CATHERINE: What?

EVE: That shingle's falling off. I might as well fix that right now. You don't mind, do you?

CATHERINE: Um . . . no . . .

EVE: (*Straightening it*) I mean, the next thing you know, there's water damage. I just love going around this place with a hammer and nails. Always something to fix. (*She starts to pound*)

CATHERINE: Eve, maybe I better just go.

EVE: Go? What are you talking about? You just got here.

CATHERINE: I know, but . . . you're so busy, and . . . I do have a standing invitation at Aunt Margaret's . . .

EVE: (*Interrupting her*) Don't be silly . . .

CATHERINE: I'm not. I just don't feel like I'm—fitting in here. I mean, this is a bar, and I come from a convent, and you're not married to the man you live with, and men keep shouting at me, and . . . Aunt Margaret would just be . . .

EVE: Aunt Margaret hasn't taken a deep breath in twenty-five years.

CATHERINE: Well, then . . . maybe Aunt Camilla . . .

EVE: Aunt Camilla is fat. And she hates men. And she hates women, too. Why on earth would you want to go see Aunt Camilla? (*Catherine pauses*) Face it, honey. I'm the only relative you got that knows how to listen with both ears. Now you sit down while I finish pounding this sucker.

(*Catherine hesitates, sits down. Eve pounds on the shingle*)

CATHERINE: At least my other aunts didn't walk out on their husband and son.

EVE: What?

CATHERINE: At least . . .

EVE: I heard you. Honey, when I walked out, it was not only for me. It was for Robert too. *And* for little Jay Bob.

CATHERINE: Jay Bob? You mean Jason?

EVE: That's right.

CATHERINE: *Jay Bob?*

EVE: Ain't it cute? That's what we call him now, while he's visiting. Jay Bob. Names just naturally get changed in Texas. Hell, I'm Eva June to most of these folks. Eva June Wilfong. Whoo! (*Pauses, admires her work on the shingle*) There now. Let it rain. I'll tell you a little secret, Catherine: Jay Bob's better off since I moved down here. You know why?

CATHERINE: Why?

EVE: 'Cause now he's got a real mother to deal with in me. Now he's got an honest-to-God human being, 'stead of just a dead hum coming out of someone else's machine. (*A beat*) It's been a real kick in the butt having him down here this summer. 'Course, he and Jim get into a fight now and then, but that's only natural.

CATHERINE: How often do they fight?

EVE: Every day. But no broken bones yet. (*Smiles suddenly*) Oh, how do you like my new accent? I forgot you never heard it before this morning.

CATHERINE: Well, it's, um . . . it's . . .

EVE: It's a dinger, ain't it? I was only here a couple months before I was talking more Texas than the Texans. Well, why not? I get along better with folks this way. Besides, Jim and I think it's good for business.

CATHERINE: Are you and Jim ever . . . going to get married?

EVE: Why should we?

CATHERINE: Well, you live together, and . . .

EVE: That's right. Living together is for having someone around. Marriage is for having someone around your neck. Jim and me share what we can about each other, and leave the rest alone. We don't mess around on the side, and we don't worry about love. 'Least, I don't.

CATHERINE: But love is . . .

EVE: Love is an evil pain in the butt. For years, I was in love with a man who had more passion for Latvian self-rule than he had for my body. You can stick love. Besides, the real treat for me down here is this place. This little tavern is just heaven for me.

CATHERINE: Why? I mean . . .

EVE: That's all right. I know it looks strange, but this here bar is one place I can *affect*. Look at that railing!

CATHERINE: What?

EVE: It's practically falling apart. I'm glad I came up. (*She straddles the railing, starts to pound*) Maintenance—that's what keeps a business alive. (*The bar door opens. We hear a bit of "Red-Neck Mother" by Jerry Jeff Walker before it closes. Eve calls down*) Hey, Joe Bill! Hey, Larry Lee! How's it going?

(*We hear voices calling up*)

VOICE: Hey, Eva June!

2ND VOICE: Don't fall off, now!

EVE: I won't! Boy, this place sure has changed. You should've seen it when I got here. I near puked. Really. There was a broken-down sign that said, "JIM STOOL'S BAR"; there was beer and broken glass on the floor; there was bikers coming in every night swearing, fighting, committing crimes of all kinds. Well, I told Jim he'd got me there all right, but if he wanted to keep me, things were going to change. So he just backed off and let me go at it. It's only been one year, but come here and look at this parking lot. (*Catherine approaches, looks down*) Asphalt. Not dirt like there was. Not one damn motorcycle, either. Pickup trucks. Solid, dependable pickup trucks. This is a workingman's bar now. (*Taking Catherine toward the door*) And look at this. (*Turning on the lights for the sign*) A new name. With a message. "NICE PEOPLE DANCING TO GOOD COUNTRY MUSIC BAR." My idea. Honey, if you call yourself nice people, nice people'll come. If you call yourself dancing, then they'll dance, instead of spreading their fat, leather-covered rears on a barstool and letting farts all night. And if you play *good* country music, well, folks'll be elevated, 'stead of teased and titillated. There's a hall-of-fame jukebox down there now. Same way on weekends, too. Dance bands. For nice people. And Jim loves it. Wasn't sure he would, but he does.

CATHERINE: Well, it's . . . it's a very nice bar.

EVE: We're going to make it a restaurant.

CATHERINE: Really?

EVE: (*Nodding, quivering with pleasure*) That's where I was all day, after I got you at the airport. Non-stop meetings with the contractors. In six months this is going to be the "NICE PEOPLE EATING TO GOOD COUNTRY MUSIC RESTAURANT." People'll pop in here like salmon up a ladder. God, I'm happy! (*Pauses*) How're you doing? I been talking all evening. What'd you do all day while I was gone?

CATHERINE: Well, I was . . . um, reading . . . up here.

(*Eve picks up the book from the chaise*)

EVE: *Sexual Advice For Teens.* Kind of a strange selection.

CATHERINE: Oh, I just . . . found it downstairs.

EVE: I got it for Jay Bob. It's kind of advanced—says sex is OK, and like that. Why were you reading it? I thought you were getting all ready to be "nunnified."

CATHERINE: Well, nuns have to deal with sex. You know— advising, and . . .

EVE: Advising against, as I recall. You a nun yet, or still a novice?

CATHERINE: Well, I've . . . been on retreat for a while . . .

EVE: Retreat? How do you retreat from a convent? Sounds redundant.

CATHERINE: It's possible.

EVE: Just shows my ignorance. But you know me. Not the world's best Catholic. Fact, I'm a Methodist now—that's how bad a Catholic I've become. (*Catherine looks at her with surprise*) I didn' t tell you about that, did I?

CATHERINE: No.

EVE: Well, I got tired of confession, but I still liked organ music. So, why were you on retreat?

CATHERINE: (*Moving toward the hibachi*) You know, I really could cook up here . . .

EVE: You dodging the question?

CATHERINE: No. I like eating simply.

EVE: It's no shame to go on retreat, is it?

CATHERINE: No, it's just . . . no, it isn't.

EVE: (*Jokingly*) I mean, it's not like them kicking you out or something. (*Pause*) Is it?

CATHERINE: They don't kick people out. That's not how they do it.

EVE: How do they do it?

CATHERINE: They ask them to go on retreat.

EVE: (*Quietly*) I see.

CATHERINE: And if that doesn't work out, they ask you if you wouldn't be more comfortable in a secular mode.

EVE: Secular mode? That sounds like IBM. Oh, honey, I had no idea . . . (*She goes to hug Catherine, who moves away*)

CATHERINE: No. I mean, I'm not unhappy. There's no need. Really.

EVE: But you always wanted to be a nun. When you were nine years old, you used to talk about it. Oh, honey. What happened? Why'd they . . . ?

CATHERINE: It was just the logical outcome of . . . certain events, that's all.

EVE: What events?

CATHERINE: Things I said.

(*The bar door opens downstairs. For a moment we hear Johnny Cash singing the first line of "Burning Ring of Fire," then silence again*)

EVE: What things did you say?

CATHERINE: Not bad things. Nothing awful, really. Just inappropriate things. Things that made people in a strict order uncomfortable.

EVE: Political things.

CATHERINE: Oh, no. No.

EVE: Reform kinds of things?

CATHERINE: No, not reform. Dirty words.

EVE: Dirty words?

(*The bar door opens again. We hear Johnny Cash still singing "Burning Ring of Fire" as the door closes again*)

CATHERINE: It's a very sort of unexpected but not entirely unheard-of syndrome I developed recently.

EVE: Dirty words, huh?

CATHERINE: I noticed it one day a few months ago. I was going to breakfast one morning—a morning like any other morning—and I passed one of the sisters in the hallway. She's a woman I saw every day, someone I'd never harbored an evil thought about. She smiled as she went by, looking serene, and I smiled back at her and said, "Isn't this a lovely morning, Sister Shit?" (*Eve laughs despite herself, covers her mouth*) I don't know where it came from. It's one of my clearest memories, though: the look on her face, the way she recovered almost at once, and asked me to excuse her, but she hadn't quite heard . . . And even *I* wasn't sure at that moment, just what I'd said. I couldn't have said what I thought I'd . . . So anyway, I smiled pleasantly and apologetically, and took a deep breath, and said, "You heard me, Fart-face," and walked on.

EVE: You didn't.

CATHERINE: I did.

EVE: Well, I'll be damned. I always wanted to say that to a nun.

CATHERINE: I swear I didn't mean to. Sister Beatrice never hurt me in her life. She was one of the ones I liked best. And it's not even a matter of that. We're in the same holy order, we're children of God.

EVE: You never heard a kid swear?

CATHERINE: Don't tease me.

EVE: I'm sorry. Why'd you do it?

CATHERINE: I had to. It just came out of me. Like speaking in tongues or something. The words just leaped out of me. They had to be spoken. That's what my psychologist said.

EVE: You saw a psychologist?

CATHERINE: Wouldn't you? I saw everybody. I saw lots of people in the Church: priests, nuns, bishops—everyone.

EVE: How'd that go?

CATHERINE: I cussed them out. All of them. Except God and my psychologist. Eve, I never meant to say any of those things. But I couldn't help it. I started swearing like a linebacker every time I saw the convent. And I'd say other things, too.

EVE: Like what?

CATHERINE: Irrational things. I'd recite the backs of Wheaties boxes. Not at breakfast—other times: during devotions, working in the garden. I didn't even know I read the backs of Wheaties boxes. It was just there, suddenly, word for word.

EVE: Why Wheaties?

CATHERINE: I don't know, it's what we ate. But other things, too. Things I'd heard on the radio, rules from games I played as a kid, bird calls, sounds from comic books: "Bam! Rat-a-tat-tat! Ka-boom!" Usually during meditation.

EVE: What did the psychologist think?

CATHERINE: That I wasn't cut out to be a nun. He said I was unconsciously trying to break out of the constraints of convent life.

EVE: He sure you don't just like dirty words?

CATHERINE: It's not the obscenity. I got no bigger thrill saying "fart-face" than yelling "red light green light" or barking like a dog. It was the impropriety of it. That's all I wanted. To shock people. To shock myself.

EVE: Guess it worked, huh?

CATHERINE: I've been numb for months. I mean, there I was—I had everything planned out. I was committed to a life of service in the Church, and suddenly it was . . . Sister Shit.

EVE: What did your folks say?

CATHERINE: Nothing helpful. I went home to explain— you know, maybe stay a week? I was there three days. They couldn't believe I'd failed at "my life's mission." They spent the whole time whimpering like a pair of lost puppies. (*Sighs*) Finally, Mom accused me of wanting to have children, and I left.

EVE: And you came down here?

CATHERINE: I didn't know where to go. Nobody up there would talk to me. And I didn't want to go see Aunt Margaret.

EVE: Well, I am glad you came to see me. What do you think you'll do now? In life, I mean.

CATHERINE: Live a normal life, I guess. I always thought I'd be special, a little more . . . something than the usual person. But I'm just the usual person.

EVE: Don't feel sorry for yourself. Hell, people don't end up what they plan to be. Except awful people. I planned to be a brain-dead housewife by now; am I?

CATHERINE: Not quite.

EVE: Stick with me, Kid. You'll become one extraordinary usual person. Why were you reading this book? (*i.e.,* Sexual Advice for Teens)

CATHERINE: What? Oh . . . well . . . no reason.

EVE: Honey, I got a whole library down there, and this is the only book that deals with . . .

CATHERINE: I was concerned about . . . mating.

EVE: Mating?

CATHERINE: Yes. Um, mating. You know, men and women and . . .

EVE: I know what it is. Why are you concerned about that?

CATHERINE: Why shouldn't I be?

EVE: No reason. Just seems like we're getting out of the convent awful fast here. How soon you fixing to mate?

CATHERINE: Not soon. It's not the physical aspects I'm worried about—I know all that . . .

EVE: You do, huh?

CATHERINE: But being around men and . . . dating. It's just that I always assumed I'd be a nun. I didn't think about boys. Now, I'll naturally begin to encounter them more. And— well, I couldn't exactly bring it up with Mom.

EVE: Bring it up with me, then. What do you want to know?

CATHERINE: Oh . . . I can read the book.

EVE: Not as good as a live witness. You still a virgin?

CATHERINE: Eve!

EVE: Well, you're a nun—figured you *might* be.

CATHERINE: What I mean is, I can't answer that.

EVE: Why not? Am I asking in Spanish?

CATHERINE: It's just a very private thing.

EVE: Kind of hard to get a read on you, if I don't know what your experience is.

CATHERINE: Nil. It's nil. I don't know a thing. OK? Just start anywhere.

EVE: OK. Let's see: men. Men are . . . not like you and me.

CATHERINE: You can go faster than that.

EVE: I better not. Men have different goals, mostly. And one of those goals is to keep as much to themselves as possible. That's why they're always turning up in other parts of town with other women, or working seventy-five hours a week, or ignoring you to watch TV till they can't even answer the simplest questions.

CATHERINE: Or reading Latvian?

EVE: (*Smiling*) And when they aren't sitting all day like a stone idol, they're heading over the hills to do whatever doesn't include you. This they call freedom, but what it really is, is them just being afraid to get to know us. Takes a man about fifteen hundred years to get to know a woman. In the meantime, all we're left with is the hills. It's like the Bible says: "The hills abideth; and the men just get lost."

CATHERINE: Well . . . what hope is there in that?

EVE: Not much. A little, though. Sometimes you find a man who's capable of improvement. Jim is. He's coming along slow, but he's coming. But I'll give you a tip: it's a good precaution to learn how to love the hills, 'cause you're going to see a lot more of them then you will of most men. That's what Houston's all about for me.

CATHERINE: I don't see many hills here.

EVE: We're standing on one. The Nice People Dancing to Good Country Music Bar.

(*The bar door opens. We hear Tom T. Hall singing, "I Love". Roy calls from below*)

ROY: (*Off*) Hey! Hey, up there! Eva June!? You around?!

EVE: (*Going to the railing*) Dear God. What is it, Roy? Can't you leave us in . . . ?

ROY: (*Off*) Let me talk to that niece of yours again!

EVE: No, I'm not going to let you talk to . . .

ROY: (*Off*) Please? I got to say something to her right now! (*Pause*) You want me to come up there? I will!

EVE: Honey? It's better'n him coming up.

CATHERINE: (*Moving to the rail*) Yes, Roy?

ROY: (*Off*) Howdy, Catherine! Listen to this! (*He opens the bar door. We hear Hall singing "And I-I-I love you, too." He closes the door*) How about that? Ready to dance now? I'm getting pretty determined down here.

EVE: You're getting pretty well oiled, is what you're getting.

ROY: (*Off*) What's wrong with right now? Come on down and take a twirl!

CATHERINE: Well . . .

ROY: (*Off*) Come on, baby!

EVE: Roy Manual, do you know who you are asking up here to "take a twirl"? A nun.

ROY: (*Off*) What?

CATHERINE: Eve . . .

EVE: That's right! My niece is a nun. You are coming on to a bride of Christ.

ROY: (*Off*) I don't care if she's the Bride of Frankenstein, send her down!

EVE: Roy! I can't believe you said that.

ROY: (*Off*) Well, you don't really expect me to believe that she's a . . . that she's a . . . (*Pause*) She's a nun?

EVE: She damn sure is. Didn't Jim tell you? (*To Catherine*) I suppose Jim wouldn't—he hates talking to Roy.

CATHERINE: Roy, I'm not a nun. I'm a novice.

ROY: (*Off*) A what?

EVE: (*To Catherine*) Quiet.

CATHERINE: (*To Eve*) Well, you're not being accurate. I was never a nun.

EVE: Accuracy ain't the point. You want to dance with him?

CATHERINE: Well, I don't know.

ROY: (*Off*) Hey! Are you a nun or not? What's the verdict?

EVE: She's a nun, Roy! She's a mother superior!

CATHERINE: (*Suddenly calling down*) No, I'm not! Uh—I'm not a nun, Roy. I used to be a novice, but I'm not even that anymore. I'm nothing. (*With an uncertain look at Eve*) And I'd be proud to dance with you.

ROY: (*Off*) You would? Great!

EVE: Are you crazy? What are you doing?

CATHERINE: I'm dancing with Roy Manual.

ROY: (*Off*) You want to come down?

EVE: (*To Catherine*) Why?!

CATHERINE: Well, why not? I've got to get started some-time.

EVE: But . . . dinner.

CATHERINE: Just one dance.

ROY: (*Off*) Or would you rather I came up?

EVE: Down, Roy! You stay down! Honey, let me talk to you first . . .

CATHERINE: Oh, Eve. It's just a dance. What's it matter who it's with? Besides, you'd rather have me dancing with the landscape.

EVE: I never meant to say that.

ROY: (*Off*) I'm coming up.

EVE: I'll break your nose, Roy! (*To Catherine*) It's just that it takes time to learn men. They're tricky. It's not a natural relationship.

ROY: (*Off*) I'm coming up!

(*The bar door opens and closes. We hear Tammy Wynette, singing, "Stand by Your Man"*)

EVE: Roy! No—Roy! Damn. You don't know what you're in for, little lady. You're about to dance with the least interesting man on the Gulf Coast.

CATHERINE: He can't be that bad, can he? (*Eve stares at Catherine*) Really?

EVE: (*Going to the door*) I'll go see if I can head him off. Save you from yourself.

CATHERINE: Well . . . don't lie.

EVE: Sure, honey. You just be a little more careful in the future.

CATHERINE: (*As she turns to go*) Um, Eve? In case someone else asks me, another time . . .

EVE: Yeah?

CATHERINE: Well, could you do me a favor? Could you teach me to dance?

EVE: I'll think about it. (*She turns again to go, stops when she hears a male voice from inside*)

VOICE: (*Off*) Can I come out?

CATHERINE: Oh, well—I'm not really sure I want to dance . . .

(*Jason enters. He's a slightly pudgy adolescent—not athletic, not intellectual. A little nervous, a little mean*)

JASON: Who asked you?

EVE: Jay Bob! What are you doing up here?

JASON: Nothing. It's my house. Till tomorrow, anyway. (*He moves around the perimeter of the deck, nervously looking down to the street*)

EVE: Jay Bob, I wonder if you'd mind taking a message down to Roy Manual for us.

JASON: No way. I'm on vacation. Besides, he's a jerk.

EVE: I thought you were helping Jim. You all done?

JASON: Yeah, kind of. Jim and me had sort of a fight, and he said I was all done.

EVE: What were you fighting about this time?

JASON: (*Looking over the railing*) Nothing. Don't tell him I'm up here. I faked like I was running outside. I don't think he's following me.

EVE: What did you do?

JASON: Nothing. I said. He just likes to persecute me. (*Picks up the book*) *Sexual Advice for Teens.* Who's reading this?

CATHERINE: I am.

JASON: They make you read it in the nun place?

CATHERINE: I found it downstairs.

EVE: Will you please tell me what's going on?

JASON: (*Shrugs*) I don't know; I don't want to talk about it.

EVE: Fine. Then you deal with it, son. I'm going downstairs.

(*Eve exits. Jason regards Catherine*)

JASON: Hey, you look OK in real clothes for once. How come you're not wearing your nun stuff?

CATHERINE: I don't want to talk about it.

(*A pause. They look out over the city. The bar door opens. We hear Johnny Cash singing, "Life ain't easy for a boy named Sue . . ." and the door closes. Jason hurries over, looks down, returns*)

JASON: False alarm.

(*They look over the city*)

CATHERINE: Don't you have something to do?

JASON: I think I'll just hang out.

(*A pause*)

CATHERINE: It's a nice view. You can see most of the city. Isn't it nice?

JASON: It sucks. This whole town sucks. Four billion people all talking like Gomer Pyle.

CATHERINE: Well, it's not Minnesota.

JASON: I'm going back tomorrow. About time.

CATHERINE: I suppose you'll be glad to see your Dad again.

JASON: Anything'd be better than here. Jim is nuts.

CATHERINE: Oh, I don't think he's . . .

JASON: What do you know? You only been here a few hours. I been here all summer. He's nuts. He makes me work in his crumby business. I'm on my vacation, and he makes me push beer cases around in the back room down there. He's a creepoid jerk.

CATHERINE: Well, I wouldn't say that . . .

JASON: 'Course not; you're a nun. Today he told me to

move twenty cases of Schlitz from the front wall to the back wall and restack 'em. It's the same twenty cases I moved from the back wall to the front wall yesterday. He can't decide where they're "the most efficient." Efficient, my roaring butt. I'm going home tomorrow—what the hell do I care where they are?! (*A beat*) Does swearing bother you?

CATHERINE: I've, uh . . . I've heard worse.

JASON: So, anyway, I'm doing all this work for him, and when I'm done he comes in and looks at it, and says he liked it better the other way. So I dumped three cases of Schlitz on his foot.

CATHERINE: You didn't.

JASON: I sure as hell did. He started screaming like crazy, and threw a bottle at my head. It missed by this much. He could've killed me, the stupid mother. Day before I go home.

CATHERINE: Maybe if you tried talking with him . . .

JASON: Advice for teens, huh? Actually, I didn't feel like waiting around to talk. There were three guys holding him down when I left. Besides, he's killed people. Did you know that?

CATHERINE: No.

JASON: He told me. Said he used to have a son by his first marriage, and the kid was always pissing him off, so he killed him.

CATHERINE: How?

JASON: With a Schlitz bottle.

CATHERINE: That's ridiculous.

JASON: How do you know? He said he did it.

CATHERINE: He was probably just trying to make you behave.

JASON: (*Picking up the flower pot, taking it to the edge of the deck just above the bar door, and sitting with it in his lap*) I behave. I'm a damn good kid. But he's pushed me too far this summer, that's all I can say. Working in the back room—how'm I supposed to meet any girls?

CATHERINE: (*After a pause*) What are you doing?

JASON: I'm going to wait for him to come out and drop this on his head.

CATHERINE: Jason!

JASON: Jay Bob.

CATHERINE: Jay Bob, you are not. That's absurd. Put that down.

JASON: You know, that's the only thing Jim ever did I liked. Started calling me Jay Bob. Jay Bob is just as stupid a name as Jason, but at least you can claim your folks didn't know any better.

CATHERINE: Look, um, Jay Bob—why do something like this? You're going home tomorrow. You'll be with your Dad again.

JASON: So what? He's not much better than Jim. Always talking to me about Latvia. He talks in a foreign language like eighty per cent of the time. Nah, it doesn't matter where I am. I'm caught in a war between the generations.

CATHERINE: How about your mother? Don't you care about her?

JASON: She sleeps with Jim. Before that she slept with Dad. I mean, it's a pattern, you know? I know what side she's on. Go back and read your book. Don't mind me—I'll be all right.

CATHERINE: I'm going down and tell Eve.

JASON: You do, and I'll drop something on you.

CATHERINE: Jason, it's my duty to warn you that Roy Manual may be up here any minute.

JASON: Roy Manual? Why's he coming up?

CATHERINE: He wants to dance with me.

JASON: What do you want to dance with him for? He's the biggest dipstick in Houston.

CATHERINE: So I'm told.

JASON: Besides, you're a nun. You can't dance. There's a commandment about it or something.

CATHERINE: Well . . . I left the convent.

JASON: How come?

CATHERINE: It's a long story.

JASON: You're not a nun then, huh? You're just, like— what—like nobody, right?

CATHERINE: Pretty much.

JASON: (*Considers this, puts the flower pot aside, stands*) You wanna dance?

CATHERINE: What?

JASON: Come on, if you wanna dance, dance with me. I'm a lot better than Roy Manual.

CATHERINE: What happened to the war between the generations?

JASON: It'll wait.

CATHERINE: Jason . . .

JASON: Jay Bob. Come on—you're not a nun anymore. Hey—that's good; that's like an oldie. (*Dancing with her momentarily, singing part of the chant from "I want to be Bobby's girl"*) "You're not a nun any-more . . ."

CATHERINE: (*Breaking away*) I'm your *cousin*, is what I am.

JASON: You're not that much older than me.

CATHERINE: Jay Bob. Listen to me. I—am—your—cousin.

JASON: So? There won't be all that getting-to-know-you crap. Come on, I've been trying to meet girls all summer. Everybody here talks like hicks. (*Approaching her again*) Come on, we'll do a close number. I'll sing. (*Softly*) "You're not a nun any-more . . ."

CATHERINE: (*Breaks away*) No! I'm going to tell your mother.

JASON: You a virgin?

CATHERINE: Jay Bob!

JASON: I am. I'm not ashamed to admit it. I've been saving myself. I get a feeling you have, too. Is that true? If we want, we could do something about it.

CATHERINE: *You shut up! Right now! Shame on you!* (*She slaps him hard*)

JASON: (*Beginning to cry*) Why'd you hit me? Geez!

CATHERINE: You are the most offensive teenager I've ever known!

JASON: (*Still in pain*) *Geez!*

CATHERINE: Well, don't cry . . .

JASON: I'm not crying! Damn grownup. Why's everybody always trying to hit me?

CATHERINE: Well, you were being so . . . aggressive.

JASON: I'm supposed to be aggressive. They said to be aggressive.

CATHERINE: Who? Who said?

JASON: The book I read.

CATHERINE: What book?

JASON: (*Pointing*) *That* book! *Sexual Advice for Teens.* Dating chapter. You just haven't gotten there yet.

CATHERINE: They said to be aggressive?

JASON: Well, kind of aggressive. I don't know. I never picked up a girl before. 'Course I'm not going to do it right the first time. *Geez!!*

CATHERINE: I'm sorry.

JASON: I'll be glad to get back to Latvia!

(*He moves to the door, and just as he gets there Roy Manual appears. He is small, but not ridiculously so. He smiles constantly. His clothes at once suggest a hard worker and a would-be fancy dresser: urban cowboy dress-shirt, dirty jeans, and work boots*)

ROY: Hey, there. It's me, Roy Manual.

JASON: (*Taking one look at him, exiting into the house*) Geez!

ROY: What's wrong with him?

CATHERINE: (*Releasing pent-up anger*) That stupid little kid! Eve was right—I've never met any children, that's why I like them. I'm going back to the convent, that's all there is to it. I'll beg them to take me back. I'm not ready for the world again.

ROY: (*Cheerfully*) Yeah, it's a bitch, ain't it? (*Catherine glowers at him*) Eve told me about your situation. Must take a lot of courage to leave your order like that.

CATHERINE: I didn't have much choice.

ROY: Still, to get back out in the world, take a look around, try and get used to things again—must take a bunch of guts.

CATHERINE: A bunch of guts?

ROY: Well, you know what I mean. I don't always express it. Did you notice me sitting down there in the bar when you came in this morning? I noticed you. Right away. Been down there ever since, hoping I'd see you again.

CATHERINE: In the bar?

ROY: (*Embarrassed laugh*) Yeah. I ain't been drinking, though. I been thinking. Thinking there's not many times in a man's life when his whole future suddenly walks by, lighting up the room around her as she goes. That room's still glowing, you should see it.

CATHERINE: (*Looking at him*) What do you do for a living?

ROY: Nothing. I mean, I'm between work. I'm normally in the trenches, though. (*Laughs*) That makes me sound like General Patton, don't it? What I mean is, utility trenches. Gas, sewer, water, underground cable—like that. I dig 'em all. But right now I'm not digging, 'cause a little while back I got buried.

CATHERINE: Buried?

ROY: Yeah. Bunch of sand, gravel—happens all the time. I was buried maybe, oh, forty-five minutes? Couldn't get any oxygen for a while. When they got me out, my brain quit working for about three weeks. (*A pause. She regards him. He smiles*) It's working again now, though. Honest. Better'n before, in fact. I go back on the job next week. (*Slight pause*) It's a good brain. I'm going to college with it. Community college. Do you like me so far? I always tell too much about myself at the start, don't you think?

CATHERINE: Roy, I'm not sure I feel like dancing to-night . . .

ROY: Well, that's OK. That was just a suggestion. Danc-ing's just an ice breaker anyway. Just a way to talk, and . . . stand next to each other, and . . . smell each other's perfume, and— well, I mean your perfume, of course, and my . . . Well, each other's *scent* is what I'm trying to say. Scent.

CATHERINE: (*Sitting on the chaise*) Maybe we could just talk.

ROY: Sure, fine. Just talk, great. No problem there. (*He sits next to her. A silence. He pulls out a package*) Beer nuts?

CATHERINE: (*Shaking her head*) I wonder where Eve went.

ROY: Eva June? I think there was some ruckus with Jim or something. She went to talk to him. They're a fine couple, ain't they? That Jim is lucky. Always was. Inherited a great place like this bar. Jim Stool's Bar—that's what they used to call it. (*Laughs*) Used to have a slogan, too: "Other towns got barstools, but only we got Stool's Bar." (*Catherine buries her face in her hands*) Something wrong? You don't like the joke, huh? Well, the place has a new name now, anyway. (*A pause*) So, uh . . . suppose it's been hard, having a spiritual failure the way you did.

CATHERINE: (*Angrily*) It was *not* a failure, it was a . . . (*Pauses, sighs*) It was a failure. That's exactly what it was. I'm not ready for the world.

ROY: (*Smiling*) Who is? I know my Daddy always used to say . . .

CATHERINE: (*Rises*) When I was a little girl, I was offended by human beings. You know that? Literally offended. I was . . . nauseated by the way they watched TV all the time and got married in Las Vegas and built ugly buildings and had mass murders and beat each other up in the park and never even thought about going to church—never sat quietly once and wondered who made their hands, for example, or . . . or anything. You know?

ROY: Kinda. But people get too busy sometimes . . .

CATHERINE: People do not get too busy. They want to get married in Las Vegas, they really do. They want to watch TV—they don't want to watch their hands. Well, I knew that as a kid, and I don't know why, but it infuriated me and I had to be away from it. I had to be a nun. For all the worst reasons. I wasn't attracted to God, I was repelled by the world He made. In a convent there's hardly any world at all, I thought; just a few walls, a few faces. But there was just as much stupidity there—that's what I found out. In those few walls and those few faces there was room for a universe of stupidity. And stupidity is like love, you know?

ROY: I . . . think I do.

CATHERINE: I mean, even the smallest amount of it suggests the whole world. To witness even one act of cruelty or anger or laziness is like . . . like being loved, if only once, by one person, for only a minute. You see? Both things transfigure experience. So that if it's love, let's say, then everything—people, animals, God Himself—everything becomes love, because love, *pure* love, in that lone act, is suddenly seen as possible. Well, the same is true for stupidity. A stupid act will . . . destroy the world someday.

ROY: Not now; they got computers.

CATHERINE: (*With a look at him*) Because stupidity *does* exist. Everywhere.

ROY: You're well-educated.

CATHERINE: (*Flatly*) There are some excellent parochial schools.

ROY: You know, I think about religion now and then.
(*Pause*)

CATHERINE: What do you think?

ROY: I think God works in mysterious ways.

CATHERINE: (*Violently*) Of course He does, as far as you can see! You're stupid! I know exactly how God works. He's created this incomparably lovely, incomparably stupid world for us to live in, and now He sits back and watches us break our hearts over it. I can't imagine how anyone can make love at night and then read the papers the next morning.

ROY: I do that all the time.

CATHERINE: *How*? How can you reconcile the two?

ROY: Making love and reading the paper? (*She nods. He pauses, shrugs*) I only do the crossword puzzle.

CATHERINE: The murders! Wars! Starvations! What about those?

ROY: They're in another section. I read them later.

CATHERINE: But you read them, And I'll have to, too. You

see? I have to remarry the whole world now. (*Points at the city*) God's world, not the convent, but the world He made, with all the cruelty and despair and deformity and . . .

ROY: (*Standing*) Are you a virgin?

CATHERINE: Why does everybody want to know if I'm a virgin?!

ROY: You are, ain't you? I could tell. You talk like one.

CATHERINE: Screw you.

ROY: (*Ignoring her*) And I can see how someone with a virgin nun background the way you got might be taken aback by the world—especially Houston. I mean, it's a pretty wide-open place, isn't it? With some pretty wide-open ways. Hell, I don't know if God made Houston or not. Either way it's a pretty rough and ready town. Got a lot of rough and ready people. (*He is standing right in front of her*)

CATHERINE: Why are you standing there?

ROY: I want to smell your perfume.

CATHERINE: I'm not wearing . . . (*He kisses her*) I'm not wearing perfume.

(*Roy smiles broadly, lets her go.*)

ROY: I'm not complaining. (*A pause. He smiles again. She turns away. He looks out over the city with pride*) You know, I don't care of Houston *is* stupid. It's growing like a damn fungus. We can't dig the trenches fast enough. All which ways, too. The city don't know what it's doing anymore—the whole thing's too big for knowing. Guess that's about as stupid as you can get. But we go ahead and dig the trenches, and lay the cables, and fill 'em back in. We figure it's all going to look like something someday. Hell, I don't even mind if you think I'm stupid, as long as you liked kissing me. You want to go out tomorrow night?

CATHERINE: Roy . . .

ROY: I ain't asking you to remarry the world, just date it a little bit. Come on, what do you say? Tomorrow night?

CATHERINE: Riboflavin.

ROY: What?

CATHERINE: What did I say?

ROY: You said riboflavin.

CATHERINE: I did? Oh, I'm sorry. I meant one hundred per cent of minimum daily requirem . . . No—that's not it, is it? I meant smelly butt.

ROY: *What?*

CATHERINE: Smelly butt?

ROY: What the hell are you . . . ?

CATHERINE: What did I just say?

ROY: I don't want to say what you just said.

CATHERINE: Oh, no, I'm doing it again.

ROY: What?

CATHERINE: I'm saying odd things. Aren't I?

ROY: You sure are.

CATHERINE: Well, don't take offense. I mean, it's not you or your tiny penis.

ROY: My what?

CATHERINE: (*Distressed*) I'm doing it again! Why am I doing it again!?

ROY: What are you doing?

CATHERINE: (*Ignoring him*) I'm not in the convent! I released the pressure.

ROY: Look, if you don't want to go out, just say so. You don't have to . . . (*Catherine barks like a dog*) What in hell?

CATHERINE: It's nothing. It'll stop. (*She barks again*)

ROY: Hey, forget I asked you. Don't know where I'd take you anyway.

CATHERINE: (*Very upset*) Why am I *doing* this?! Because I'm in the world? I can't leave the world. (*Turning to Roy, speaking deliberately*) Don't worry. I'm under control. My doctor told me to stay calm, and breathe slowly, and . . . not talk. (*She sits glumly*)

ROY: What does not talking do?

CATHERINE: It keeps me from calling you a . . . (*She slaps her hand over her mouth*)

ROY: I see. You want me to go get Eva June?

CATHERINE: (*Slowly removing her hand*) No, no. I'll be all right. Just let me rest.

ROY: OK.

CATHERINE: I'll be fine.

ROY: Good.

CATHERINE: I just need to get used to the world a little more. Too much all at once, I think.

ROY: Would you like a glass of water?

(*Jason hurriedly re-enters. He is clearly frightened, striving to hide it*)

JASON: 'Lo again. (*He hurries to the rail above the bar door, looks down*)

ROY: Hey, Jay Bob. Anything wrong?

JASON: No. Jim's kinda mad again, but . . . Say, Roy, could you help me with this? (*Jason starts to lift the flower pot*)

ROY: What do you want with a dead plant?

CATHERINE: Dead plant?

JASON: Just want to lift it up to the rail here. Come on.

CATHERINE: Jason . . .

JASON: Come on, Roy.

ROY: Well, I don't know . . .

CATHERINE: Jason, put that down.

JASON: *Come on, Roy!*

(*The bar door opens. We hear Gogi Grant singing "The Wayward Wind" for a moment*)

JASON: Roy!

VOICE: (*Off*) Jay Bob! Come down here!

ROY: (*Looking over the rail*) Oh—hey, Jim!

JIM: (*Off*) Jay Bob! You hear me?!

(*Pause*)

JASON: What do you want?

JIM: (*Off, booming*) *Come down here!*

(*A pause*)

JASON: No.

JIM: (*Off*) That does it, I'm going to kill him. (*We hear male voices attempting to dissuade Jim*) No, damnit—he's not getting away with it. Jay Bob—stay right where you are. I'm coming to kill you.

(*Sound of male voices again. The bar door opens and closes. Same song. Jason runs to the door, stops*)

ROY: He don't mean it, Jay Bob.

JASON: How do you know? (*Moving around the perimeter*) I can't jump; it's too high.

CATHERINE: What's he mad about now?

JASON: Nothing much. I called him kind of a bad name.

CATHERINE: What?

JASON: If I told you, your whole head would probably turn blue, OK? Anyway, he took it wrong. So come on, get me out of here.

CATHERINE: How?

JASON: I'm going up on the roof.

ROY: Need a boost?

JASON: Yeah.

(*Just as they begin this, Eve enters*)

EVE: Where are you going?

JASON: For a walk.

ROY: Hey there, Eva June.

EVE: Shut up, Roy. Get down here. Come on, get down. (*Jason pauses, does so*) This has gone just about far enough. Where's Jim?

ROY: He's on his way up. He was just down there, and he . . .

EVE: Shut up, Roy. (*To Jason*) We'll just calmly wait for him to join us, then. (*To Catherine*) You should've heard what this boy said to Jim. (*To Jason*) Language has plenty of conventional weapons. I don't know why you always got to go nuclear with it. (*To Catherine*) Honey, even you would've been shocked. Things'll be all right, though. I'll calm Jim down. I always do.

ROY: She always does.

(*Jim enters. He is powerfully built. Menacing at his nicest, he is at the moment not very nice—a dark cloud of imminent catastrophe in low-riding jeans and a black T-shirt*)

ROY: Hey, Jim. How's it going?

JIM: (*Deadly serious, to Jason*) Take it back.

JASON: What?

JIM: You know what.

EVE: Now Jim, you know I don't like coming between you two, but it seems to me we can talk this over . . .

JIM: You been mouthing me all summer, boy! Now, you got just three seconds to say you're sorry.

JASON: Or what?

JIM: Or you'll die.

ROY: (*With a forced laugh*) Hey, Jim . . .

(*Jim glares at Roy, who shuts up*)

JASON: You won't kill me. They'd electrocute you.

JIM: It'd be a pleasure, knowing I got you first.

EVE: This is ridiculous. Jay Bob, apologize. That's all he wants.

CATHERINE: Apologize.

JASON: (*Pausing*) No. I'm on vacation, I don't have to.

JIM: (*Going for him*) Good enough.

EVE: (*Interposing herself*) Don't be stupid, Jay Bob.

JASON: (*To Jim with bravado*) You don't dare kill me!

EVE: That's right, it doesn't make sense. Say you're sorry, Jay Bob.

JASON: Hell I will. I meant every word—you're a low-bellied, puke-faced . . .

(*Jim lifts Jason high in the air*)

JIM: Time's up. (*He takes Jason over to the railing above the bar door*)

ROY: Hey, Jim . . .

CATHERINE: Jim!

JASON: You're bluffing!

EVE: Set him down, Jim!

JIM: (*To the others*) Get back! (*They do so. Jim stares at Jason*) Well?

JASON: You're not a real cowboy. (*Jim throws Jason over the railing*) Ji-i-i-i-m-m-m-m!!!!!!

EVE: Jason!

CATHERINE: God!

ROY: Hey now!

(*They rush to the railing, where Jim has remained. Jim begins a slow, deep laugh as we hear male voices from below hooting with derision*)

VOICE: (*Off*) Hey, boys—look who dropped in. It's Jay Bob!

VOICE: (*Off*) Howdy, Jay Bob. What's the matter? Thought you were gonna die?

(*Wild laughter from below. Voices make comments such as,* "Thought he was gonna die!" *and* "Did you have a good flight?")

ROY: A blanket. They caught him in a blanket!

JIM: 'Course they did. You didn't think I was going to kill him, did you?

ROY: Well . . . I wasn't sure . . .

JIM: Hell, he's all right. Hey, Jason—how you doing?

JASON: (*Off*) You crazy son of a bitch! I'm gonna kill you!

JIM: See? He's fine. Think I'll go down and buy him a drink, now that we understand each other better.

CATHERINE: (*Slowly recovering from her shock, to Jim as he goes*) You're going to buy him a *drink*? You just threw him off the . . . and now you're going to buy him a drink?

JIM: Why not? He can hold it. Come on, Roy—I'll even treat you.

(*Jim and Roy exit*)

CATHERINE: (*To Eve, who is still looking over the railing, her back to the audience*) Are you going to let him *do* that? Eve, why don't you say something?

EVE: (*Turning*) 'Cause I can't stop laughing, that's why. (*Indeed, she is laughing*)

CATHERINE: Eve!

EVE: Oh, you should see him down there now. I never saw anybody that mad in my life. His face is so red—I wouldn't be surprised if his head explodes.

CATHERINE: I can't believe this!

EVE: What?

CATHERINE: How can you talk that way? That man just threw your son off a balcony.

EVE: So what? He didn't mean to hurt him.

CATHERINE: Jay Bob didn't know that!

EVE: (*Laughing despite herself*) Well, he knows it now.

CATHERINE: Eve!

EVE: Look, honey. I know how far Jim'll go, and how far he won't go. I admit he had me worried there for a second, but when I looked down and saw Jay Bob bouncing in that blanket—well, it was just funny, you know?

CATHERINE: No. I don't know.

EVE: (*Smiling*) Don't be a drip. You've never had kids, that's all. My God, I can't tell you how good it felt to see somebody sending that boy over a balcony. About time. I'd 've done it myself, 'cept he's been too big ever since he was ten. Hey, come on. Let's go to dinner.

CATHERINE: Dinner?

EVE: Yeah. Aren't you hungry?

CATHERINE: (*Sitting*) I know what my problem with the world is. I know what it is.

EVE: You do? What is it?

CATHERINE: I'm trying to understand the world. That's my problem.

EVE: Honey, you're just not used to the frontier sense of humor.

CATHERINE: I'm going to forget about trying to understand anything. I'm going to sit here and stare at Houston.

EVE: (*Looking out over the city*) It gets prettier as the lights come on.

CATHERINE: I mean, why should the world explain itself to me?

EVE: Hell, the world never explains itself to anyone. You just got to make something up. That's what I did. I made up a whole new way of life. Even built a sign to celebrate the fact: NICE PEOPLE DANCING TO GOOD COUNTRY MUSIC. You just got to make something up, honey, and go on from there. Hell, I think you already got a good start on it, you want to know the truth. You managed to pick out your single favorite person in the whole family, right in the middle of all your trouble and everything. Why not stick with that a while? You can use Jay Bob's room after tonight. Stay all winter if you want. Never know. You may get to like it here.

CATHERINE: Roy Manual wants to take me out tomorrow. If I don't bark.

EVE: Well, go, if you want to. Roy's no fun, but he's no harm either. And you're just starting.

CATHERINE: I think he wants to go dancing. Does it matter if I can't dance?

EVE: With Roy? Nah. Come on—let's get something to eat. (*Catherine smiles, rises. They move toward the door*) Houston's got a lot of great restaurants. I know a place where the food just fights to get into your mouth.

CATHERINE: Sounds great.

EVE: Yes, it is. And we can work more on our men lessons, too. I swear, it's a lifetime study.

(*They exit as the bar door opens below. We hear Hank Williams singing, "The silence of a falling star/Lights up the purple sky . . ." and so on from "I'm So Lonesome I Could Cry." Slow fade until all we can see is the dimly glowing neon sign. Then it too fades to black*)

The End

Casey Kelly
THE OTHER WOMAN

Casey Kelly

When Casey Kelly's full-length play *Grand's Finale* premiered at the Delaware Theatre Company in Wilmington in March of 1983, *State News* critic Joyce Mullins observed, "Mastery of craft is what Kelly has attained with this work, and it wouldn't be surprising to find this play or another of hers on Broadway soon. . . . She treads very skillfully on the tightwire balance between comedy and drama and ties up all the loose ends as neatly as a plastic surgeon." *Grand's Finale* was subsequently produced at the Quaigh Theatre in Manhattan.

Another of Casey Kelly's full-length plays, *Ready or Not*, has been produced by the Pennsylvania Stage Company in Allentown; Tiffany's Attic Theatre in Kansas City, Missouri; Celebrity Playhouse in Birmingham, Alabama; and The Gallery Theatre in Bellingham, Washington. Ms. Kelly has also written a new drama, *Errand of Mercy*, and a musical entitled *Streeterville*, which was a finalist in the University of Chicago's Sergel Drama Prize competition. Other works of hers have been sold to television and film producers.

The Other Woman, which appears in print for the first time in this anthology, was first produced by Joan See with Barbara Moss at the Three of Us Studios in New York. It was directed by Duane Sidden and featured Elizabeth Ward as Ginny, Memrie Innerarity as Virginia, Gerald Kline as Hank, and Jayne Bentzen as the Woman. The playwright, who resides on Roosevelt Island and writes in Manhattan, dedicates *The Other Woman* to her daddy, Melvin R. Elliott, Sr.

Cast of Characters:

GINNY GIBBS, *age twelve*
VIRGINIA, *her mother, slightly plump, age thirty-five to forty-two*
HANK, *her father, a salesman, age thirty-five to forty-five*
WOMAN (JENNY), *beautiful, in her twenties*

Time:

September, this year

Place:

Ten miles past the last house in Sedalia.

An evening in September, this year. The stage is spare but suggests a rural home. There are no dividers between the rooms, only plumbing and wiring to show where the kitchen and a child's bedroom would be. The kitchen sink stands alone, appearing to be supported only by the gooseneck pipe; it is an old fixture. Other furniture— a kitchen table and chairs, a child's bed and desk—might be only black boxes. A print coverlet is on the bed, and a substantial doll collection is on a shelf, with a favorite doll on the bed. The bedroom area has a window frame, if only suggested; doors lead into a bathroom and to the kitchen. The kitchen area has an outside door and a door leading to the rest of the house.

As the lights come up, a pre-adolescent girl and her mother are seated at the kitchen table, shucking peas.

GINNY: But why do I have to shuck peas?
VIRGINIA: If you don't learn now, you'll never learn.
GINNY: But why do I have to learn at all? I can't really see any advantage in it, when I hate peas.
VIRGINIA: There doesn't have to be an advantage to everything you do.
GINNY: Why not?
VIRGINIA: There just doesn't. Break it with a snap—it's faster. Throw them out when they're shriveled like that. (*She*

notes that Ginny has propped one leg up in her chair) Ginny, I see stars.

GINNY: Oh, Mama.

VIRGINIA: Put your leg down. You're too old for that. Your drawers show.

GINNY: You've seen them before.

VIRGINIA: It's not ladylike. Anyway, Hank'll be home in a minute.

GINNY: Daddy's seen them before, too.

VIRGINIA: Ginny! Now you just sit up straight and finish what you started.

(*Ginny puts her leg down and they continue shucking a moment*)

GINNY: Do you like this?

VIRGINIA: What?

GINNY: Shucking peas—do you actually like it?

VIRGINIA: I don't mind.

GINNY: Then why is your mouth all pulled down like that?

VIRGINIA: It isn't. See. (*A fake smile*)

GINNY: That doesn't look real.

VIRGINIA: Will you just finish your peas?

GINNY: I don't even like peas.

VIRGINIA: Then finish them for me.

GINNY: Do you like peas?

VIRGINIA: They're good for you.

GINNY: But do you like them?

VIRGINIA: I don't think one is supposed to like peas. One is only supposed to eat them.

GINNY: But who *said*?

VIRGINIA: I don't know. I suppose my mother told me.

GINNY: How did she know?

VIRGINIA: Her mother told her, I suppose.

GINNY: What if they were all wrong—your mother and her mother and her mother and her mother? I mean, did any one of them ever ask a real scientist?

VIRGINIA: You make me so weary, sometimes.

GINNY: How come?

VIRGINIA: Don't ask me any more questions. Not today.

GINNY: But why?

VIRGINIA: Because I'm weary.

GINNY: You're always weary. Will I be weary when I grow up?

(*Virginia's lips tighten at the question*)

VIRGINIA: Ginny! I see stars again.
(*Ginny lowers her leg. Sound of wheels on gravel*)
GINNY: Daddy's home!
VIRGINIA: Don't yelp like that! It's unladylike.
(*Ginny runs to the screen door and hollers out*)
GINNY: A Hank a hair a
rag a bone!

>   HANK: (*Offstage*)   Don't
>   come out here—wait just a
>   minute. Go on.

(*Ginny backs in the door expectantly. Hank enters and picks her up—she's a little too old for this. Virginia turns away*)
HANK: What's your name?
GINNY: Puddnin' tane—ask me again and I'll tell you the same.
HANK: What's your name?
GINNY: Puddnin' tane—ask me again and I'll tell you the same.
VIRGINIA: Hank, Ginny hasn't finished her share of the peas.
GINNY: I hate peas.
HANK: Well, I'm relieved. No woman of style and grace ever liked peas.
VIRGINIA: Hank . . .
GINNY: I'm never going to be that kind of woman.
HANK: You are, my beautiful puddnin' tane.
GINNY: I'm not beautiful.
HANK: Virginia, would you have this girl's eyes checked?
VIRGINIA: If she doesn't learn household skills now . . .
HANK: Shuck those peas. Your mama's right. If you don't do a few things you hate, right now, while you're young, well, what'll you have to reject when you're older?
VIRGINIA: Hank . . .
HANK: Oh come on, Virginia.
GINNY: What's outside?
HANK: Oh, just a little something.
GINNY: What?
HANK: Sugar and spice and everything nice.
GINNY: Come on, daddy. What?
VIRGINIA: Hank . . .
HANK: Run on to your room, honey. I gotta talk to mama first.

GINNY: Is it something for me?

HANK: Could just be.

GINNY: Give it to me now, OK?

VIRGINIA: What have you gone and done?

HANK: (*To Ginny*) I'll call you in a minute. (*Ginny exits to her room*) I got the greatest thing for her birthday. She's going to fly to the moon.

VIRGINIA: Her birthday's over—you got her too many presents anyway.

HANK: Well, what's the next thing up? Halloween. This is perfect for Halloween. Too big to store, though. Guess I'd better give it to her now.

VIRGINIA: I give up with you. I just give up. You're never going to own your own warehouse, if you keep spending every extra cent on . . .

HANK: Hold it, hold it, hold it. First of all, we've got a contract from the new shopping center.

VIRGINIA: I know, but . . .

HANK: Have you seen this contract?

VIRGINIA: Of course, but . . .

HANK: And did you satisfy yourself that I hadn't forged it?

VIRGINIA: Oh, Hank.

HANK: And did I not show you that that same shopping center had indeed broken ground?

VIRGINIA: But it's so far off. If something should happen, we'll need that money you squander . . .

HANK: Would you like to know how much I squandered on this present?

VIRGINIA: How much?

HANK: It didn't cost me a cent. (*Kiddingly*) But it's sure been a pleasure arguing with you. Now wait here and turn around. Even you're going to get a kick out of this one.

VIRGINIA: What is it?

HANK: Just keep an open mind. (*He exits, slamming the door*)

GINNY: Can I come out now?

VIRGINIA: No, Ginny. He's still getting it.

GINNY: Can I keep it?

VIRGINIA: Sure. It's your present.

GINNY: Did he give you a hint?

VIRGINIA: No.

(*Hank enters carrying a nude female mannequin*)

HANK: She'll just need a little work.

VIRGINIA: Good God; no! Where did you get that thing?

HANK: She'll clean up real pretty. I'm going to touch out those nicked places—and I thought you could help me with this.

(*He hands her a disheveled wig; she recoils from touching it, and he puts it on the table. She removes it to a chair, a little disgusted. Her reserve contrasts sharply with his joy*)

VIRGINIA: Not on the table. Who gave you this?

HANK: Fate. I was driving along Highway 14—I never go that way—but something inside me made me. When I came around the bluff and saw this . . . Ginny, are you listening?

GINNY: No, sir! Honest.

HANK: Then how'd you hear me?

(*Her face registers "Oops"*)

Go on in the bathroom and close the door. I don't want to spoil the surprise.

(*Ginny does; he waits for the door to close*)

Anyway, I came around the bluff to the old Daniels place, and you know who it turns out he sold out to?

VIRGINIA: Neiman-Marcus?

HANK: (*Laughs heartily*) No—the city! And that's where I got this.

VIRGINIA: From the city.

HANK: They didn't want her. I came around the bluff, and there she was, leaning casually against the tree, her shoulders just catching the light, like the statue of Venus, only slim. And there were a whole pile of arms off to the side—they just screw on. I gotta take you and Ginny back there, Virginia—it's a sight to behold. Lots of worthless torsos and arms and legs in a pile . . . but this one gorgeous specimen standing there, complete.

VIRGINIA: But what use could the city have for . . . (*It dawns on her*) . . . wait a minute—what's the city using the land for?

HANK: You know . . .

VIRGINIA: The city dump? (*Hank nods*) Get that damn thing out of here this instant!

HANK: But Virginia . . .

VIRGINIA: We'll all have the plague.

HANK: It's a very clean dump. There's hardly anything there yet. No garbage to speak of—just a bunch of old department store fixtures, boxes, a couple of warped counters. I mean, it hasn't even had time to get dirty.

VIRGINIA: Lice—did you think of lice? (*She pitches the wig out the door*)

HANK: It's plastic—plastic doesn't get lice. Can you imagine how thrilled that kid'll be to get a life-size doll?

VIRGINIA: I don't want her to have it. It's not healthy. And even if it were antiseptic, it's obscene.

HANK: Well, I planned to put clothes on her. That's why I sent Ginny out.

VIRGINIA: What clothes?

HANK: `I just thought, if you wouldn't mind . . .

VIRGINIA: Not my clothes.

HANK: If you had something old, that you didn't want any more.

VIRGINIA: Hank, I'm really opposed to this.

GINNY: (*Offstage*) Daddy, is it ready yet?

VIRGINIA: No, Ginny.

HANK: Don't break her heart.

VIRGINIA: You really have me in a bind.

HANK: I had to, honey. It's the only way to get you to try anything new. Come on—you've got a pile of stuff you never wear any more.

VIRGINIA: I'm going to wear them again. When I lose weight.

HANK: I know, I know. We'll take good care of them. Maybe something really old . . . so you won't worry. Like that— remember that black and red number, with the little fluffy . . . (*He describes a flounce with his hands*) . . . you know.

VIRGINIA: Flounce.

HANK: Do you still have it? It's probably the right size— weren't you about this size once?

VIRGINIA: You can't expect me to look like that. I've had a baby.

HANK:　I don't expect you to look like that.

VIRGINIA:　I know you're thinking that after twelve years, I should have shaped up by now, but . . .

HANK:　Virginia. You're fine like you are. Did you save that dress?

VIRGINIA:　It's in the cedar closet. (*Hank starts to go*) Wait . . .

HANK:　Do you mind using that one?

VIRGINIA:　(*Pause*) I guess not. You always did like it better than I did.

HANK:　I know—I bought it for you. You looked scrumptuous in it.

VIRGINIA:　It really wasn't me. No, I'll get it. You clean that thing up. And spray it with Lysol.

(*As Hank starts to work, Virginia starts toward the back of the house but is stopped by Ginny's call. Ginny pokes her head out from the bathroom door*)

GINNY:　Mama, could I have something to eat while I wait? I'm starving.

VIRGINIA:　You'll ruin your dinner.

GINNY:　Could I have my dinner in here, then?

VIRGINIA:　That's disgusting, to eat in the bathroom.

GINNY:　I was going to eat off of a plate, not the potty seat.

VIRGINIA:　Just get your mind on something else.

GINNY:　But there's nothing to do. I can't go to the bathroom for tomorrow, or anything.

VIRGINIA:　Go back in your room then. We'll be careful not to give you any more clues.

GINNY:　Just tell me one thing—it isn't another doll, is it? (*Pause*) Well, is it?

VIRGINIA:　Just let me say

that it's . . . well . . . not like anything else you've ever gotten.

GINNY: Goody!

(*Meanwhile, Hank is having fun cleaning up the mannequin. He treats her mechanically for a few beats, but as he soaps the shoulders a change comes over him. He realizes he's having carnal feelings, but he shakes them off by whistling. It doesn't work for long. He scrubs the back with no problem, pauses at the buttocks, then skims over them and on down the back of the legs, around to the front of the legs. He pauses and takes a breath, left with the breasts and groin area: suddenly, he charges them and completes the task as quickly as possible, his whistle now reduced to blowing air. He dries her as Virginia enters with a dress, speeding up the process when he sees her. She turns away quickly when she sees what he's doing, as though she had stumbled into the bedroom of lovers*)

HANK: Welp, she's all spic 'n' span. Oh, you found it.

VIRGINIA: I should get rid of some of that stuff, really. Maybe all of it. (*Eyes mannequin*) Maybe I should just admit that I'm fat.

HANK: You're not fat. She's emaciated.

VIRGINIA: Hardly.

HANK: Here and there.

VIRGINIA: Did you clean her everywhere? (*He nods*) Even the . . . cracks?

GINNY: (*To herself*) Cracks? What has cracks?

HANK: Well enough. Wherever I could reach.

VIRGINIA: Including the . . .

HANK: (*Toying*) The what?

VIRGINIA: You know, the . . .

HANK: No, what?

VIRGINIA: . . . the . . .

HANK: Just say it.

VIRGINIA: (*Softly*) Groin area.

HANK: I can't hear you.

VIRGINIA: (*Very softly*) Groin.

HANK: I can't hear you.

VIRGINIA: Groin!

HANK: I will if you want me to.

GINNY: Groin? Groin. (*She gets the dictionary and looks it up*) G . . . G-R . . . G-R-O . . .

(*Hank tries to act casual around Virginia, but this is no casual matter for either of them. He approaches the mannequin's groin*)

VIRGINIA: No. That's probably a, uh . . . temptation for you. I should do it myself.

HANK: Your hands are littler anyway. (*Virginia fumbles a bit: this embarrasses her enormously*) You know, there's probably no dirt to speak of in there anyway.

VIRGINIA: Little girls are very susceptible to infection. Get the Lysol.

HANK: It's the same kind of dirt that's on the outside, for chrissake!

VIRGINIA: I know that.

HANK: If she gets anything, it'll be Lysol poisoning, not VD.

VIRGINIA: Hank.

(*Virginia gets the Lysol and sprays between the mannequin's legs, then does the entire mannequin, front and back. Hank has gone outside for the wig and has returned. Virginia points at the floor*)

VIRGINIA: Put it there.

(*She sprays the wig without touching it, then puts the lid on the Lysol and starts to put it away. She has a second thought, takes the lid off, and re-sprays the groin area well. Satisfied, she puts the Lysol away. They dress the doll. Meanwhile, Ginny has been consulting the dictionary*)

VIRGINIA: There really should be something under this.

HANK: Virginia.

GINNY: Bet I can guess what it is.

HANK: Bet you can't.

GINNY: Bet I can.

HANK: Never in a thousand moons.

GINNY: It's jenny-tall-ya.

HANK: Spell it.

GINNY: G-e-n-i-t-a-l-i-a.

(*Pause. The adults catch on together. Virginia runs into Ginny's room*)

VIRGINIA: Ginny, what are you reading?

GINNY: Just the diction-
ary. Y'all gave me a clue.
"Groin: the fold where the
thigh joins the abdomen at the
jenny-tall-ya."

VIRGINIA: Oh.

GINNY: But what's "jenny-
tall-ya"? I know, "Look it up."

VIRGINIA: You don't have
to this time. (*She takes the dictionary*) We're almost ready for
you.

(*Virginia returns to the kitchen, looking ferocious*)

HANK: I heard.

VIRGINIA: This is just the beginning of all this if you give
her that thing. (*Pause*) Ginny, are you listening?

(*Ginny puts her hand over her
mouth to keep from revealing
herself twice*)

HANK: I think you have to unscrew the arm to get the
sleeve in. Yeah.

VIRGINIA: You just intend to go ahead with it? With no
thoughts of the hornet's nest it can stir up?

HANK: I'm going to need you to hold the sleeve so it doesn't
get pinched. (*She does*)

VIRGINIA: I just want to go on record . . .

HANK: It is duly noted, and you shall have the honor of
the first "I told you so"—if it comes to that.

VIRGINIA: When your daughter asks you more questions
than you'd care to answer, about things she's too young to
care about . . .

GINNY: (*To herself*) I can't
wait.

HANK: It's a goddamn doll, for chrissake! Not a hooker!
(*Pause*) Ginny?

VIRGINIA: Ginny?

(*Ginny runs to bathroom and
flushes toilet. They look relieved. Ginny returns*)

GINNY: (*To herself*) A
goddamn doll. (*Shrugs*) At least
it's not a plain doll.

VIRGINIA: It's starting already. Your language.

HANK: (*Pointing at mannequin*) She didn't make me curse—
you made me curse.

GINNY: (*Aloud*) Can I just
get this over with?

HANK: Don't spoil it for her. (*Virginia gives a half-concili-
atory shrug*) Come on in, honey.

(*Ginny moves toward the door, pauses a moment to work up an
appropriately pleasant presentation of herself, despite her disappointment about the doll. She enters, says hello to the mannequin
on the way to Hank*)

GINNY: Where is it?

HANK: You don't know? Our guest will give it to you.

(*Ginny turns and starts to speak, recognizes that it's a giant doll,
and drops her jaw in awe. For her, this is a mystical experience.
She walks around the doll several times, without hearing her parents*)

HANK: Well, whaddya say, sweetheart?

VIRGINIA: You don't have to keep it if you don't want to.
I wouldn't want to.

(*Hank signals her to shush. Awestruck, Ginny slowly reaches out
to touch the mannequin but withdraws her hand*)

GINNY: She's so beautiful.

VIRGINIA: Well, you don't look very happy about her.

GINNY: No, I am.

HANK: You're sure you like her, now? If you don't, it's
OK with me. Honest.

GINNY: I love her, Daddy. I honestly love her.

VIRGINIA: Hank, she's crying.

HANK: Shhh. What is it, honey? Don't you want her?

GINNY: I love her. She's beautiful.

HANK: But do you want her?

GINNY: (*Unconvincingly*) I do.

HANK: Well, she's yours. Forever. Come on, show me where
you want her.

GINNY: Can't we just keep her in here?

VIRGINIA: Absolutely not.

HANK: What's the big deal?

VIRGINIA: I spend most of my day in here.

HANK: So?

VIRGINIA: I like being alone. Look, if Ginny doesn't want
her, get rid of her.

GINNY: No, I do! (*Pause*) I guess she can stay in my room.

HANK: Do you want to take her? She's lighter than she looks.

GINNY: No, you take her.

(*Hank takes the mannequin into Ginny's room and she follows: Virginia watches them a little sadly, then continues preparing the evening meal*)

HANK: OK, where do you want her? (*He sets the mannequin by the window*) How 'bout here?

GINNY: She doesn't like the sun. She likes the dark.

HANK: This corner then. It's the darkest, don't you think?

GINNY: No, that's not right.

HANK: Here then. How's this?

GINNY: She wouldn't like it there, either.

HANK: Your friend is very picky. (*Ginny nods*) Where, then? Show me the exact spot.

GINNY: (*Anxious*) It's so hard to decide. There's an exact right spot, but I don't know where.

HANK: You just take your time deciding, puddnin' tane.

GINNY: Please don't call me that. (*Hank looks confused*) Maybe we'll just leave her here for now. Until she's sure.

HANK: You really like her, huh? Really? It is just another doll, I know, but special, don't you think? Something no other kid has, I'll bet.

GINNY: It's . . . too much.

HANK: What's too much?

GINNY: Something I don't understand.

HANK: She's just so beautiful, isn't she? It's hard to be around something that beautiful.

GINNY: Do you understand, Daddy?

HANK: Boy, do I.

GINNY: I don't want to hurt your feelings, but I think I know where she wants to be.

HANK: Where?

GINNY: In the closet.

(*Hank looks disappointed, then recoups*)

GINNY: Unless you would mind.

HANK: No, I think the closet is where she'd most like to be.

VIRGINIA: (*From the kitchen*)
Ginny!

GINNY: Tomorrow she might have changed her mind.

HANK: We wouldn't want to rush her. (*Ginny enters the kitchen*)

GINNY: I'm not very hungry.

VIRGINIA: Put the silver on, please.

(*As Ginny sets the table, quietly, Hank starts to pick up the mannequin—but he has humanized her a bit in his mind. Now that she is dressed, he doesn't want to put his hands anywhere she would disapprove of, yet at the same time he wants to. He opens the closet, but it is full. He moves things around to make room and wedges her in in front. Virginia comes to the door, unseen. Hank closes the closet door, then reopens it after a beat, gazes at the mannequin as though she were the most beautiful thing he'd ever seen, then reaches out and touches her shoulder, pauses, then shuts the door. Virginia moves to the stove*)

VIRGINIA: Hank, dinner's ready.

HANK: Coming.

(*They take their customary seats at the kitchen table*)

GINNY: I'm not very hungry.

VIRGINIA: You have to eat.

GINNY: I'm not hungry at all.

HANK: Otherwise, you won't grow into a lovely lady like your mannequin. Or like your mother.

GINNY: I'm never going to be a lady.

HANK: Of course you will. But you've got to get meat on your bones.

GINNY: It's hard to believe I'll get breasts from meat loaf.

VIRGINIA: Ginny Gibbs, I'll wash your mouth out with soap. (*To Hank*) And don't you laugh.

GINNY: I'm sorry.

HANK: (*To Virginia*) Sorry, doll.

(*There is a long pause, while Hank and Ginny await a signal from Virginia*)

VIRGINIA: Ginny, you say grace tonight.

GINNY: Yes, ma'am. "Bless us, O Lord, for these thy gifts which we are about to receive from the bountiful hands of Christ, Our Lord, Amen." Oh, and thanks for bringing me my new doll, Jenny. Amen again.

HANK: You are quite welcome, on behalf of myself and God. So, you've named her Ginny?

GINNY: Not Ginny. Jenny, with a "J."

HANK: How come?

GINNY: I got the idea from y'all's hint. Jenny Tellya. Isn't that pretty, Daddy? Much prettier than "groin."

(*Virginia shoots an angry look at Hank*)

HANK: Uh, yes. Quite pretty . . . as a word. Nice melodic flow . . . but maybe not just the name for a doll.

GINNY: Jenny isn't a doll—she's a woman. Jenny's a nice name for a woman, isn't it?

HANK: It's fine.

VIRGINIA: Hank. Ginny, "genitalia" refers to your private parts.

GINNY: Which private parts?

VIRGINIA: You know very well which private parts. And we don't discuss private parts at the dinner table. Or name toys after them.

GINNY: She's not a toy—she's a woman.

VIRGINIA: All the more reason.

GINNY: What if I just didn't tell anybody her last name is "Tellya"?

VIRGINIA: Ginny.

GINNY: Jenny Gibbs, then.

HANK: That's pretty too. Almost sounds like you.

VIRGINIA: Nobody's eating. Ginny, I see stars!

(*Ginny puts her leg down*)

GINNY: I'm not hungry. May I be excused?

HANK: Sure.

VIRGINIA: Hank . . .

(*Ginny goes to her bedroom and stares at the closet door*)

HANK: It won't hurt her this once. She's just excited. You're not eating either.

VIRGINIA: I'm on a diet.

HANK: Since when?

VIRGINIA: Since today. (*Realization*) Since Ginny was born.

HANK: Not on my account, I hope. (*He reaches over and touches her shoulder, as he had the mannequin's; the similarity isn't lost on her*) You know, I sure would like to hold you right now.

VIRGINIA: You haven't eaten.

HANK: Want to go on back to our room?

VIRGINIA: I have to do the dishes.

HANK: They're practically clean.

VIRGINIA: And put away the food, if nobody's eating. (*She rises*)

HANK: It would be nice, though, wouldn't it? Just to tell Ginny we're going to bed early and not to come out until in the morning. We haven't done that for ages.

VIRGINIA: She's used to us kissing her goodnight.

HANK: We can do that now, and she can put herself to bed at nine.

VIRGINIA: But she'll be so lonesome.

HANK: Naw, she'll want to play with her new friend, I'll bet. Give her some more of those dresses, and I'll bet she plays for hours.

VIRGINIA: That woman doesn't have any panties on. Or a slip.

HANK: She doesn't need them. She doesn't have any "private parts." Get those dresses? Hmmmm? (*Virginia exits, and Hank enters Ginny's bedroom*) Puddnin' tane?—Ah! I mean, Ginny. Your mom and I are going to bed early tonight.

GINNY: It's only seven o'clock.

HANK: Your mother's tired, and I've had a long day.

GINNY: It's because of her, isn't it? (*She points at the closet. She's right, Hank knows*)

HANK: How could it be because of her?

GINNY: I just had a feeling. Daddy, I'm not sleepy this early.

HANK: Well, your mother and I thought you might like to read . . . or, if you're ready for it, you can try some more clothes on Jenny Gibbs.

GINNY: Her name isn't really Jenny *Gibbs*.

HANK: Well, that'll be our little secret, OK?

(*Ginny nods. Hank gets the doll out, trying to appear nonchalant, but Ginny can sense something*)

GINNY: I'm not sure I want to play with her tonight.

HANK: Why not?

GINNY: It might be too soon.

HANK: Just give it a try. Start with the small stuff and see how you feel. (*She nods*) So, what'll you need? Hats, purses, scarves, and stuff?

(*Ginny doesn't react. Hank exits. Ginny stares at Jenny warily*)

HANK: (*Offstage*) Virginia, mind if I give Ginny the old stuff in the coat closet?

VIRGINIA: (*Wearily, off-stage*) Whatever you want.

HANK: You finding anything?

VIRGINIA: I'm coming.

(*Virginia enters with a plain print housedress, which she hands to Ginny. Obviously Ginny didn't have this in mind, but she doesn't want to hurt her mother's feelings*)

VIRGINIA: Your father thought you might want to play with this.

GINNY: You wear this.

VIRGINIA: It's about shot anyway.

GINNY: I wasn't going to change her dress tonight anyway.

VIRGINIA: Tomorrow then. You can have it for keeps.

GINNY: What about those old dresses—in the cedar closet?

VIRGINIA: I want those. I'm going to wear them again someday.

(*Hank enters with hats, purses, and scarves*)

HANK: Oh, don't give her that thing. Jenny Gibbs is a classy chick. Never does a lick of housework, right, doll? (*He winks at Ginny*)

GINNY: I don't know. (*Virginia's feelings are hurt. She goes into the kitchen to put food in the Tupperware*) You hurt Mama's feelings.

HANK: Did I? Oh . . . (*He goes into kitchen, still carrying the paraphernalia*) Did I hurt your feelings about your dress?

VIRGINIA: It was old anyway.

HANK: It looks fine on you. All your dresses look fine on you.

VIRGINIA: Fine.

HANK: Fine, yes. They're just housedresses. If you want to look great, you could wear that red housecoat I gave you.

VIRGINIA: It isn't me.

HANK: I'm not sure these functional things are "you" either.

VIRGINIA: I'm functional.

HANK: (*A compliment*) You are functional as hell—and then some. A great housewife, a nice home, nice meals, nice daughter. What more could a man want?

VIRGINIA: That other woman. (*The mannequin*)

HANK: Jenny Gibbs? (*He laughs and proceeds to put the hats and scarves on Virginia*) Well, I tell you about Jenny Gibbs. She has a great body, but it's all show and no go.

(*Singing*)
"Oh, you beautiful doll
You great big beautiful doll
Let me put my arms around you . . ."

(*Ginny watches from the door*)

VIRGINIA: Cut it out.

HANK: I'm so happy that
I found you, Oh, oh, oh, oh—

VIRGINIA: Stop it.

HANK: Oh, you beautiful
doll.

(*Virginia looks ridiculous, and a little humor crosses her face. Hank kisses her and fondles her breast. She pushes his hand away, Ginny steps back into her room, affected*)

VIRGINIA: She'll see us.

HANK: Come on. (*He enters the bedroom*) Good night, honey.

GINNY: Good night, Daddy. (*He bends over to kiss her, but she pulls away*) Good night.

HANK: (*Sensing something*) Good night. (*He passes by Virginia in the kitchen; she is putting away the food*) Coming?

VIRGINIA: Couple of things left to do here.

HANK: Sometimes it takes you so long.

VIRGINIA: . . . wipe off the counters, and uh . . .

HANK: I'll help.

VIRGINIA: No, I'll do it.

HANK: I'm not going to fall asleep this time. I'm waiting as long as it takes.

(*She nods and wipes the counter faster. As soon as he exits, she takes the domed cake plate down from the refrigerator, cuts a small piece, and eats it while putting cake and milk on a tray for Ginny. Ginny hears her coming and hops up to act as if she's been playing with the mannequin. She puts a wonderful hat with feathers that complement the dress on the mannequin*)

GINNY: Mama?

VIRGINIA: I didn't want you to go to bed hungry.

GINNY: Was all this stuff yours? (*Virginia nods*) You must have been beautiful.

VIRGINIA: I was passable.

GINNY: Daddy says you were beautiful. Your honeymoon picture is beautiful.

VIRGINIA: Well, all brides are beautiful.

GINNY: When does a person start being beautiful, Mama? And when do they have to stop?

VIRGINIA: (*Disturbed*) They don't have to stop . . .

GINNY: Then why did you?

VIRGINIA: I haven't stopped.

GINNY: Are you just taking a little rest, or what? (*Virginia is disturbed and starts to exit. Ginny is disturbed, too, and calls after her*) Wait, Mama. When will I be beautiful?

VIRGINIA: You're beautiful now. Good night.

GINNY: No, beautiful. Like you were.

VIRGINIA: (*Fleeing*) Any day now. Any time. Night.

(*She exits to kitchen, starts to put the lid on the cake plate but instead takes a big hunk of cake*)

HANK: (*Offstage, sweetly*) Virginia!

(*Both Virginia and Ginny know what his call means. Virginia pauses a moment, puts the cake up, and reluctantly exits. Ginny pointedly looks at the mannequin, but when she hears her mother's door close, turns away and lies on her bed, fondling a very old doll. But the gaze of the mannequin seems trained on her. Ginny sits up*)

GINNY: What do you want with me? I can't do it yet. It's too soon.

(*She lies down, puts her thumb in her mouth, than withdraws it, disgusted with herself; it doesn't fit any more. The doll gives her no satisfaction, either. She addresses the mannequin finally, without looking at her*)

Tell me what you want, then.

(*She rises and walks to the mannequin, unbuttons her dress, and is disappointed at the incomplete breasts*)

You're a fake too. Like me. You don't have them either. Why do you act like you have them if you don't!

(*She sits at her desk, turned away from the mannequin*)

I don't want them, anyway. I hope I never get them. Nobody wants them. I don't know why they come if nobody wants them.

(*Ginny stares at the wall for a few beats, then wheels in the direction of the mannequin*)

Okay, goddamnit!

(*She roots through her crayon cannister for the right color and bites her lips to keep from crying as she draws nipples on the mannequin*)

But I don't want them. You're the one who wants them. And if anybody blames me, I'll tell them you made me do it. They won't believe me. They'll think I wanted them. There, are you satisfied?

(*She starts to button the dress, but stops, thinks of something overwhelming*)

No! Please don't make me. Please.

(*She looks into the fixed gaze of the mannequin, sees it's no use arguing. She goes back to the crayon tin, gets another color, and returns to the mannequin. She pauses a moment, puts the crayon in her mouth to free her hands, and finishes unbuttoning the mannequin's dress. She takes the crayon out of her mouth, kneels, and starts crying as she draws on pubic hair. By the time the job is complete, she is in full sob: she re-buttons the mannequin's dress and puts her in the closet, closing the door. She turns out the light, gets into bed, and pulls up the coverlet, her sobs diminishing by degrees. A soft light remains on her face as night lighting and moonlight at the window fade in. Moments pass. Presently, the closet door opens and a beautiful woman enters, wearing the mannequin's clothes. They look similar, but the mannequin's vinyl hair is now soft and real, and the clothes fit the woman well. She regards Ginny with compassion for a moment, bends over her to stroke her hair, but decides not to wake her. She removes her hat carefully and hangs it on the bedpost. She lies down beside Ginny, her head propped on her arm, smiling contentedly and looking into Ginny's face. Suddenly Ginny's eyes open*)

JENNY: I wanted to thank you for that. I know it wasn't easy.

GINNY: You couldn't possibly have wanted them.

JENNY: I wanted them.

GINNY: Why?

JENNY: Because they're me. I was just waiting for me to happen.

GINNY: I don't want to happen.

JENNY: You're already happening.

GINNY: It has to be stopped.

JENNY: It can't be stopped.

GINNY: You could stop it if you wanted to. You have the power.

JENNY: You have the power to let it happen.

GINNY: But I don't want it! (*Jenny reaches for Ginny, but she jumps out of bed*) Don't you touch me!

JENNY: I know, baby. I know. I know.

GINNY: Please help me.

JENNY: I will.

GINNY: You'll stop it, then?

JENNY: No—I'll help you want it.

GINNY: But I don't want to want it.

JENNY: You will.

GINNY: When?

JENNY: Whenever you're ready. We have all night.

GINNY: But I want longer. Way longer.

JENNY: No, Ginny.

GINNY: Just a year or two?

JENNY: No.

GINNY: A few months, then. Just until I get used to the idea.

JENNY: No.

GINNY: I hate you. I hate you. I hate you. (*Jenny holds her arms out*) No. I hate you. I mean it.

JENNY: I know.

GINNY: Why did you come here, anyway?

JENNY: You invited me. Remember? (*Jenny starts to unbutton her dress*)

GINNY: No! I remember. (*Jenny moves away to give Ginny space. She sits in a rocker, rocking peacefully with the moonlight on her face. Ginny can't look at her*) Those little lumps—I found them before my birthday. Is that it starting?

JENNY: Uh huh.

GINNY: They're not so terrible, if they just don't race ahead.

JENNY: They'll give you all the time you need.

GINNY: I wouldn't want them to come all at once.

JENNY: They won't.

GINNY: What before dawn then? You said tonight. (*Jenny nods*) Not the rest. Not the red, sticky rest. (*Jenny nods*) No! I'm only twelve. Mama was fifteen. She promised I would be fifteen.

JENNY: She didn't have the power to promise.
GINNY: She lied to me.
JENNY: Yes.
GINNY: Damn her.
JENNY: She didn't mean to, Ginny.
GINNY: I just wasn't expecting it, that's all. I'm too young to have the curse.
JENNY: It's not a curse.
GINNY: It is too.
JENNY: Says who?
GINNY: My mother told me.
JENNY: And who told her?
GINNY: Her mother, I suppose. Look, she ought to know.
JENNY: What if they were wrong—your mother and her mother and her mother and her mother? I mean, did any one of them ever ask a real scientist? (*Ginny softens as she hears her words turned on herself*) Facts aren't curses . . . they're just facts. Come here.
GINNY: I don't want you to touch me.
JENNY: I won't until you want me to. Just come look. (*Ginny moves cautiously toward the window, taking care not to step into the moonlight*) See that moon up there? (*Ginny nods*) What do you see?
GINNY: The man in the moon.
JENNY: Who said it was a man?
GINNY: My daddy.
JENNY: And who told him?
GINNY: I know. His daddy and his daddy and his daddy.
JENNY: We can't blame them for naming the moon for themselves. She's just so glorious. But it's us who are connected to the moon. The tides of the great seas—and women—both take our rhythms from the moon. I bring you a secret song, not a curse.
GINNY: I wish I could believe you.
JENNY: You might as well. It'll make the next thirty years a lot happier. Come here. Let the moonlight fall on you.
GINNY: I'm afraid of her.
JENNY: She knows. But come. Don't be earthbound. (*Jenny's outstretched arms become very compelling, and Ginny steps into the moonlight, eyes closed tightly. After a moment, she opens them and her expression softens*) You're so beautiful now.
GINNY: Me? I am not. I'm never going to be.

JENNY: Oh, says who? The same people who decide what curses are, get to say what beauty is? Nope, we're just going to decide for ourselves. (*She studies Ginny's face in the moonlight*) Yep, you're beautiful all right. And it's here to stay. Definitely.

GINNY: I don't want that either.

JENNY: Beauty?

GINNY: If it never comes, then it won't hurt so much when it goes.

JENNY: Who says it has to go? You have to throw beauty away with both hands to get rid of it. It's easier just to keep it.

GINNY: Could you tell my mother that?

JENNY: She has to find it from within. But maybe you could help her. Oh, and while you're about it, remind her that chocolate causes pimples in adolescents. (*Ginny laughs, then throws her piece of cake in the trash can. She looks at Jenny for approval, gets it, then runs into the kitchen and gets the chocolate cake. Jenny laughs*) Proceed at your own risk. (*Ginny takes the cake into the bathroom, throws it into the toilet, and flushes a couple of times*) Your mother might not think too highly of this.

GINNY: (*Offstage*) I'll blame it on you.

JENNY: Don't you dare.

(*While Ginny finishes, Jenny goes back to the bed and lies down. When Ginny re-enters, Jenny's arms are outstretched to her. Ginny pauses in the door a moment, then sets the cake plate on the desk*)

GINNY: I wish you were my mother.

JENNY: I'll be your best friend.

(*Ginny runs to Jenny, lies beside her, and holds her for dear life*)

GINNY: OK, I'll do it. But only if you'll stay with me.

JENNY: Oh, I plan to.

GINNY: Until dawn?

JENNY: Until hell freezes over.

GINNY: I love you.

JENNY: I love you.

(*Ginny soon relaxes into sleep. Jenny, head propped up on arm, strokes her hair. Darkness, immediately punctured by a call offstage*)

VIRGINIA: Ginny! School day. We're running late.

(*Lights up. The bed is empty. Virginia enters, wearing a pretty red kimono quite unlike her previous dress*)

VIRGINIA: Ginny! I over-slept... (*She knocks on the bathroom door*) Ginny?

GINNY: (*In bathroom*) I'm up.

VIRGINIA: Have to hustle this morning—I overslept. (*She sees the empty cake plate*) Ginny! Did you eat all of this cake?

GINNY: No, Mama.

VIRGINIA: Where is it, then?

GINNY: I cannot tell a lie.

VIRGINIA: Where?

GINNY: I flushed it.

VIRGINIA: Ginny Gibbs!

GINNY: It causes zits in adolescents.

VIRGINIA: In adolescents. You're just a kid.

GINNY: Could you come in here, please?

VIRGINIA: I've got to get your father's breakfast.

GINNY: I've got to show you something.

VIRGINIA: Is it impor-tant?

GINNY: *Mama.*

(*Virginia enters the bathroom. Hank has just entered the kitchen, notes the coffee water isn't on, and fills the kettle—something he doesn't usually do. Virginia leaves the bathroom and passes through the kitchen*)

HANK: Hey, you wore it! Let me look.

VIRGINIA: Just give me a minute. (*She exits and is back in a split second, hiding toiletries for Ginny in a fold of the kimono. She is very fidgety but proud of her daughter's womanhood*) Ginny needs me a minute.

(*Hank calls at her on the way by*)

HANK: You're sure beautiful this morning.

VIRGINIA: (*Loving it*) Oh, I'm not. Stop.

HANK: Thank you for wearing it.

VIRGINIA: It really isn't me.

(*She disappears into the bathroom, while Hank takes money out of his wallet and puts it on the counter. Virginia comes out of the bathroom, closing the door behind her*)

> VIRGINIA: Holler if you need me.
>
> GINNY: (*Offstage*) Don't tell Daddy.
>
> VIRGINIA: I won't.

(*She enters kitchen*)

HANK: Don't tell Daddy what?

VIRGINIA: Shhhhhh.

HANK: You two got a secret? I'll have to charm it out of you, I guess.

VIRGINIA: Wait. It's private to her.

HANK: Should have held out for a boy. I've got nobody to have secrets with around here.

(*Virginia smiles at him lovingly. She sees the money*)

VIRGINIA: I've got the grocery money.

HANK: It's not for groceries.

VIRGINIA: What then?

HANK: I would consider it a great favor if you would go out and buy yourself something that *is* you. I'm dying of curiosity as to what that is.

VIRGINIA: My diet . . .

HANK: Virginia . . . you're beautiful now. You're just not size nine.

VIRGINIA: I am. It's under here.

HANK: I know, I know. But will you just buy one pretty thing that fits, for now. Something you feel lovely in.

(*She rushes into his arms*)

VIRGINIA: Hank, please love me.

HANK: I do love you.

VIRGINIA: I'm not size nine.

HANK: You have a womanly figure. That's all I want from a woman.

VIRGINIA: I'll never be that size again.

HANK: Congratulations, honey. (*She smiles at him, then stuffs the money in her pocket. He beams*) Virginia . . .

VIRGINIA: I want to be beautiful again.

(*He holds her. Ginny emerges from the bathroom in a robe and stands in the kitchen door*)

GINNY: Morning, Daddy.

HANK: You have a beautiful mother, did you know that? (*Ginny nods. Hank does a double take at her. There is a womanly quality he hadn't seen before*) Ginny, I think I know your secret.

GINNY: Mama!

VIRGINIA: I didn't . . .

HANK: She didn't say a word. And nobody has to confirm anything. (*He takes more money out of his pocket*) How would you like to go shopping with your mother today—for a new dress?

GINNY: For me? Oh, yeah. Thank you.

VIRGINIA: It's a school day . . . oh, the heck with it.

HANK: (*To Ginny*) And, for God's sake, get something that's "you."

Curtain

David Higgins
PARTNERS

David Higgins

A hit at the 1982 Actor Theatre of Louisville SHORTS Festival and carried over for the 1983 Humana Festival of New American Plays, *Partners* drew plaudits from *Newsweek* theatre critic Jack Kroll: "David Higgins' *Partners* is an explosive vignette about three young dope-dealing friends who've become murderous enemies through the vicissitudes of the underworld." Commenting on the premiere of the play at the SHORTS Festival, Louisville *Courier-Journal* critic Owen Hardy raved: "For pure theatrical dazzle, Higgins' *Partners* would be difficult to beat . . . it's a taut, totally engrossing spellbinder. . . . [T]he play depicts its characters with depth and uncanny authenticity. It also keeps one on the edge of his seat until the shocking ending." *Partners* appears in print for the first time in this volume.

A native of Pittsburgh, David Higgins has used his background in a trilogy of screenplays on youth in western Pennsylvania. The three plays are entitled *Bad Humor, Kid Billy,* and *Angles.*

Also a musician, Mr. Higgins plays drums for the Buddy Hall Band and has combined his musical and dramatic interests in *Bix*, a screenplay based on the life of jazz cornetist Bix Beiderbecke and in *Bad Dreams and Be-bop,* which explores the life and death of a jazz drummer in the 1950s. The latter play was a full-length finalist in the Actors Theatre of Louisville's 1981 Great American Play Contest.

Mr. Higgins is currently working on *Airgood,* a new short play that pays homage to detective films of the 1940s that featured private investigator Amos Airgood. The play has been commissioned by the Actors Theatre of Louisville.

Characters:

TROY BaDEAU
PETE
AL
THE MANAGER

Time:

The summer. About 10:00 P.M.

Scene:

A room at the Edison Hotel in Pittsburgh, Pennsylvania.
    The setting is a dilapidated hotel room with peeling wallpaper, worn furniture (dresser and two armchairs), a rickety night table, a window that provides access to a fire escape, and an old, metal-framed bed on which Troy BaDeau reclines as he prepares his dinner by pouring a generous serving of bourbon into a cup of plain yogurt. Troy is in his late twenties. He wears blue jeans and boots, no shirt. The wide-eyed, casually disturbed look on his face suggests that behind this expression there exists the soul of a mad-man. It's an accurate suggestion.
    His belongings are strewn all over the room. An opened leather suitcase at the foot of the bed looks as if it has vomited its contents onto the floor. Four or five liquor bottles cover the top of the dresser, and an ice chest is on the floor next to the night table. In between gulps of the bourbon-yogurt concoction he reaches for a mound of darts that lies on the night table next to the phone. After selecting a dart he takes careful aim and hurls it across the room in the direction of the door where he had previously attempted to draw a target with a black magic marker. He misses the door. Disgusted, he throws the next dart into the toe area of his left boot. He frowns, sets the yogurt cup down, picks up the phone, and dials.

    TROY: *(On phone)* Yeah. Is Wendy around? *(Pause)* Oh, she is? How much longer . . . ? *(Pause. A knock on the door. Troy flinches, thrusts his hand under the pillow, removes a gun, and aims at the door)* OK, I'll call back. *(He hangs up)* Yeah?

PETE: (*Outside the door*) Troy?

TROY: Pete?

PETE: Yeah.

(*Troy puts the gun under the pillow, gets up, and limps to the door. He opens it, and Pete enters. They stare at each other for a moment before shaking hands*)

TROY: Long time, Peter.

PETE: How ya doin', Troy?

TROY: Fine, fine. Where's Al?

PETE: Parking the car.

TROY: So is that a project? There's a goddamn parking lot across the street.

PETE: It was full, so I told him to drop me, and I'd go ahead up and see if you were still around.

TROY: Where am I gonna go? I told you I was here.

PETE: (*Nervously*) That's true. I don't know. I just thought . . . or we just thought . . . I don't know.

(*Pause*)

TROY: Have a seat. (*They sit down*)

PETE: (*Noticing the dart in Troy's boot*) The fuck . . . ?

TROY: Yeah. You hear about that?

PETE: Yeah. Had some trouble, huh?

TROY: Hey, I'm lucky to be here. The guy with the shotgun ain't bush-league, then I'm a dead man. I mean, it was pointblank, from the other side of the room. My buddies weren't that lucky.

PETE: That's what I heard.

TROY: And that got back here?

PETE: Yeah, well, it had to. Guys are blowin' back and forth all the time. (*Pause*) I was real sorry to hear about that.

TROY: What can you do? Right? I just gotta look at the positive side. At the good things.

PETE: Good things?

TROY: Like, for instance, it gave me an excuse to quit jogging. Or when I say, "Knock on wood," I don't have to look all over creation for something . . . and all you see, you know, whenever you say that, is Formica, or metal, or fuckin' Styrofoam, or . . . you know what I mean? I can reach down (*He reaches down and taps his wooden leg with his knuckles*) like that. Everybody thinks it's funny when I do that.

PETE: Knock on wood?

TROY: Yeah.

PETE: But it's not.

TROY: What? Wood?

PETE: No. Funny.

TROY: Hey, I don't give a shit. It's history. I can't do anything about it now. (*Troy pulls the dart from his foot and throws it into the floor*) You guys still go to the Mayflower to do some throwin'?

PETE: Not much. Maybe three, four times since you left. You were always the dart fanatic. Me and Al didn't care one way or the other. (*An awkward pause. Pete sniffs the air and frowns*) I hate to say anything.

TROY: Yeah, I know. It's pretty bad.

PETE: What is it?

TROY: I don't know. Maybe it comes with the room. The sick-sweet smell of success, no extra charge. You'll get used to it. (*Pause*) Surprised to hear from me?

PETE: Goddamn right. When'd you get in?

TROY: Couple days ago. (*A beat*) You knew that. (*Pause*)

PETE: We didn't know where you were, though.

TROY: But you knew I'd call.

PETE: I didn't know shit. I told you I was surprised. Especially when you said you were staying in this rat-hole.

TROY: It's not that bad. Got a nice bar downstairs . . . good show . . .

PETE: Yeah, I know all about their fucking shows. You got a half-dozen derelicts sittin' around with hats and newspapers in their laps and maybe another three or four with baggy pants and pup tents that spend the whole night pole vaultin' back and forth to the bathroom.

TROY: You kidding me? You're talking about the dark ages, for Christ's sake. They got a classier clientele than that.

PETE: Maybe they do. I haven't been for a while.

TROY: There's a lot of white collar jerk-offs down there now. Fuckin' guys with ties and briefcases . . . *Wall Street Journal* tucked under their arm. You know the type. Glasses . . . little security mustache . . .

PETE: Yeah.

TROY: They come down after work to suck down a few beers and look at the snapper. It's a nice atmospher. You wanna go down tonight?

PETE: I don't know.

TROY: Or better yet, I was talking to this one stripper this afternoon, they do a matinee, y'know . . .

PETE: (*Sarcastically*) Of course.

TROY: The chick's a sleaze, naturally. Her face don't look so hot, like she had acne real bad when she was a kid. Looks like a goalie for a dart team. But her body's great. Nice tits, got one of those nigaboo asses that sticks out, like a little trailer, like she stopped at U-Haul on the way over . . . lips that look like they've applied a little suction in their time. What can I say? The chick's ready. So I told her I might have some buddies stopping over tonight and if she'd mind, for a nominal fee, of course, doing an impromptu bump and grind for the boys. And then I asked if she just danced or what, and she said if the price was right I'd be surprised what she'd do, and I said I doubt if I'd be surprised but I'll give her a buzz anyway.

PETE: I don't know . . .

TROY: What? I thought you enjoyed abusing a pig every now and then. Degrade 'em a little bit . . . squirt on their face an' shit . . .

PETE: I know. But if the chick's a waffle face, then I don't know.

TROY: Yeah, but see, that's what I find . . . provocative about her. Reminds me of this widow lady used to live in my neighborhood. Probably killed her husband with an intense hum job made his heart explode. I don't know . . . she was forty, forty-five. Used to like young guys. So she hired me to clean out her garage for a five-spot, which I thought was a lot for moving around a couple boxes and lawn chairs and dumpin' some Ajax on her oil spots, which doesn't help much anyway.

PETE: I know.

TROY: But she didn't give a rat's ass about the garage. And she had a face like a lunar relief map but a body like one of those old pigs they stick in a stroke book every once in a while, you know, as a change of pace. Give some incentive to the younger chicks that just because you turn thirty or forty or whatever, you don't have to let yourself go, next thing you know you can use their ass for a roadblock.

PETE: Yeah, but chicks don't read stroke books.

TROY: Sure they do, some of them. Some of them'll do anything. Like this lady. She was one of those "I'll try anything" chicks. I think she had a thing for Dobermans . . . the sky was the limit with her. And talk about a hyper piece of ass. Moved like an asphalt tamper on full throttle. I thought she was a fuckin' epileptic. First time, she scared the shit outa me. I kept saying, "You all right, you all right?" And she'd say (*He maneuvers his Adam's apple to get a vibrato effect*), "Ye-e-e-e-es. Do-o-o-o-on't st-o-o-op." (*Laughs*) Used to clean her garage about once a week.

PETE: I know. I heard this story before.

TROY: You did?

PETE: About fifty times.

TROY: Why didn't you stop me?

PETE: I never knew how. Why do you think I heard it so many times?

TROY: Sorry.

PETE: That's OK. Haven't heard it in a while.

TROY: But you can understand why I might be attracted to someone like that.

PETE: I don't know as to whether I understand it, but . . . whatever you're into.

TROY: Maybe she has some friends . . .

PETE: It doesn't make any difference. It's all low rent down there, anyhow. Those are the kind of chicks you have to clean off before you touch 'em. Get out the garden hose. Go through some kind of fuckin' . . . decontamination thing . . .

TROY: So you're not interested?

PETE: I'll pass.

TROY: Remember, one you pass up is one you don't get.

PETE: That's OK. I'll make it.

(*Pause*)

TROY: I didn't want to just blow into town, y'know. I wanted to try and keep a low profile.

PETE: Don't worry. You stay here, and your profile don't get any lower.

TROY: Hey, you know me. If I have a choice between flea-bag decadence or that Holiday Inn no-suprise bullshit, I'll go with the flea-bag every time. Fuck the screwed-in artwork and the paper across the toilet seat. This joint here, this is me.

(*Pete sees the yogurt concoction on the night table*)

PETE: Still having trouble?

TROY: Not really, but, you know, once you have an ulcer, you're not real anxious to have it flare up again. It's a precaution. I don't eat anything that I think's gonna give me trouble. Like onions or garlic. They give me heartburn enough to launch a fuckin' space shuttle. Everything's gotta be bland. I'm a bland freak.

PETE: Sounds like fun.

TROY: What difference does it make? You are what you eat, right? I'm goddamn . . . whiskey and yogurt. What're you?

PETE: Anything I want.

TROY: Lucky bastard.

(*Pause*)

TROY: You think Patsy knows?

PETE: Knows about what?

TROY: Where I am.

PETE: Well, you know we wouldn't say anything.

TROY: Hey, I know that.

PETE: I'm just sayin'.

TROY: I know.

PETE: He has other sources.

TROY: He always did.

(*Pause*)

PETE: Nah. He knows about it, then you'd know about it.

TROY: That's what I figured.

(*A knock on the door*)

PETE: That's Al.

TROY: (*Calling*) Al?

AL: (*Through the door*) Yeah. How ya' doin'?

(*Troy opens the door. Al enters and they shake hands*)

TROY: The fuck you doin', buddy?

AL: Good, good. How about yourself?

TROY: I'm great. Never been better. Come on in. Can I get you guys a drink? I'm sorry, I forgot to ask you, Pete.

PETE: That's OK. Don't worry about it.

AL: What do you got?

TROY: Got some beer in the ice chest . . . scotch, J.D., vodka, Myers' Dark . . .

AL: Jack Daniels sounds good.

PETE: Yeah, that's good for me too.

TROY: OK. What? On the rocks?

PETE: Yeah.

AL: Rocks are fine.

TROY: That makes it easy. You guys sit down, I'll get these. I think there's a couple glasses in the bathroom. (*He exits to the bathroom. Al grimaces*)

AL: What the . . . fuck is that smell?

PETE: You noticed it too, huh?

AL: How can you help it? Stench's enough to knock you on your ass.

PETE: You'll get used to it. I'm starting to.

AL: I don't know if I want to. What is it?

PETE: I don't know, he don't know . . .

(*Troy enters, carrying three glasses*)

AL: (*To Troy*) Sorry to hear about your wheel.

TROY: It's no big deal. I was just telling Pete how it coulda been a lot worse. (*He starts to fix the drinks*)

PETE: What was that all about, anyway?

AL: Yeah. I heard something about some Cubans.

TROY: Fuckin' sand niggers, I tell you what, doing business with them's like this . . . (*He mimes pressing a gun against Al's temple*) You're doing this to each other, sayin', "Give me yours and I'll give you mine." It's ridiculous. So me and my three partners put this thing together, we're walking away with about three-fifty, moving pounds. So it's with these four Cubans. We meet at this beach house right outside Lauderdale, and no sooner did we make the switch then three more blow in and start sprayin' the room.

PETE: Machine guns?

TROY: A couple. It was a miracle I didn't get hit with any of that, but then there's seven other guys picking up my share. So this one motherfucker with a sawed-off drills me. And I go down, my knee is gonzo, ground beef, no support whatsoever. I don't know what was holding my leg together, but it sure as hell wasn't my knee. So I black out, and one of my buddies lands on top of me. That's what saved my life. They thought they got everybody, no doubt. (*Pause*) Those bastards had it all cased out. They blew in and out in a matter of seconds, walk away with the coke and the three hundred and fifty thou.

AL: They don't fuck around, huh?

TROY: Not even a little bit. (*Troy hands them their drinks and raises his glass*)

TROY: Here's to good things in hell and space.

(*They drink. Pause*)

TROY: You guys still go up State College?

PETE: Now and again. Haven't been for awhile.

TROY: How about you, Al?

AL: I haven't been but maybe once or twice in the last year. Which reminds me, you remember John Holshue?

PETE: (*Under his breath*) Shit.

TROY: The bartender?

AL: Yeah.

TROY: At Ace's.

AL: At Ace's, right. Well, he got canned from there because Ace found out he was doing some dealing out of the bar. A little Mickey Mouse. Some weed, reds, gorilla biscuits . . . Ace got pissed about that.

TROY: So what about him?

AL: He got killed. Guy shot him at a party we were at.

TROY: No shit? What happened?

AL: Case of the ol' irate boyfriend with the short fuse.

PETE: Guy blows in looking for Franky Andelmo. You remember . . .

TROY: Yeah. I know Franky.

PETE: Anyway, Andelmo brought this chick to the party over at his place, and he puts her up for grabs. 'Course, that's what he called her for. She's one of them ones you call if you don't want to go home with a newspaper or if you're having a party and you need something to entertain the troops.

AL: A real oinker. Bitch had a snout instead of a nose.

PETE: And she's got this boyfriend with honorable intentions who doesn't know her track record . . . thinks she's Snow White. And he finds out about it, and it turns out he was a little nuts.

AL: The guy was a sick unit, no doubt about it. Usin' a .45 revolver with hollow points, for Christ's sake.

PETE: Fuckin' cowboy.

TROY: And what? Holshue was with her when the guy blows in?

PETE: Yeah. He was battin' around cleanup. And you know how those parties get up there. A lunatic storms in off the streets . . .

TROY: And nobody notices.

PETE: Right.

AL: Well, I noticed. Guy blew right past me like shit through a tin horn. But I figured I don't know this guy, whether he's nuts or what. Just leave me alone and we'll get along fine.

PETE: So he finds them upstairs and drills Holshue right as he's pullin' out to see who the fuck kicked the door in. Shot him in the back, blew his heart out his chest, and put a pattern on the wall you wouldn't believe. Like a tie-dye.

AL: And the bitch of it is, the guy thinks it's Franky that's working over his old lady at the present time so . . . you know, it's dark, what the hell does he know and what difference does it make anyway?

TROY: Right.

AL: So he starts screaming, "Andelmo, you mother-fucker," or words to that effect, right before he drills him. (*Laughs*) That's the last thing poor John heard . . . someone calling him by the wrong name.

TROY: Ah, well, what's in a name? (*Pause*) But a nice party otherwise?

PETE: That kinda put a damper on it.

TROY: It's always something, you know? That place, though . . . I don't know. I miss it. (*Pause*) Should've finished as long as I was there. I was only six credits shy when I dropped out.

AL: We all dropped out.

TROY: Yeah, but six credits . . .

AL: So what? Fuckin' B.S. in sociology. Big deal. A piece of paper, that's all it is. You can't do anything with it.

PETE: Well, maybe one thing.

AL: Nah. It's too rough for toilet paper.

TROY: Yeah, but I'm just sayin', as long as I was up there . . .

AL: Then you should've finished. Who was stopping you?

TROY: No one. It just seemed ridiculous at the time since I was making more moving weed than I'd probably ever make with my degree.

AL: Then you made the right decision. Why waste your time with that shit?

TROY: Yeah, but still . . . It would've been nice to have something to fall back on.

AL: Maybe. Never thought about it much.

(*Pause*)

TROY: We were kings up there, huh?

AL: We coulda been kings here.

TROY: You think?

AL: Sure. Good place for business, even in a recession. Things are depressing enough that people need a blow now and then and not quite so bad that they can't afford it.

TROY: Perfect economic climate.

AL: Right.

(*Pause*)

PETE: So . . . how long you home for?

TROY: For good.

PETE: Huh?

AL: What do you mean, "for good?"

TROY: I mean for good, to stay, indefinitely, whatever you want to call it.

(*Pause*)

AL: I hate to tell you this, Troy, even though it shouldn't be news, but you stick around here, and "for good" won't be very long. I'll give you another day at the most and Patsy'll know where you are.

TROY: You didn't tell him?

AL: If I told him I wouldn't be talking to you now.

PETE: (*To Troy*) That's what I told you . . .

AL: He knows you're in town, but not where.

PETE: Yeah. I tell you we didn't tell him, and we didn't.

TROY: Doesn't he think that I might try and get in touch with you?

AL: No. He probably figures that you figure that we're pissed too.

TROY: Are you?

AL: What went down's between you and him.

TROY: And he's still pissed off?

AL: Pissed off ain't the word for what he is. Pissed off's what you get at your old lady when she goes apeshit with the Master Charge, or your car when it breaks down. Trivial shit like that. Pissed off doesn't describe what he feels about you. He burnt your house down, for Christ's sake. As soon as he found out you split, your fuckin' crib was a foundation. No, he's more than pissed off.

PETE: He even hears your name and he goes nuts.

AL: Yeah. He's real pissed off, Troy.

TROY: Fuck 'im if he can't take a joke.

PETE: Why'd you do it, first of all? I never could figure it out. Did you just snap all the sudden, or what?

AL: That was the most weight he ever trusted with anybody.

TROY: I told him I could move it. (*Laughs*) And I was right. That should teach him to be so trusting.

AL: It did. That's why we should be pissed off.

TROY: Yeah?

AL: Goddamn right. He's real careful now. He checks everything out real careful, and I don't like it.

TROY: Tell him about it.

AL: What am I gonna tell him?

TROY: That you don't appreciate him checking up on you. (*Al shakes his head*) Just tell him. You don't like something, then tell him.

AL: You don't tell Patsy DeBartolla anything. He tells you, you don't tell him.

TROY: Bullshit.

AL: You think?

TROY: Yeah, I think. What, do you guys bow when he walks in the room? Raise your hand to go take a leak? I don't understand this hero worship crap, not with that bastard. Sure, it might've been pretty easy bucks with him, at least compared to what we were used to. Driving to Youngstown with a trunk full of Columbian in a goddamn Mercury with air shocks. Sure, that was a pain in the ass, but just because we didn't have to do that kind of thing anymore, why should we always take our cut and like it when we knew he was skimming . . .

AL: Right, we knew. So what? He had a lot of class acts, and we weren't driving all over Bumfuck, Egypt with a lot of weight. He was setting everything up, so why not overlook a little skim here and there?

TROY: Why didn't he just say he was taking a little more for his trouble?

AL: Maybe he thought we knew.

TROY: How would we know? He didn't say anything.

AL: He didn't need to. You knew about it.

TROY: Yeah, well . . . I had to figure it out.

AL: OK, you figured it out, then you know, then you should have understood why.

TROY: I didn't understand why he didn't just tell us from the git-go . . .

AL: I don't know, I don't care. As far as I was concerned it was worth it.

TROY: Whether it was worth it or not doesn't matter. The motherfucker was trying to get over on us.

AL: He wasn't trying shit. That's in your mind. He probably didn't think anything about it. Probably took it for granted.

TROY: That's what I mean. You can't have one guy taking something for granted when it comes to money. That's not what a partnership is . . .

AL: Who cares?

TROY: I care. I'm self-employed, and if I work with some guys, then they're self-employed with me, which means we're partners, which means it's an even cut all the way around unless we decide otherwise.

AL: I'm not gonna worry about a few bucks' difference . . .

TROY: It's not the money, it's . . .

AL: The principle. Christ! I knew you were gonna say that.

TROY: I know. You finished my fucking sentence.

AL: (*To Pete*) Here's a guy that'd sell a gram to a sixth grader talking about principle.

TROY: The fuck you talking about, a sixth grader?

AL: I'm not saying you would.

TROY: You just did.

AL: It's an expression.

TROY: Oh, yeah? I never heard that one before.

AL: I'm just trying to make a point. We're not in the kind of business that you worry about principle. Principle is way the fuck on the back burner. Besides, him skimming a little bit is no reason to steal his weight.

TROY: That's for me and him to work out, and as far as that goes, he wants me . . . he can come and get me.

PETE: Said the fly to the spider.

TROY: That's real cute, Pete.

AL: Sounds about right, though, doesn't it? (*Pause. Troy walks to the telephone and picks up the receiver*) What're you doing?

TROY: I'm gonna make it easy on him. What's his number?

PETE: Don't be an asshole, Troy.

TROY: What's his number?

AL: C'mon, Troy, put the phone down. It won't do any good, anyway. He's not home.

TROY: He's not?

AL: Hasn't been all day.

TROY: How do you . . .

AL: Because I've been trying him all day.

TROY: What about?

AL: It didn't have anything to do with you. Hang up and relax.

(*Troy hangs up*)

TROY: I'm curious about these things. I can't help it.

PETE: I'd be curious too, I was you.

TROY: I just want to know who's in my corner.

AL: I'm not in anybody's corner, and if I was, it wouldn't be yours.

TROY: Thanks.

AL: Hey, you know what I mean? The fuck? You got yourself into this thing. All we can do is get you out of town immediately if not sooner because Patsy finds out, and he'll have your balls slung over his rear-view like foam rubber dice.

TROY: Aw . . . come on, Al. Give me a break. If I was worried, I wouldn't be here.

AL: Then why'd you take off in the first place? Why didn't you just steal his weight and say, "come and get it"?

TROY: Not being afraid and being stupid aren't the same thing.

AL: Sometimes they are.

PETE: Like now.

TROY: You know, it irritates me the way you guys talk about him like he's a god or something.

AL: He's not a god, he's just real good at getting even. You remember Jimmy Hung?

TROY: The fuck does he have to do with anything?

AL: You remember him?

TROY: Guy that used to do old man Lee's shit work.

AL: Yeah.

TROY: Right. So what?

PETE: You remember what happened to him?

TROY: Yeah. Again—so what?

AL: He was a nasty motherfucker, Troy.

PETE: From a Hong Kong Triad, no less. I mean, you don't get no nastier than that.

AL: That was Lee's ace. His twenty-game winner. That's why he got the call when Lee wanted Patsy taken out.

TROY: I just said I know all about this shit. I remember it well. Next day someone drops a bowling ball bag off at Lee's restaurant, and Lee hasn't bothered him since.

PETE: That's how Patsy operates.

TROY: Of course, he's a showman. See, that's one thing you guys never understood about him. You got this Chinaman going into Hazelwood looking to do bodily harm to one of that community's finest. That's Patsy's back yard. Custer had a better chance. I don't care how nasty Hung is. So Patsy's laying for him and takes him easy. Then he thinks, "What can I do that's gonna make an impression on those piss ants that work for me? Especially that smart-ass BaDeau. What can I do that will forever discourage them from getting too ambitious while they're in my employ?" And that's what he came up with. A head in a bowling bag.

PETE: It worked for me.

TROY: (*Laughs*) I gotta admit, that was funny. A chink head in a goddamn bowling bag. East meets West. Sure, it worked for you, Pete. (*To Al*) And it worked for you too, even though you probably won't admit it. But I can detect bullshit theatrics that are supposed to make an impression, and I took it as an insult.

AL: I guess we don't go that deep.

TROY: If you ever want to get anywhere in this life, Al, you have to be willing to go deep.

AL: You picked the wrong guy to go deep on.

TROY: No, I picked the perfect guy.

AL: Why's that?

TROY: Because I don't like him.

AL: Looks to me like you might've been a little desperate.

TROY: You think?

AL: Well, seeing as that boat deal went down the tubes.

TROY: What're you gonna do? It was a shot.

PETE: You weren't shrugging it off then.

AL: That's right. And you were out . . . what? Fifty thou?

TROY: Seventy.

AL: Seventy?

TROY: I sub-farmed another twenty.

AL: Oh yeah, that's right. So all the more reason to do something stupid. Plus you were putting a lot up your nose . . .

TROY: Your ass.

PETE: No, hey, you were. You probably didn't notice it . . .

AL: They never do. The guys doing two grams a day never think it matters. They think it's just a buzz. (*To Troy*) If it's just a buzz, they never would've taken it off the market. That shit . . . any kind of shit, it makes you irrational after awhile.

PETE: Weed doesn't.

AL:　No. Weed makes you senile. Fuckin' sittin' in a bar, next thing you know there's a puddle of drool between your glass and your change.

TROY:　You guys can both kiss my ass.

AL:　Why don't you admit it? Things weren't going too well. That boat gig didn't go down, you were hurtin'. You probably had a habit, but you didn't know it, which . . . still, you should've known something. I mean, Beth apparently noticed it . . .

TROY:　She didn't have anything to do with anything.

AL:　(*To Pete*) They never do.

TROY:　Fuck you.

AL:　All right, forget about all that. Fact is, you were hurtin', and you needed some quick bucks and maybe you didn't like Patsy too much, but the main reason was you wanted to make a lot in one shot.

PETE:　And two hundred thou's a lot for one shot. At least for us.

AL:　Yeah. Besides, Pete and I were in on the boat for fifty each our own selves. We took a bath, too. But you didn't see us stickin' Patsy and runnin' off with his toot.

TROY:　It wasn't something I planned. Just seemed like a good idea at a bad time. (*Pause*) Got to the point where everything I'd try to do on my own turned to shit. And I had to get away from Patsy, from being one of his niggers, no offense. And . . . there wasn't any reason for me to stick around here. With Beth gone . . . it didn't make much sense. (*Pause*) She did the best thing, I guess. She went deep too, only it was in the wrong direction. And coke didn't have anything to do with her, except for what it was doing to me. She stayed away from it most of the time. It's just . . . everybody fights with their old lady once in a while. But with us once in a while got to be more and more often, and finally it was constant. And I came home that day, and she's crying and shaking and carving my name in the coffee table with a fingernail file, and I knew it was time for her to abandon ship. Save herself . . . get the fuck away from me.

(*Pause*)

AL:　She was a good chick.

TROY:　Probably still is.

AL:　Yeah. (*Pause*) She still live in Cleveland?

TROY:　Yeah.

PETE: Shit. Cleveland. The mistake by the lake.

AL: Why don't you go up there for a little while? Stay with her. She'd probably be glad to see you.

TROY: She might. I doubt if her husband'd be too thrilled.

PETE: She got married?

TROY: Yeah, to a lawyer, of all things. Kind of a dork-wipe.

PETE: You met him?

TROY: Nah. Talked to him on the phone once. He answered and wanted to know who I was, and I told him. He didn't sound too pleased and started getting kinda shitty, like he didn't want me calling there. So I asked him, matter-of-factly, if Beth takes out her false teeth when she administers oral gratification or was she still shy about it, and hung up.

AL: Oral gratification?

TROY: I tried to word it the way a lawyer would appreciate.

PETE: Wait a minute. She has false teeth?

TROY: No, of course not. But it gave him something to think about.

PETE: Bet it did.

(*Pause*)

AL: Still, you'd be safer there. Anyplace'd be safer than around here.

TROY: That's one thing I can't understand, why I was so safe in Florida. I mean, if Patsy's such a dangerous person why didn't he have me taken care of down there?

AL: I don't know. I'm sure he had his reasons.

TROY: He probably did. That's what I mean.

AL: What's what you mean?

TROY: That he had a reason.

AL: What're you getting at?

TROY: I'm just saying, maybe he thinks I'm as nuts as he is.

AL: Are you?

TROY: I don't know. You'd have to ask him.

(*Pause. Al is getting annoyed*)

AL: Look, it's not advisable for you to stay in town. You want to, there ain't dick I can do about it, but if you're smart . . . you need a few bucks? I can help you out, take you to the airport. You rent a car?

TROY: No. Took a limo.

AL: We can drive you over.

TROY: No, I'm all right. Don't worry about it.
AL: OK. That's the last I'm gonna mention it.
TROY: Good.
AL: You're not being sensible, but . . .
TROY: What?
AL: You never were.
TROY: No, not too, I admit. But instinct . . .
AL: What about it?
TROY: *That* I got.
PETE: You can't have instincts.
(*Troy and Al turn to Pete*)
TROY: I can't?
PETE: People don't have instincts. Just animals.
TROY: Why's that?
PETE: I heard it somewhere.
TROY: That makes it a fact, you heard it somewhere?
PETE: Made sense to me. It was a guy on Carson, I think.
TROY: Oh, well . . . fuck . . . excuse me.
PETE: I'm just sayin' . . .
TROY: I know.
PETE: Making conversation.
AL: What the fuck you think me and him been doin'? Having a circle jerk and exchanging recipes? We're making goddamn conversation. I'm trying to convince this asshole, in case you didn't notice, that his homecoming isn't gonna be . . . well, there ain't gonna be ticker tape all over the fuckin' place.
TROY: Hey Al, I know what I'm getting into, so let's drop it.
AL: I'm done.
TROY: Good.
AL: Why should I care if you don't?
TROY: And I don't, so you shouldn't.
AL: But you should.
TROY: But I don't.
AL: If you say so.
TROY: I knew you'd understand.
AL: Fuck you.
TROY: Don't get hostile.
AL: No, well, you talk about insults, this is a fuckin' insult. I'm your friend. I get concerned and go out of my way to do

more than just take an interest, and all you can do is be sarcastic.

TROY: I'm sorry.

AL: You're taking this way too lightly.

TROY: I know.

AL: This is serious.

TROY: I know, I know. So let's not be.

AL: You're not. That's my point.

TROY: I'm not trying to be. I wanted to get together with you guys and have a few laughs. It's been two years, for Christ's sake. I don't want to talk about this shit.

(*Pause*)

AL: OK. You want to go out?

TROY: You think it's safe?

AL: I thought you didn't care.

TROY: Just being cautious. I'm always cautious. That's why I'm still around. (*He reaches down and taps his wooden leg*) (*Pause*)

AL: Then what do you suggest?

TROY: We might as well stick around here. I got plenty to drink. Got some coke . . . (*He takes a thermos out of the dresser and tosses it to Al*) Try some of this. It's pretty nice even though it was hit a couple times, but what're you gonna do? By the way, what's this I hear about the coke around here?

AL: What'd you hear?

TROY: I met a guy in Key West said he stayed about three months up here last winter and, well, he likes to toot. He's good for an eighth or so now and then, but he says they have garbage up here. Says he tried everywhere, friend of a friend, this and that, said at best he figured it was fifty cut, but most of it was closer to seventy-five.

PETE: So, he was dealing with Mickey Mouse.

TROY: Not always, I'm sure. The fuck? He said he was jumpin' all over.

AL: C'mon Troy, you know Patsy don't go for more than twenty-five per cent cut. It ain't twenty-five or less, then it doesn't go out. At least not with us. We're dealing with good people, executive types, fuckin' patent attorneys, that kinda thing. We start cutting too much, they'll pick up on it right away, and they won't even bother.

TROY: I figured he must've scored with you guys at least once.

AL: Not if he said he was getting garbage. (*Pause*) I don't even want to talk about it. (*He tosses the thermos back to Troy*) It's an insult.

TROY: (*Laughs*) Another insult? Holy fuck, Al, you and I aren't getting along too well. I thought maybe Patsy was slippin', was all I meant.

AL: No chance.

TROY: Then sorry I brought it up. Anyway, I was telling Pete about this chick, this dancer downstairs. She said she'd stop up if I called.

AL: And do what?

TROY: What do you think?

(*Pause*)

AL: I don't care. It's your party.

PETE: If the chick's low rent though, you know . . . I'll let her suck me off, but that's about it. Go stickin' it in something like that, you don't know where it's been and what's been in there, your cock ends up looking like a zucchini.

(*Pause*)

AL: Maybe we should go out.

TROY: I don't wanna go out.

AL: C'mon, Troy. What do you want to stay here for?

TROY: I just said. It's safer.

AL: Safer than what?

TROY: I think you know.

AL: You think I know what? What're you talking about?

TROY: You want the truth, Al, I don't give a rat's ass if you stay or not. You've been on my shit ever since you got here.

AL: Did it ever occur to you that maybe why that is, is because I like you?

TROY: Is that why?

AL: Yeah.

TROY: Then I apologize.

AL: So do I. I'm just nervous, y'know? This is a bad situation, this here. Pete and I are caught in the middle of this shit, and it's frayin' the fuck out of my nerves.

PETE: Me, too.

AL: I mean, you can understand that we're on the spot . . . (*Troy is nodding his head impatiently as he picks up the phone and dials*) What're you doing?

TROY: Calling the chick.

AL: Now? I'm right in the middle of some emotional shit here.

TROY: Yeah, I know. But I have to catch her between shows.

AL: Oh, well ... fuck it then. Why should I ...

TROY: Shhh! (*On phone*) Hello? Yeah, is Wendy around? (*Pause*)

AL: (*To Pete*) This is ridiculous. (*Pete nods*)

TROY: (*On phone*) This is Troy BaDeau from 514. She wanted me to call her. (*A beat*) OK. (*To Al and Pete*) She went to get her. Wait'll you see this sleaze.

PETE: Her name's Wendy?

TROY: Yeah. Wendy the Whip Lady.

PETE: (*To Al*) Whip Lady?

TROY: (*On phone*) Who's this? (*Pause*) I know who I am, who are you? (*Pause*) Her manager? That's nice. The fuck's she need a manager for to stick a whip handle up her snatch? (*A beat*) Hello? Hello?

PETE: (*To Al*) Great. We don't have time for this, Al.

TROY: (*As he hangs up*) Asshole. That man has no sense of humor.

AL: You offended somebody?

TROY: I think so.

PETE: Her manager?

TROY: That's what he said.

PETE: Is he coming up, you think?

TROY: I don't know. Depends on what kind of guy he is. He might be the kind that'll let a remark slide. But then he might be a hard ass that you say anything to, it's like you pissed in his cornflakes.

AL: How'd you ever live this long? I swear to God, you make more enemies just by opening your big mouth. You bitch about me being hostile, but you can't get enough. You have to call room service.

TROY: That guy ain't coming up.

AL: How would you know? You don't know who you just talked to. You don't know his history. He could be a time bomb. People been dumpin' on him all his life, and he's about at his breaking point. He's starting to get goofy. He might get his rocks off sitting at home shaving the scales off his goldfish with a razor blade. You don't know ... because you don't know his history.

TROY: His history? The fuck do I . . . I don't wanna know his history. I just talked to the guy for ten seconds, and I can conclude that he's an asshole already. So why would I want to know more than that?

AL: You might not have a choice. That might be his wife, the whip lady. If he comes up sayin' shit like, "That's my wife, motherfucker," then you learn something about the guy.

PETE: Yeah. That he's got a wife with waffles that grind-fucks a whip handle . . .

AL: And he doesn't like guys calling her up and then questioning him about the necessity of his job. (*To Pete*) Waffles?

TROY: What kinda guy has his wife up there? Come on, let's be serious. It was an innocent phone call, it's no big deal. Nothing's gonna come out of it, believe me. Because I tell you what, these so-called managers, these guys just take their fifteen or twenty per cent off the top and maybe cop a little head now and then, but that's it. When it comes to defending the honor of their clients . . . there's nothing to defend. What the hell do they expect you got this pig doin' pelvic thrusts in front of some deviate with slobber on his chin who hasn't got it up in years but thinks he's starting to so he takes a dive at her bush right there on the stage. They have to put up with that shit all the time. So why should this guy get bent out of shape over a remark on the phone?

(*A loud pounding on the door*)

PETE: I guess this guy's a little different.

TROY: How come nobody has a sense of humor anymore? (*The pounding continues*)

MANAGER: (*Through the door*) Open the fuckin' door before I break it down!

TROY: Sounds like he means it. (*He walks to the door*) Got any suggestions?

AL: I'm dry.

PETE: Don't look at me.

(*Troy opens the door and the manager, red-faced and furious, walks into the room*)

MANAGER: (*To Troy*) You the one that put in the call downstairs?

TROY: Hey, come on pal, where's your sense of humor?

MANAGER: Do you think this is funny?

TROY: Well . . . no. I guess not.

MANAGER: Then why the hell should I have a sense of humor?

TROY: I think it would help, considering the circumstances.

MANAGER: What circumstances?

TROY: Well, you're outnumbered, for one thing. And these two gentlemen here, they are on a mission of sorts, and they need as little interference as possible and you, my friend, are interference. (*To Pete and Al*) Isn't that right, gentlemen?

AL: I don't know what you're talking about.

TROY: Don't you?

AL: No, I don't.

TROY: Either you're a liar, or I made a mistake.

AL: I think you made a mistake.

TROY: I don't think so.

AL: Think what you want, Troy. Go ahead and think what you want.

TROY: So I'm right, then. That's the same thing as saying I'm right.

AL: Think what you want.

TROY: I am thinking what I want, and I don't like what I'm thinking.

AL: That's your problem, then. How can I help . . .

MANAGER: (*Impatiently to Troy*) All I want to know is, was it you that called Wendy?

TROY: I thought it was pretty obvious.

MANAGER: Then this is between you and me. (*To Al*) Is that OK?

AL: I don't give a shit.

MANAGER: Thank you.

(*The manager sucker-punches Troy and knocks him to the floor, where he lies, moaning. Pete and Al do not move*)

MANAGER: (*To Troy*) I think you need a little lesson in manners . . . (*Mockingly*) friend. (*He kicks Troy in the ribs*)

AL: (*To the manager*) OK, buddy, you made your point. Now why don't you go back to whatever it was you were doing and leave us alone.

MANAGER: I ain't finished yet.

AL: I think you are.

MANAGER: In case you haven't noticed, I ain't exactly worried about the odds.

AL: I noticed, and I'm impressed. But unless you leave right now, you can start.

MANAGER: Start what?

AL: Worrying.

MANAGER: Is that right?

(*The manager moves toward Al but stops when he sees Pete draw a gun from inside his coat*)

PETE: I think you better go. (*He grabs the manager, who is quite frightened, and pulls him away from Al*)

PETE: Go back to the whip lady and forget you ever came up here. OK?

MANAGER: Hey look, I don't know what this is all about, but . . .

AL: But you don't want to know. If you're smart you want to leave. Right?

MANAGER: Yeah, sure. I don't want no trouble with you guys.

PETE: I thought you weren't worried about the odds . . .

AL: Never mind that shit, Pete. No sense rubbin' his face in it. My man fucked up. (*To Manager*) Didn't you?

MANAGER: Yeah.

AL: But we won't hold that against you because you look like a smart guy. And if you are, then you know that it would be to your definite fuckin' advantage to forget what we look like real fast. You understand what I mean?

MANAGER: Yeah . . . I think so.

AL: What?

MANAGER: Huh?

AL: What am I talking about?

MANAGER: I was never here.

AL: That's the idea. (*He nods to Pete, and Pete shoves the manager toward the door*) Be a good boy and you'll never see us again.

(*The manager exits*)

PETE: I don't trust that guy.

AL: Neither do I. Looks like the type that holds a grudge, you point a gun at him. He'll mumble and apologize his way out of a situation like this, then go down to his car and get a grenade launcher out of the trunk.

TROY: (*With some difficulty*) You always expect the worst, don't you, Al?

AL: That's what it's all about, Troy. Expect the worst, and you won't be surprised. That's the key.

TROY: Key to what?

AL: Longevity. To staying around longer than the other guy. (*Pause. He turns to Pete*) I think the fire escape is our best bet. Better than waltzing him through the lobby.

PETE: What do we got out there?

AL: An alley, I think.

PETE: I'll take a look.

(*Troy attempts to get to his feet*)

AL: (*To Pete*) Wait a minute. Help me up with him.

(*They help him up*)

TROY: Let me sit on the bed. I don't feel too good.

AL: OK. No problem.

(*They sit Troy down on the bed. Al sits beside him. Pete stands with his gun aimed at Troy*)

TROY: Think I got a rib stuck in my lung.

AL: Nah. It ain't that bad.

TROY: The fuck would you know?

(*Pause*)

AL: I'm sorry, Troy.

TROY: I kinda figured this. You couldn't wait to get me outa here.

AL: That was the plan.

TROY: Well . . . just so it's not personal.

AL: It's not. We're just looking out for our partner.

TROY: Your partner?

AL: Patsy.

TROY: He's your partner? He's not your partner. In no way, shape, or form is he your partner.

AL: I'm not talking about who does what or who calls the shots. I ain't even talking about whether or not I like the guy. The point is we work together, and we do all right. He doesn't fuck us, we don't fuck him. Now, you stuck it up his ass for five pounds. You stuck him, not me, not Pete. But he's our partner, and he never stuck us. So, that being the case, don't you think we ought to help him do something about it?

TROY: Why the hell would I think that? I mean, considering my position at the present time.

AL: I don't mean think that. I mean, you understand why we might be obligated?

TROY: Oh, sure, I understand. Do unto others as they might do unto you.

AL: Well, in a way . . . yeah.

TROY: And I guess money didn't have anything to do with it.

AL: What do you mean by that?

TROY: C'mon, Al. What am I worth? (*Pause*) Don't tell me you're doing it for nothing.

(*Pause*)

AL: Why'd you come back, Troy? You really put us on the spot.

TROY: (*Laughs*) Why'd I do this, why'd I do that? The fuck do I know? (*Pause*) I just do things. (*Pause*) I came back because I wanted to. I was homesick, maybe. I was losing my edge, the home-field advantage. Maybe I knew that if I didn't come back now, I never would, and I didn't want that. (*Pause*) I like it here. That's why I came back.

AL: You should've talked yourself out of it.

TROY: Why the hell would I do that once I made up my mind what I was gonna do? You put doubt in the back of your mind, and eventually it eats its way to the front, and next thing you know your commitment goes right down the shitter.

PETE: Commitment?

TROY: That's right, goddamn commitment. You commit yourself to something, and that's it. It's gotta be tunnel vision. Point A to point B. You don't think about the consequences. You don't worry about what . . .

AL: That's your problem, Troy. You don't think and you don't worry.

TROY: What do I have to worry about? Dying? (*Laughs*) I fucking doubt it. There's bound to be things worse than dying, and one of them might be waking up in a goddamn hospital ward with an itch on the bottom of your foot that you can't scratch because you don't have that foot any more. Especially when I got this old bastard next to me in constant pain that's screaming for doctors and nurses and Jesus H. Christ Almighty at the top of his lungs. You think that didn't get on my nerves, hearing the Lord's name in vain at two hundred decibels every ten seconds? And he's throwing in a middle initial that doesn't even belong there. So I figured it must've been the six years I went to Catholic schools that conditioned me to want to get up and throttle that fucker. But I had to lie there and listen to it and wish to God that they would've named him something that didn't have those violent "J" and "K" sounds, so people wouldn't even want to use it in vain. Something like . . . like Barry Manilow. (*Pause. Pete and Al exchange confused glances. Troy continues*) That's when you know that nothing really matters any more. I have one and a half legs, an imaginary itch, and two feds strolling around out in the hallway like a couple of vultures ready to grill me as soon as the doctor says it's OK, and all I can think about is how nice it would've been if our savior was named after a sissified piano player that wouldn't even be born for another two thousand years. (*Pause*) How worse off am I gonna be than that, that I gotta think everything out before I do something? I'm not that concerned about survival, and that's to my advantage, don't you think, Al?

AL: I don't know, Troy. You lost me after the itchy foot part.

TROY: It's a hard thing to explain, I guess.

PETE: (*To Al*) We don't have time for this.

AL: (*Annoyed*) Then go check the fuckin' window.

PETE: Hey, you don't have to get shitty with me.

AL: You're getting on my nerves, Pete. I can't help it. You do that to me sometimes. You want to check the window, then check the window.

PETE: I'll check the window, then.

AL: Good. Check the window.

(*Pete mutters something under his breath as he walks to the window, opens it, and looks out. Al turns to watch him and when he does, Troy, in a single motion, removes his gun from beneath his pillow and places the tip of the barrel at the base of Al's neck. Al stiffens. Pete is oblivious to this action*)

PETE: You were right, it's an alley.

AL: Uh . . . never mind, Pete. Forget about it.

PETE: What're you talking about, forget about it? Let's get . . . (*He turns around to face them*)

TROY: Put it down, Pete. On the end of the bed. Real slow. (*Pete doesn't move. He keeps his gun aimed in the direction of the bed*)

AL: Do it, Pete.

PETE: He don't have the balls to use it.

AL: I don't want to debate about whether he's gonna

use it or not when he's got it to my fuckin' head! Now put it down!

TROY: Real slow, Pete.

(*Pete places his gun on the bed*)

TROY: Now back up to the wall.

(*Pete backs up to the wall on the other side of the room. Troy frisks Al with his free hand and removes a gun from inside Al's coat*)

TROY: OK, Al. You go over with Pete.

(*Al gets up and walks over beside Pete*)

PETE: Where'd he get the piece?

AL: He sleeps with it.

PETE: Figures.

(*Troy picks up Pete's gun and places it, along with Al's gun, on the night table*)

TROY: Got myself a regular arsenal here. How quickly the tide turns, huh? You should've left it like you said, Al. What went down was between me and Patsy.

AL: Seems that way.

TROY: I was hoping that was the case.

AL: Why's that?

TROY: Because I thought maybe, like a fucking idiot, that we might get together again.

AL: The three of us?

TROY: Sure. Why not?

PETE: For one thing, there's no way you could work around here again. No one would trust you.

TROY: You know, I think trust is overrated. If you're careful enough, you don't have to worry about trusting anyone. That's one thing about Patsy is he gets careless too often. He's careless, and he trusts people he shouldn't trust.

AL: Like you.

TROY: Like me. Exactly. It's a hard habit to break, being careless, and Patsy, try as he probably did, never quite broke it.

AL: That sounds like the pot calling the kettle, don't it Pete? Guy gets sucked in by some Cubans, loses a leg, and talks about being careless.

TROY: You don't know what the circumstances were. Down there it's easy to get into the high roller lifestyle where you're blowin' five bills a night at a fucking bar and scoring enough pussy to sink a ship and then find out the next day that a guy you were partying with two weeks ago, they found him in a swamp with his tongue pulled through his throat. You can only be so careful.

AL: I'm just sayin' . . .

TROY: If you don't know of what the fuck you speak, then why bring it up? I try to learn from my mistakes. Problem with Patsy is . . . he doesn't think he makes any.

AL: I don't see him setting his leg next to the bed every night, though. You may learn from your mistakes, but at least his body's intact.

(*Troy smiles and sets the gun down*)

TROY: Sleep on it, why don't you?

AL: You mean we can go?

TROY: What the fuck am I gonna do with you? Hold you hostage? Start blasting away and wait till the cops show up, so they can find me with two guys bleeding all over the floor? There isn't anything I can do. You said it wasn't personal, right?

AL: Right.

TROY: Then I won't take it personal. You were just looking out for your partner, if you want to call him that, and . . . that's OK. I can't bitch about it. I'd expect the same if you guys were working with me. One thing about this business, and I don't give a shit who you are, you need guys that are gonna back you one hundred per cent, or you're done. Might as well fold up the tents and go hustle life insurance or something ridiculous like that, be making two-fifty a week if you're lucky. (*Pause*) But, like I said, think it over. It could be like old times. Al, you'd be a good right hand like you were with Patsy. And Pete . . . well, you're about as intelligent as a potted plant, but you'll go where you're pointed.

PETE: Fuck you.

TROY: (*Shrugs*) Suit yourself.

AL: There's no way . . . I don't think, Troy.

TROY: Just say you'll think about it.

AL: I'll think about it.

TROY: What about you, Pete? (*Pete glares at him*) This guy's real true blue, isn't he, Al? What happened? Did Patsy remove a thorn from his paw?

AL: He'll think about it, too. But you still got Patsy to worry about.

TROY: I don't worry, remember? Besides, I think I have that situation handled.

AL: You think?

TROY: Yeah, I do.

AL: If you say so.

TROY: You don't have to take my word for it. I know what it takes to make an impression around here. And that reminds me, I want you to take something off my hands.

AL: Like what?

TROY: Something I should've told you about before, but I was waiting for the right time.

AL: And this is the right time?

TROY: Whether it is or not doesn't matter any more. I've been keeping it around all day, and I'd appreciate it if you could dump it somewhere. See, it kinda makes the air . . . unpleasant.

(*He reaches under the bed and removes a bowling ball bag. He tosses it to Al*)

AL: What the . . .

(*Al and Pete wince as the smell becomes overwhelming. Al runs his hand along the bottom of the bag where it appears to be wet and flinches so suddenly that he drops it on the floor. It lands with a sickening, squishy thud. They back away, staring at the bag in horror*)

TROY: It's Patsy. (*Laughs*) Your partner.

(*He continues laughing as Al and Pete stare at the bag*)

Blackout

John McNamara
PRESENT TENSE

John McNamara

When composer Stephen Sondheim was president of the Dramatists Guild in 1981, he initiated a program to select and produce the work of aspiring young playwrights. Limited to writers eighteen and under, the first Young Playwrights Festival drew 732 entries from thirty-five states. Ten of these scripts were selected for presentation at the Circle Repertory Company in New York. The success of the event in quality as well as quantity prompted the Dramatists Guild to take on the project as an annual event, and results continue to be impressive.

One of the remarkable talents discovered in the 1982 Festival is John McNamara. Eighteen years old at the time he submitted his play *Present Tense*, he had already been writing plays for five years. To facilitate production of his earlier works, Mr. McNamara had organized his own production company in his hometown, Grand Rapids, Michigan. In New York *Present Tense* drew plaudits from the critics. Robert Massa of the *Village Voice* reported: "John McNamara's *Present Tense*, the brightest of the comic plays, is a monologue with fantasy vignettes in the James Thurber-Woody Allen vein. It concerns a teenage boy who is convinced his girlfriend is about to rush back into the arms of her ex, the surly captain of the football team. There are some hilarious lines and the writing is buoyant throughout." And John Patterson, reviewing the play for *The Villager*, reflected: "McNamara's tight dialogue, loving though amused point of view, and detailed drawing of Norm keep our attention throughout. By play's end Norm Prescott is a welcome guest in both our memories and imaginations."

After Mr. McNamara's first success, the North Light Repertory Company of Chicago produced his *The Early Male Years*, a trilogy of one-acts that included *Present Tense*, and in 1983 CBS-TV Afternoon Playhouse presented his *Revenge of the Nerd*. He also participated in the 1983 Writers' Guild Television Comedy Class, conducted by Lee Kalcheim. Continuing to study as he wrote, Mr. McNamara recently was graduated from New York University. We look forward to more fine work from this accomplished young playwright and from the Young Playwrights Festival that helped to discover him.

Characters:

NORM PRESCOTT
ANN ALLEN
JERRY MELNICKER
A BLONDE
MARGIE EATON
DOUG WILLARD
MOTHER'S VOICE

Scene:

We are in Norm Prescott's bedroom. It is the typical bedroom of a seventeen-year-old American male. Various movie posters surround a single bed—which is unmade—a dresser, a table and chair, and a closet. On the dresser is a picture of a pretty girl about Norm's age. Strewn about the room are various items of clothing, books, papers, dirty magazines, etc.

The lights come up and we see Norm lying on the bed, holding the telephone on his chest. He tips his head upward, looks us over for a moment, and then addresses us.

NORM: Excuse me, but how many people here are virgins? I know that's a really embarrassing question, and there's no reason to raise your hands. Especially for the people here on their first date. It's just that a lot of things have been on my mind lately, and basically one of them is sex . . . I've got nothing against sex. But unfortunately it's got nothing against me either. (*A nervous laugh. He clears his throat*) Which is part of the problem, but not really. You see, I've got this girlfriend, Ann Allen. (*Picks up her picture and shows it to us*) This is her. She's a knockout, right? And she's also nice and wonderful and sweet and very smart. Let's face it, she's the light of my life, and I never want to change the bulb. Everyone tells me how lucky I am. I think I heard one person tell Ann how lucky she is. My mother. Anyway, we've got this really wonderful teenage relationship . . .

(*Lights fade and come up center stage only. Ann Allen, indeed a very pretty girl of seventeen, comes on. She eyes Norm lovingly and sighs*)

Hi, Ann.

ANN: Oh, Norm, I've missed you so much. (*She kisses him*) You look so handsome today. So virile, so . . .

NORM: Masculine.

ANN: Oh, yes, yes. Have I told you how lucky I am to have you?

NORM: Not since lunch.

ANN: I am. I'm so lucky to have someone so handsome. So virile, so . . . so . . .

NORM: Masculine.

ANN: Oh, yes, yes, yes . . .

NORM: (*Addressing audience; Ann freezes*) Oh, who am I kidding? Let's face it, it's not a wonderful teenage relationship. It's fraught with guilt, despair, hopelessness, jealousy, pity and fear. I feel like I'm living in a Dostoyevsky novel.

(*Lights fade to black. We hear two bodies rustling. Then:*)

ANN'S VOICE: Don't.

NORM'S VOICE: Why not?

ANN'S VOICE: Because.

NORM'S VOICE: Because why?

ANN'S VOICE: Because . . . because. (*Silence*) Please, Norm.

NORM'S VOICE: But I'm not doing that any more.

ANN'S VOICE: I don't like what you're doing now, either.

NORM'S VOICE: Okay, why don't we draw up a series of boundaries, like the United Nations. Everywhere I can't go is Communist territory.

(*Silence again*)

ANN'S VOICE: Norm . . . !

NORM'S VOICE: OK, that's it! Revoke my visa!

(*The lights come up. Ann is sitting on the bed, buttoning her blouse. Norm is downstage addressing us*)

NORM: Every time! This happens every time! The Battle of the Blouse! And I know what you're all thinking. That I'm just one of these Joes out for a good time. Love 'em and leave 'em. And I realize I may seem very suave and devil-may-care to you, but I love Ann. I mean, I've been out with other girls before. Like . . . er, uh . . . Mary Jo Jenkowski, who is so huge she's getting curvature of the spine. And Sally Billings, who invented a whole new strain of social disease. The point of this being, I've been around, I'm no kid. But with Ann it's different. It's like I want to . . . to . . . own her. I think of her every minute of the day. When I'm walking, talking, sleeping, eating. Once I sculpted her face in my mashed potatoes. But what makes it rotten is, I have no idea if she feels the same way about me. Okay, she *is* my girlfriend and she's never turned me down for a date—except the time she had her wisdom teeth removed. She said she didn't want to bleed on me. Other than that, though, dating is really good. But we never talk. Well, we talk, but it's never about anything . . .

(*Ann is holding a newspaper, scanning the movie section*)

ANN: What about a comedy?

NORM: I want to see a love story.

ANN: I hate love stories. Let's see a war movie.

NORM: Do you love me, Ann?

ANN: Did you get your allowance this week? Can we go to dinner, too?

NORM: If you don't love me, say so. I want to hear it. I can take it. When I kill myself, I'll make it look like an accident so you won't be embarrassed.

ANN: Nut. (*She shakes her head and laughs*)

NORM: You do love me.

ANN: Let's see a monster movie.

(*Lights on Ann fade. Norm talks to us*)

NORM: You see how distant she is? How she sidesteps even the subtlest questions? I could never figure out why. Until two weeks ago, when . . .

(*Lights come up on Jerry Melnicker, a friend of Norm's*)

JERRY: (*Chewing on a piece of gum*) Hey, Norm, guess what I heard? You know Ann? You know, your girlfriend? You know who she used to go out with? Doug Willard, for like six months. Isn't that bizarre? Who'd think any girl who had Doug Willard would ever want to go out with you? (*Laughs. Pause*) What? . . . What are you getting so upset about? . . . Oh, yeah, well so's your mother.

(*Lights fade and Jerry disappears*)

NORM: I know he's an idiot. I know he shouldn't bother me. But . . . do you know who Doug Willard is? He's the captain of the football team, the captain of the swim team, the captain of the baseball team. The Commander-in-Chief of interscholastic sports.

(*Doug Willard appears in a spotlight, dressed in only a bathing suit. He is tall, blond, and good-looking. He smiles a dazzling smile, and his muscles ripple*)

NORM: But the worst part is, I know him. I see him every

day. In addition to everything else, Doug Willard is the editor of the school paper, and as an editor he makes one hell of a swimmer. But I don't want to get into personalities, particularly since Doug is somewhat lacking in that area. OK, yeah, you could say he's relatively attractive in a physical way but I . . . I've got . . . heh, heh . . . I . . .

(*Ann comes on in a spotlight of her own. She eyes Doug lustfully. She crosses to him and throws her arms around him*)

NORM: I've got nothing! What have I got? I'm pale, I'm skinny, I can't use aftershave because it gives me pimples.

(*Doug grabs Ann. They fall to the floor, moaning. Lights fade on them. Norm sits and stares straight ahead for a long time*)

NORM: It's stupid, right? Jerry didn't tell me he caught them in the back of a Thunderbird, he told me they *used* to go out together. It's over. (*He stands*) Oh, yeah? Well, then why hasn't she called yet? Huh? Can you tell me that? Because tonight is the night of the prom. I mean, this is something that Ann and I have been planning for weeks. And do you know what she told me last week?

(*Ann appears, holding a telephone. Norm holds one also*)

ANN: . . . oh, and also I've kind of got some bad news.

NORM: Oh, yeah? What's that?

ANN: Well, I'm not sure I'm going to be able to make it to the prom Saturday night. (*Pause. Norm looks as if he might throw up*) Norm? Are you there?

NORM: Uh huh.

ANN: I'm not sure or anything. It depends on if my Aunt Gladys gets better. You know the one who lives in Kalkaska? She's got bad gallstones, and we might have to go up and visit her. But I won't know for sure until Saturday morning. (*Pause again*) Norm?

NORM: Mm, hm.

ANN: Are you mad?

NORM: No, no. Saturday's fine.

ANN: OK, well, I'll see you in school tomorrow.

NORM: Right. 'Bye.

ANN: 'Bye. (*Lights on Ann fade*)

NORM: Do you know what time it is? Noon. It is no longer Saturday morning, it is Saturday afternoon. And guess who hasn't called? (*He crosses up near the bed and looks at a tuxedo hanging there. It is a typical prom tux; white with lots of blue ruffles and trim*) I explained the whole thing to the guy at the tuxedo shop. You know how it's sometimes easier to spill your guts out to a total stranger? And he was very compassionate, let me have a special deal. I'm renting it by the hour. (*Looks at his watch*) Yep, there goes another two-and-a-quarter. Okay, sure, I know what you're saying. They broke up, it's over. But I know it wasn't a real break-up. It was just a scene in one of those torrid Warner Brothers relationships.

(*Lights up on Doug and Ann, each dressed in a trench coat and felt hat. There is the sound of a train whistle in the distance. A blast of steam shoots out across the stage*)

DOUG: This is it.

ANN: Yes.

DOUG: Any regrets?

ANN: A few. But you know I'll always love you. Even if I start going out with some little schmuck who tries to take my bra off on the couch.

(*They both turn and look at Norm*)

DOUG: What do you say? One more for old times' sake?

ANN: Sure.

(*They fall to the floor and tear each others' clothes off*)

NORM: Stop it! Stop it! Haven't you two got any sense of decency? (*Lights come down on Doug and Ann*) OK, so I'm a little paranoid.

MOTHER'S VOICE: Norm!

NORM: Yeah, Mom?

MOTHER'S VOICE: Your friend Jerry is here to see you.

NORM: All right, send him up.

JERRY: (*Off*) Norm, hey, Norm . . . (*Jerry enters*) Hey, Norm, y'know tonight? What are you doing tonight?

NORM: (*A glance at the tux*) I don't know. Why?

JERRY: Great, great. There are these two girls I met last night, they go to the junior college and, y'know, we were talking, and they want to go out tonight. But you know how girls are, they want to go together, so I've got to find somebody else, and I thought, "Hey, your old buddy Norm'll help you out," soooo . . .

NORM: Aw, I don't know, Jerry.

JERRY: Hey, you think they're ugly, right? Well, I've got a picture of them right here. (*He takes a snapshot out of his back pocket and hands it to Norm*) I told them that I was gonna have to go around looking for another guy to go out, so I made them take that picture in the Foto-Now Booth at the mall.

NORM: Which one would I get?

JERRY: Either one. They don't care. Y'know, I was thinking, halfway through the night we could switch off . . .

NORM: (*Looking at the picture*) Wow. Boy, Jerry, they really
are—What am I saying? (*Hands the picture back*) I can't go out
with other girls. What about Ann?

JERRY: Oh, Ann, schmann. You shouldn't tie yourself down
the way you do.

NORM: No, Jerry. I'm sorry. I can't do it.

JERRY: But, Norm . . .

NORM: It just wouldn't . . . feel right.

JERRY: Norm, how long have we known each other?

NORM: A long time, Jerry.

JERRY: That's right, a long time. I'm your buddy, Norm.
Do you think I like seeing you like this? You think I haven't
noticed the way you've been acting? Mumbling, moaning,
twitching. You're like an ad for Preparation H . . . I'm not
saying Ann's not great. I think she's a great girl, Norm. Everybody thinks she's the best.

NORM: What does *that* mean?

JERRY: It's just an expression . . . But Norm, Ann is not
the earth and sky; you're not stranded with her on a desert
island. (*Jerry has made his way around to where the tuxedo is hanging. He eyes it for a moment, looks at Norm, raises an amazed eyebrow,
then continues*) Look, I'm gonna go home and try and get my
dad's convertible. Give me a call if you change your mind.
And remember. These are junior college girls. A once-in-a-
lifetime chance. (*Jerry gives Norm one last look, turns, and walks
out of the room*)

NORM: Once-in-a-lifetime is right. How could I be so stupid? Ann's never gonna call. God, you should have seen that
girl. The blonde one . . . (*A blonde appears. She looks at Norm*)
Her body was so . . . geometric. She probably would have been
really dumb, and really easy. (*The blonde moves toward Norm.
He gives her what he thinks is a sexy look*) Hey, baby. Come here
often?

BLONDE: Beat it, creep. (*She struts off*)

NORM: I can't even have fun in my imagination. It's better
than real life, though. Speaking of which, there's something
you ought to see, something that happened the other day. It
was in school . . .

(*Lighting change. A bell rings. We hear voices, as if we are in a hallway. Several lockers appear. Ann walks on. She leafs through a textbook. Doug comes from behind the lockers and runs into Ann. She drops her books. Doug picks them up for her)*

ANN: *(Surprised)* Doug, hi.

DOUG: Hi, Ann. How are you?

ANN: Fine. I haven't seen you around school much lately.

DOUG: Oh, I've got all my classes in the morning.

ANN: That explains it. I've got most of mine in the after-noon.

DOUG: Yeah.

ANN: Well . . .

(There is an awkward pause)

DOUG: Well . . .

ANN: I've got to get going.

DOUG: I'll see you later, then.

ANN: 'Bye.

(They walk off in opposite directions)

NORM: Looked perfectly innocent, didn't it? Yes, to the untrained eye that was the chance meeting of two people who hadn't seen each other in a long time. But to the expert . . . *(Doug and Ann come back on, moving as if they were a film being run backward at high speed. They go quickly and silently through every movement in reverse. When Doug is back behind the lockers, they begin to move forward again at normal speed. Doug comes from behind the lockers and runs into Ann. Norm, pointer in hand, freezes the action)* Exhibit A, Doug running into Ann, a lame excuse so that two bodies lusting for one another can touch for a brief moment . . . *(Action proceeds. Ann drops her books. Doug reaches down, picks them up, and hands them to her)* Let's take that again, in slow motion. *(Action is rewound. Then, in slow motion, Doug reaches down and picks up the books)* Notice how, as he bends over, his eyes toil over her legs, how her eyes stare at his back. And as he gives her the books, his hand is passionately drawn to hers. Now the conversation.

ANN: *(Playfully, a smile)* Doug . . . hi. *(Bats her eyes)*

DOUG: *(Very macho)* Hey, Annie, how are you?

NORM: "How are you?" clearly translates to, "May I put my hand on your knee?"

ANN: Fine. I haven't seen you around school much.

NORM: . . . "But I'd like to."

DOUG: *(Moves close)* Oh, I've got all my classes in the morn-ing.

ANN: That explains it. I've got most of mine in the afternoon.

DOUG: (*Grins*) Yeah.

ANN: (*Expectantly*) Well . . .

DOUG: (*Eyeing her*) *Well* . . .

ANN: I've *got* to get going.

DOUG: I'll see you later, then.

ANN: 'Bye.

(*They stop, stare at one another, and . . . fall to the ground and tear each others' clothes off*)

NORM: For Christ's sake, will you stop already??? You guys ought to have your hormones removed. (*They fade out. Norm sits and breathes a heavy sigh*) Why doesn't she call? What's really going on? Why am I sitting here slowly going out of my mind? (*Norm stands and begins to pace*) Maybe if I was more like Doug. God, you should see the way he is with women. There's this one girl who works on the paper. Margie Eaton . . .

(*Doug appears, wearing a button-down shirt and glasses. Margie Eaton, eighteen and beautiful in a cheerleaderish sort of way, walks on*)

DOUG: Uh, Margie . . .

MARGIE: Yes?

DOUG: About this article you wrote for the school paper . . .

MARGIE: Did you like it, Doug?

DOUG: Oh, yes, very much. You've got a teriffic sense of the language.

NORM: (*A short laugh*) I wonder who read it to him.

DOUG: But I think it'll need a rewrite.

MARGIE: Oh?

DOUG: I think we should . . . go over it together.

MARGIE: (*Smiles big*) Oh. (*She moves close to him*)

DOUG: My place? Eight o'clock tonight?

MARGIE: Sure.

(*Then, all at once, Margie reaches over and tears Doug's shirt open, revealing a Superman "S." At the same time she slips the glasses off and smiles dynamically. Norm turns and looks at us, just as surprised as we are. Doug and Margie fade out*)

NORM: . . . I've really been spending too much time alone . . . (*He flops down on the bed*) Why doesn't she call? Even if it's bad news, I'll be out of my misery. God, I'd give anything for it to be the way it was. I mean, Ann and I have had some pretty good times.

(*Ann appears*)

ANN: Hey, Norm, close your eyes; I've got a big surprise for you.

NORM: What is it?

ANN: Close the eyes and you'll find out.

(*Norm closes his eyes. Ann moves toward him. Her hands are behind her back*)

NORM: (*Opening his eyes*) No, forget it, I don't trust you.

ANN: Don't trust me? Norm, what is an emotional commitment? What is a relationship? It's *based* on trust. If you're committed to me, you have to trust me. (*Norm closes his eyes. Ann takes out a toy gun and squirts water in Norm's face*) Happy April Fools' Day.

NORM: It's not April Fools' Day.

ANN: Every day with you is April Fools' Day.

NORM: (*Mock tough*) Oh, yeah? Well, you listen to me and listen good . . . You better gimme that gun, see, because I know that you know that we both know that you killed Lee No, the Chinese bookie . . .

ANN: (*Laughing*) Keep away, creep-o, or I'll . . .

NORM: You want to shoot? Go on. I got a high rate of saturation. (*Ann shoots again*) Now you are going to get it . . . (*He starts to chase her. She runs out of the room*)

MOTHER'S VOICE: Norm!

NORM: Yes, Mom?

MOTHER'S VOICE: There's someone here to see you.

NORM: Probably Jerry again. I told him I didn't want to have anything to do with him and the Bobbsey Twins . . .

(*Suddenly, Doug Willard appears in the doorway. Norm jumps as if seeing a ghost, and we realize this is no fantasy*)

DOUG: Hey, little guy, how ya doin'?

NORM: Ah, Dou-Dou-Dou . . . uh . . .

DOUG: Mind if I come in?

NORM: Ah, n-n-n . . . uh . . .

DOUG: Nice room, very nice.

NORM: Ah, w-w-w . . . uh . . .

DOUG: (*Sees the tux; unconvincingly*) Nice tux. (*Norm sits on the bed, very weak. Doug picks up on this and slaps a hardy hand on his shoulder*) You feel okay? (*Norm manages a nod. Doug opens a notebook he is carrying*) Listen, the reason I stopped by was, I want to talk to you about this article you wrote for next week's issue.

NORM: Article.

DOUG: The football article. You remember.

NORM: Oh. Yeah. That.

DOUG: Well, only one thing bothered me about it. And I'm a little embarrassed to mention it, but . . . you don't mention me once in the article. Well, I mean after all, I am the quarterback, and I think that entitles me to a, uh, passing reference. (*To Doug Willard this is extremely clever. He laughs heartily*)

NORM: I guess it depends on your view of football. Do you really see the quarterback as the key to the game?

DOUG: Absolutely. You see, this is a good article, but it's got just one flaw.

NORM: What's that?

DOUG: It's boring. I think sports articles should be exciting, should encompass the thrill of the game. Now take that pass I made in the second quarter. The way I faded back, ignoring the three linemen coming at me. Then I just tossed that ball . . .

NORM: . . . to one of the linemen coming at you. He intercepted and made a touchdown.

DOUG: (*Clearing his throat*) Well, I think you get the idea anyway. I'd like to see a redraft on Monday. (*Hands Norm some papers*) Hey, by the way, do you have a bathroom I could use? It was kind of a long drive over here.

NORM: Oh, yeah, sure. (*Goes to door, points*) It's right down the hall there.

DOUG: Thanks. (*He exits*)

NORM: Boy, this is something I never expected. But do you see what I mean? He's got all the brain power of a corn flake. And he wants me to rewrite the article . . . rewrite the article . . . that's funny, he never stopped by to ask me to rewrite an article before. What the hell is he up to? It's got to have something to do with Ann. This is just too much of a coincidence. First that meeting in the hall. Then her Aunt Gladys gets sick. Hah! Who does she think she's kidding? Nobody has an Aunt Gladys.

(*Doug and Ann appear in a spotlight*)

ANN: At last, darling, we'll be together.

DOUG: Yes.

ANN: Try not to hurt him too much. For a skinny little wimp he's pretty nice.

DOUG: I'll just tell him the truth. That I dumped you for another girl but now I want you back, and since he means absolutely nothing to you, you never want to see him again. And if he ever comes near you, I'll push his face through the back of his head.

ANN: Oh, you're such a romantic.

DOUG: I know.

ANN: (*Breathing heavily*) Oh, Doug, oh, Doug, oh, Doug . . .

DOUG: Ann, Ann, Ann, Ann . . .

(*They paw at each other, grope, grab, kiss, fall to the floor and . . .*)

NORM: Stop it, stop it, stop it, stop it!!!!!! (*Lights fade on Ann and Doug, and they exit*) Jesus, I'm driving myself crazy!!

MOTHER'S VOICE: Norm!

NORM: What is it??!!! (*Takes a breath*) Uh, I mean, yes, Mom?

MOTHER'S VOICE: Someone else here to see you.

NORM: OK. Ann, Ann, Ann, why don't you call?

(*Ann appears in the doorway*)

ANN: Hi, Norm.

(*Norm screams and jumps*)

NORM: What are *you* doing here?!

ANN: Well, I would have called but . . .

(*From offstage, a toilet flushes*)

ANN: Oh, do you have company?

NORM: Company? Oh, God, company, that's right . . . Oh, no, here it comes. The big axe, the final scene.

ANN: Norm . . .

(*Doug comes into the room. He is zipping up his pants*)

DOUG: You know something, little guy . . . (*Sees Ann*) Ann . . .

ANN: Doug . . .

NORM: Why couldn't I live in a room with a back door?

ANN: (*to Doug*) What are you doing here?

DOUG: Me and the little guy are working on a football article. I didn't know you and Norm were friends. (*Ann smiles*) So . . . how's everything?

ANN: Good. How about you?

DOUG: Great. Listen, I was just leaving. Can I give you a lift?

ANN: No, I just got here.

DOUG: Oh. Well, I'll wait. Say, why don't we have lunch?

ANN: Doug, I don't think you . . .

DOUG: I know this great hamburger place . . .

ANN: I came to see Norm.

(*A pause as Doug considers this*)

DOUG: What do you mean? You mean you came to . . . *see* Norm? (*Ann nods. Doug gives a short laugh*) What are you guys? Going together or something?

ANN: Yes. We are.

(*The laughter becomes hysterical. Doug can hardly contain himself as he looks at Norm and Ann*)

ANN: What is so funny?

DOUG: Nothing . . . nothing.

ANN: No. I want to know what it is you find so humorous.

DOUG: (*Managing a straight face*) No, no. It's nothing really. Listen, I've really got to be going but, uh, you can call me sometime, Ann. (*A last hooting laugh escapes before Ann speaks*)

ANN: Oh, can I? Well, I don't think I will, Doug. And I don't want you to call me, either. In fact, I don't ever want you to speak to me again, because if you do, I'll push your face through the back of your head.

(*A double take from Norm*)

DOUG: Hey, Ann . . .

ANN: Go on, leave. I didn't come to see you.

NORM: Yeah, that's right. And one more thing, Doug. I don't ever want you to call me "little fella" again, because I happen to have a norm, and it's "Name."

(*Doug has exited. Norm, standing by the door, realizes his mistake. He shoves his hands into his pockets and looks at Ann*)

ANN: Can you believe the nerve of that guy? What a jerk.

NORM: Yeah. Tell me, despite the fact that he's tall, muscular, and handsome what did you ever see in him?

ANN: Sorry I'm late.

(*Norm crosses over to the tuxedo on the wall, tries to stand nonchalantly in front of it so Ann can't see it*)

NORM: Oh, that's OK. I was just kind of sitting around, anyhow, not doing much.

ANN: Well, I just stopped by to say that if you want, I can go to the dance tonight.

NORM: Your Aunt Gladys is all better?

ANN: The gallstones turned out to be gas.

NORM: (*Taking the tux off the wall*) Then I'll pick you up around seven.

ANN: OK. (*She leans over and kisses him. He starts to kiss her back, but she breaks away with a laugh*) I'd better get going. I've only got six and a half hours to get ready.

NORM: Well if you work straight through, you should be able to make it.

ANN: I'll see you tonight.

NORM: (*Sitting down on the bed with the tux*) 'Bye.

(*Ann goes out the door, then comes right back in. She pauses for a moment, then goes to Norm*)

ANN: Hey, Norm?

NORM: Yeah?

ANN: I have a confession to make.

NORM: Oh?

ANN: You asked me what I saw in Doug? Well, something I never told you was one day while Doug and I were still going out, I was in the hall at school. And I saw this guy trying to open his locker. He wasn't exactly what I'd call handsome, but he was definitely cute. And he stood there, spinning and spinning the dial of the lock, trying and trying to get that locker open. Then he started kicking it. Then hitting it. And when that didn't work, he started talking to it like it was a real person . . . "C'mon, will you please open up?" he said. "Look, I'll share my lunch with you if you just let me hang my jacket up . . ." I laughed so hard there were tears rolling down my eyes, and I thought right then, forget Doug Willard and meet this guy.

NORM: Wow. (*Ann hugs him and leaves*) Wow. Wow, what a great girl . . . what an *intelligent* girl. To . . . to fall in love with me at first sight. I always knew Ann was something special, something terrific. To just see me in a hall and fall immediately and completely in love with me. My gosh . . . (*Pause. Suddenly worried*) . . . my gosh. To fall in love with me after just seeing me? How many guys does she see in a day? A hundred? Two hundred? She must fall in love two hundred times a day . . . with every guy I know . . .

(*Suddenly, Jerry ambles onto the stage in a spotlight. Ann appears at the opposite side of the stage*)

ANN: (*To Jerry*) Oh, God, the way you walk. It drives me mad.

(*Jerry looks confused at first*)

NORM: Oh, no. Oh, no. It's happening again.

(*Ann crosses to Jerry like a panther stalking its prey. With one hand she pushes him back and sprawls him on the floor*)

ANN: I love you.

NORM: Oh, no, I can see it coming.

ANN: I love you. I love you. (*She starts to close in on Jerry*)
Use me, abuse me, toss me away like an old Kleenex.

(*They fall to the floor, tearing each others' clothes off*)

NORM: HEEEEEEEEEEEEEEEEEEELLLLLLLLLLLLPPPP
PPPPP!!!!!

Blackout

Romulus Linney

F.M.

Romulus Linney

When Romulus Linney's *F.M.* premiered in May 1982 at the Philadelphia Festival Theatre in a production that Mr. Linney also directed, Nels Nelson of the *Philadelphia Daily News* hailed him as "a luminous creative spirit touched by so superior a gift that we would cheerfully knight him on the spot." The Philadelphia audience responded with a standing ovation for this tale about a college creative writing course in which a Faulknerian talent is discovered and two Southern women students of antagonistic dispositions leave in a huff (to the delight of the teacher and her gothic protégé). Not since Thomas Wolfe's hilarious spoof (in *Of Time and the River*) of George Pierce Baker's famous playwriting class at Harvard has anyone so successfully satirized the conflicting egos in a creative writing class. This, the first publication of *F.M.*, joins Mr. Linney's Obie winner *Tennessee*, which appeared in the 1980 edition of *Best Short Plays*.

Born in Philadelphia, Pennsylvania in 1930, Romulus Linney grew up in Madison, Tennessee and spent his summers in North Carolina. He was educated at Oberlin College, where he received his B.A. in 1953, and the Yale School of Drama, where he earned an M.F.A. in 1958.

Mr. Linney is the author of two highly regarded novels, *Heathen Valley* and *Slowly, by Thy Hand Unfurled*. He has written many plays, including *The Love Suicide at Schofield Barracks*, which was produced on Broadway in 1972; *Democracy; Holy Ghosts;* and *Old Man Joseph and His Family*.

His best-known play is *The Sorrows of Frederick*, a psychological drama about Frederick the Great. Its many stage productions include the 1967 premiere at the Mark Taper Forum in Los Angeles with Fritz Weaver in the title role. Subsequent productions were staged in New York with Austin Pendleton, in Canada with Donald David, and in Great Britain with John Wood and later, Tom Conti. *The Sorrows of Frederick* also was performed at the Dusseldorf Schauspielhaus in Germany and at the Burgtheater in Vienna, where it successfully played in classical repertory through the season of 1969–70 in a production that won two Austrian theatre awards.

Mr. Linney has written extensively for television and has published a number of short plays and fiction in numerous

literary magazines. An opera was made from his short play
The Death of King Philip.

Mr. Linney received two fellowships from the National Endowment for the Arts and from 1976 until 1979 served on its literary panel. In 1980 he received a fellowship from the Guggenheim Foundation.

He has taught playwriting at many schools, including Columbia University, Brooklyn College, Connecticut College, and, currently, the University of Pennsylvania and Princeton University.

His most recent plays include *Childe Byron*, produced in New York by the Circle Repertory Company, in Louisville by the Actors Theatre, in Costa Mesa, California by the South Coast Repertory, and in London by the Young Vic; *The Captivity of Pixie Shedman*, performed at the New York Phoenix Theatre and the Detroit Repertory Theatre; *El Hermano* and *Goodbye, Howard*, staged at The Ensemble Studio Theatre in New York; *April Snow*, produced at the South Coast Repertory; and *A Woman Without A Name*, performed at the Empire State Theatre in Albany, New York.

As a director, Mr. Linney recently staged his own plays for the Philadelphia Festival of New Plays, the Actors Studio in Manhattan, the Alley Theatre in Houston, and the Actors Theatre of Louisville.

A New York Production of *F.M.* in April 1984 received critical acclaim.

Characters:

CONSTANCE LINDELL
MAY FORD
SUZANNE LACHETTE
BUFORD BULLOUGH

Time:

Fall 1981.

Place:

A small Southern college near Birmingham, Alabama.

Scene:

A dreary classroom in a small Southern college. The room contains a long seminar table and chairs sitting about at random.

Enter Constance Lindell, a woman in her thirties, attractive and intelligent. She stares at the room bleakly.

CONSTANCE: Wonderful. (*She shrugs, smiles, drops her briefcase onto the seminar table, opens it, takes out a class list*) One, two, three. And me. (*She smiles again and sets up chairs, one at each end of the table and two in the middle. Enter May Ford. She is a nervous woman in her forties, wearing a flower-print dress*)

MAY: Creative Fiction?

CONSTANCE: That's right.

MAY: Are you Constance Lindell?

CONSTANCE: I am. How do you do?

MAY: Oh, my goodness. What a pleasure. I'm May Ford. I'm taking the class.

CONSTANCE: Good. Come in. (*She smiles at May, takes her briefcase to one end of the table. She opens it and takes out a notepad and a pen and the class list*)

MAY: It is such a privilege to have you here. With your wonderful books. Everybody here is just . . . well, truly excited. Really we are.

CONSTANCE: (*With a smile*) All three of you.

MAY: Three?

CONSTANCE: That's the class.

MAY: My goodness. And here you are, so distinguished. Oh, this college. They just don't get the word out the way they should. They really don't. Could I sit here?

CONSTANCE: Please do.

(*May takes one of the chairs in the middle of the table. She removes a small manuscript from a tote bag whose side is decorated with prints of flowers. The manuscript is neatly clipped into a colored binder, which is also decorated with flower prints. Next May pulls out a small thin vase and sets it by the manuscript. She then takes from her bag tissue paper in which is wrapped a rose. She puts the rose into the vase and smiles at Constance*)

MAY: Isn't this silly? But you know, when I work, I need some small part of God's beautiful natural world to look at. I mean, when writers write, they have to face reality, don't they? I mean, they certainly need escape, don't they?

CONSTANCE: They certainly do.

MAY: I use flowers. What do you use?

CONSTANCE: Oh, this and that.

(*Enter, precisely on time, Suzanne Lachette, a very attractive young woman, neatly dressed and smiling a very pleasant smile*)

SUZANNE: Good evening.

CONSTANCE: Good evening.

MAY: Good evening.

(*Suzanne takes the other chair in the middle of the table. She puts down a manuscript in a black spring binder and sits*)

CONSTANCE: Suzanne Lachette?

SUZANNE: That's right.

CONSTANCE: May Ford, Suzanne Lachette, and according to this class list, a Buford B— (*Pause*) Buford "Bulla." (*Pause*) I suppose that's the way you say that. Not here yet.

SUZANNE: It is time, isn't it?

CONSTANCE: Yes, but let's give him a minute. Since there are only three of you.

SUZANNE: (*Pleasantly*) Only three? Well, good. We can work in depth. Dig in. But I do think people ought to be on time. (*To May*) Don't you?

MAY: Well, I think, yes, of course, any class should begin when it should begin. It is a mark of respect for the subject and for the other pupils enrolled, but, on the other hand, perhaps Mr. Buford Bullough hasn't found the right room,

or maybe some car trouble? I'm sure he'll be here soon, and
we can all get right off to a wonderful start. (*She bends over
quickly to smell her flower. Suzanne looks at her pleasantly, smiling*)

SUZANNE: I bet you wouldn't say that if his name was Betty
instead of Buford.

MAY: I beg your pardon?

SUZANNE: Never mind.

CONSTANCE: Women are used to making excuses for men?
Is that what you mean, Suzanne?

SUZANNE: Well, aren't they?

CONSTANCE: I suppose, some.

SUZANNE: More than some, I think. And I think we ought
to start the class.

CONSTANCE: All right, if you wish. This is an extension
program course in writing fiction. One semester. Wednesdays,
six to nine-thirty. My name is Constance Lindell.

(*May applauds. Suzanne stares at her*)

SUZANNE: Is there something I don't know about?

MAY: Her wonderful books! Haven't you read them?

SUZANNE: No. (*To Constance*) Should I have?

CONSTANCE: Not at all.

SUZANNE: How many books are there?

CONSTANCE: Two.

SUZANNE: Both novels?

CONSTANCE: One collection of short stories.

MAY: And they're just wonderful! Every last story! Simply
wonderful and—marvelous! Really fine!

SUZANNE: I'm sure they are. I look forward to working
with you, Constance.

CONSTANCE: And I with you, Suzanne. The course will be
conducted as a workshop, without lectures. I work more like
an editor than a professor, which, I must warn you, can mean
slow, painstaking, and unglamorous labor. You both have
manuscripts in progress?

SUZANNE: I certainly do.

MAY: So do I.

CONSTANCE: Good. I usually try to begin without any grand
statements or aesthetic pronouncements about writing, except
maybe it's a way of life more than anything else.

SUZANNE: (*Politely*) Excuse me. But what does that mean?

CONSTANCE: Not very much, forget it. In any case, neither
I nor anyone else can teach you how to write. What I can do,

perhaps, is help you to teach yourself. What I can do certainly is encourage you to pay close attention to each other's work. To each other's struggle to write well. A class can often have insights deeper than its teacher, and within writing that seems awkward and even preposterous, real talent is sometimes buried. Our criticism must be candid but, I hope, always supportive. We are here to help each other.

MAY: That is simply inspiring! I am ready!

SUZANNE: (*Smiling*) *Help* each other? *Writers?*

CONSTANCE: Why not?

SUZANNE: Because two writers in one room are like two scorpions in one bottle. And teacher makes three.

CONSTANCE: You've taken a writing class before.

SUZANNE: I sure have, in this room. With the dummy they got last year, from God knows where. After that fool, you're lucky anybody showed up.

CONSTANCE: I see. So, to begin, what we need is a bit of background on each of us, including me. Let me ask you who you are, where you are from, what you are working on, and why you write. May?

MAY: My name is May Ford. I'm from Fontana, ten miles away. My husband is in the furniture business. I have three children, eleven, thirteen, and fourteen, and my hobbies are roses and needlepoint.

SUZANNE: (*Quietly*) And writing.

MAY: Yes, I suppose you can call it a hobby. The book I am working on is a novel. It is called *Hollyhock Road.* It's about a woman who finds herself in middle age, and at the end of all pleasure, and who is redeemed by the beauty of the natural world she discovers around her. I *am* having a little trouble with it.

SUZANNE: (*Quietly*) I bet you are.

MAY: Why do I write? Well. (*Pause. May thinks about it carefully*) Because I need to. I need to believe that, in spite of everything, there is the same purpose and goodness in human beings that there is in God's wonderful natural world, and if we seek, we will find.

CONSTANCE: Thank you. Suzanne?

SUZANNE: My name is Suzanne Lachette. I live here in town. I work at the University Medical Center, as a lab technician. Divorced, at last. One child, a female, thank God. I am also writing a novel. It is about a woman ending her marriage and facing life as it is. The title is *Scaulded Dogs*. It's coming along fine. Why do I write? That's easy. Writing is the only way I can say something and keep it the way I said it. How's that?

CONSTANCE: Just fine. I'm Constance Lindell, from Chapel Hill, North Carolina. Also divorced, remarried, my husband teaching this term in another school. No children. I am working on a novel, too, no title yet, and at the moment anyway, I think I became a writer because I couldn't do anything else. Henry Miller said somewhere, if you just get desperate enough, you'll write, and I think that is what happened to me.

SUZANNE: You read Henry Miller?

CONSTANCE: With pleasure.

SUZANNE: Yuck.

CONSTANCE: (*Smiling*) What's wrong with Henry Miller?

SUZANNE: (*Smiling*) He wrote with his penis.

MAY: Oh! I mean, well, people will write for all kinds of reasons, won't they?

SUZANNE: Henry Miller was the worst example of male arrogance in all literature. He thought women were bathrooms. I'm surprised you enjoy him.

CONSTANCE: Well, I do. The procedure of this workshop is simple. A chapter, or a section ten to twenty pages long, is read aloud, then discussed.

MAY: Read aloud? But isn't that vulgar?

CONSTANCE: Vulgar, May?

MAY: Maybe not vulgar, exactly, but common, surely. I mean, the whole purpose of writing is to say beautiful things in silent print, instead of just blabbing about it like everybody else, isn't it? So to read what's written aloud is to make it back into what you didn't want it to be in the first place. Isn't it?

CONSTANCE: (*Slowly*) I think I see what you mean. But reading manuscripts aloud in class is the only practical way we can focus on it together, at the same time.

SUZANNE: Excuse me. We could read them before we came in.

CONSTANCE: That means copies have to be made, for one thing, and manuscripts don't get read, for another. I prefer we read them together, here. It takes up the slack.

SUZANNE: And lots of class time. But all right. I see your point. Fine with me.

CONSTANCE: One more thing. When a manuscript is read,

before we jump in with critical judgments, I ask for a period where only questions are asked. Logistical matters. Who was where, when what happened, and so on. To clear things up, so that what is not clear gets all sorted out and we know what the writer was trying to do, even if he didn't always succeed.

SUZANNE: Or she.

CONSTANCE: Or she.

SUZANNE: I have a question now.

CONSTANCE: All right.

SUZANNE: How many other courses have they got you teaching?

(*Pause. Constance stares at Suzanne a second, takes a deep breath*)

CONSTANCE: Three.

SUZANNE: Freshman comp?

CONSTANCE: Two. One survey of world lit. For sophomores.

SUZANNE: That must be difficult. Plus office hours, I would think, and plenty of advising.

CONSTANCE: Add it up, Suzanne.

SUZANNE: Certainly. You're not exactly an artist-in-residence here, are you?

CONSTANCE: I think I said before that writing is a way of life more than anything else. Plenty of good writers, like me, thank you, are in exactly the same boat. But that isn't the point. The point is, am I going to conduct this course, or are you?

SUZANNE: You, if you can. Frankly, I'm doubtful.

MAY: Do we get to have coffee breaks, or anything like that? I sure could use one.

CONSTANCE: We break after something is read. And I suppose Mr. Bullough isn't coming after all, so let's start. Who would like to go first?

SUZANNE: I defer to any novel as much about plants as people. Go ahead, May.

MAY: Oh, no! *Scaulded Dogs* is such a brilliant title. I know it will be just overwhelming. I'd be scared to death to go before that. You first, please.

SUZANNE: No, you first. I insist.

MAY: I don't think I can. We *know* you can. So, please do.

SUZANNE: I wouldn't think of it. Gridlock. (*She smiles at Constance*) Constance? (*Ready for her, Constance flips a coin*)

CONSTANCE: Heads, May. Tails, Suzanne. (*She catches the coin, slaps it onto the table, looks at it*) It's tails. Suzanne.

MAY: Thank God.

SUZANNE: Let me see that, please. (*She gets up and peers over at the coin*) Very well. (*Suzanne goes back to her seat and prepares to read her manuscript. She checks her chair and gets set in her position at the table. She centers her spring binder in front of her. She thinks a minute. She clears her throat and begins to read aloud*) *Scaulded Dogs.* Chapter One.

"Frank came in the door without ringing the bell, of course. The familiar lurch showed Laurinda that he had already been drinking, although her mother's clock on their fireplace mantlepiece pointed to only four in the afternoon.

" 'I wasn't expecting you,' she said gently.

" 'It's still my house,' " he said, sneering. " 'Even with you in it.' "

"Laurinda felt like the head of a big kitchen match, rasped across a hot stove, struck into sulphur and fire. But she bowed her head and said nothing."

(*Constance puts one hand briefly over her face and summons up powers of endurance. May radiates a look of serious appreciation*)

MAY: Oh, that's wonderful. Powerful. That match thing. What a metaphor.

SUZANNE: It's a simile, not a metaphor. (*To Constance*) I beg your pardon, but we *do* get to read uninterrupted, don't we?

MAY: Oh, I'm sorry! (*She claps her hands over her mouth*)

CONSTANCE: Yes, you do.

MAY: I won't say another word!

CONSTANCE: It's all right, May. Sometimes it is useful to take notes while someone is reading, so you can remember what to ask about. Go ahead, Suzanne.

(*May takes her notepad and pen and is quickly poised to take her notes. Suzanne continues reading her manuscript*)

SUZANNE: (*Reading aloud*) "Frank looked at the open ledger book into which Laurinda had just listed their common possessions.

" 'What you get and what I get, eh?' he said, squinting at her hard work with contempt. 'Bet I know how that works out.' "

"Since Laurinda had been scrupulous in her fair division

of their property, this stung her bitterly, but she put it behind her, to face as bravely as she could a more vital issue.

" 'You didn't come for the children yesterday, when you said you would. They were expecting you.'

"He dismissed her words with one wave of his hand.

" 'Well, something came up,' he said, minimizing the wounds he had inflicted on his own children. 'I have to make money, after all. To keep you in ease and comfort, not to mention your lawyer. Ha ha.' " (*Constance stares into space, determined to keep listening. May makes industrious notes*)

"That was his idea of a joke. Laurinda stared at him. To think she had once given him her love and thought him capable of its return. What treachery. There he stood, a smug, self-satisfied, domineering drunk. An intolerant, arbitrary bully. A superficial, narrow-minded, short-sighted, besotted, provincial bigot. A self-indulgent, flatulent, gruesome eyesore of a man, odious and repellent, a repulsive buffoon."

(*Enter Buford Bullough, with a lurch and a stagger. He carries a cardboard box and a battered portable phonograph.*

(*Buford is a wreck. He is possessed by intermittent and terrific jerks that convulse him, sending his chin diving to his shoulder. He sweats. His eyes bulge, and stare ildly ahead of him, as if seeing somewhere in space, something astounding. He wears a worn hunting shirt and jeans and a jacket, heavy boots, and a baseball cap. His hair is all unkempt.*

(*He puts the box down at one end of the table and sits quickly. In one hand he carries a can of jumbo size soda, open. He drinks from it deeply, pulls a kerchief from his pocket, and wipes his brow. The three women stare at him, speechless*)

BUFORD: Sorry ah'm late. Just pay me no mind.

CONSTANCE: Mr. Bullough?

BUFORD: Bull-loo. Bewford Bull-loo.

CONSTANCE: Mr. Bullough, then. May Ford. Suzanne Lachette.

BUFORD: Hidy.

SUZANNE: Good evening.

MAY: Hello theah.

CONSTANCE: Go ahead, Suzanne. (*To Buford*) First chapter of a novel.

BUFORD: Ah see.

(*He puts his chin on his hand, elbow on the table, and stares at Suzanne with fierce concentration*)

SUZANNE: (*Reading aloud*) "So once again Laurinda saw there was no possible way to communicate with Frank. None at all.

" 'Frank,' Laurinda said. 'I had hoped you would think of the children if not of me. Some tincture of grace I had hoped for, to color this bitter medicine we must take.' "

(*Buford's attention span snaps. He reaches down and with one hand opens the top of the cardboard box. He sees Suzanne glaring at him and pays attention again*)

" 'Correction,' said Frank. 'You must take. I am still a healthy human being.' "

"It was hopeless. 'Very well,' she sighed. 'What do you want, Frank?'

" 'I want what's mine,' said Frank. 'And a lot of it is in this room right now.' "

(*Buford looks at the cardboard box*)

" 'All right, Frank,' said Laurinda, patiently. 'I have done my best. You look and see what you think should be yours instead of mine. I'll consider any changes you may suggest.' "

(*Buford reaches into the cardboard box*)

" 'You'd better,' said Frank. 'I just might take it all. Or smash it all, every stick. How would you like that, lady?' "

(*Buford takes out a bottle of bourbon. Turning slightly and holding the bottle below the table, he pours bourbon into his soda can*)

"Oh, Laurinda thought, the brute. The coarse, insensitive, sadistic brute. Why had she married him?"

(*Buford puts the bottle back in the box and takes from the box a huge manuscript, tied by a rope. It is composed of many sections, each novel length, held by a rubber band. He puts the manuscript on the table and stares at it*)

"There he stood, his whiskey breath plain as the scent of a skunk, still weaving in front of her, a slack-jawed, leering, childish, smart-aleck of a man, a swine absolute and unmitigated, a boorish, filthy-minded . . . " (*Suzanne stops reading and slams her spring binder shut*) Since it is blatantly obvious that Mr. Bullough does not care to listen to my work, I will not continue to read it!

MAY: Oh, Suzanne! Don't stop! That was all just wonderful!

SUZANNE: May, you try it. It's a bit difficult to read aloud the deepest meditations of your heart and soul with a man unpacking a suitcase, like somebody going fishing. Not to mention slipping whiskey into a soda can. What is it, Bullough? Corn whiskey?

BUFORD: Bourbon. Ah need it.

SUZANNE: I'm sure you do.

BUFORD: Lady, ah certainly am sorry if ah bothered you.

SUZANNE: My name is not Lady. It is Suzanne Lachette. La - *chette*!

BUFORD: Miz Lachette, ah certainly didn't mean to. Ah was listening.

SUZANNE: Oh, please!

BUFORD: It's just that, well, you see, ah'm here to do it, and ah, well, it's just inside me all the time like a drum going boom-boom-boom all the time. It don't never stop, so ah have to get ready, you see. I mean, boom-boom-boom! Hit's awful. You will understand.

SUZANNE: If your writing, Mr. Bullough, is no more illuminating than your speech, that is not very likely.

CONSTANCE: (*To Suzanne*) You're sure you won't continue?

SUZANNE: Positive.

CONSTANCE: Would you like us to discuss what you've read?

SUZANNE: Hardly. I cannot at this moment allow my work to be pawed over by a man obviously interested in nothing but himself.

CONSTANCE: Very well. May?

MAY: (*Terrified*) What?

CONSTANCE: Would you read instead?

MAY: You mean out loud right now?

CONSTANCE: You're next. Why not?

MAY: Oh, no! I better wait a little while. I mean, like the flowers I always seem to write about, my story is delicate and needs a little sunshine, and good weather, you see.

BUFORD: (*Explosively*) Well, me then! Ah'm willing to read! Ah'm willing to read!

SUZANNE: What a surprise.

BUFORD: Ah mean, if hit's my turn. Ah don't want to step out of line or nothing.

SUZANNE: Out of line or nothing. Jesus Christ.

CONSTANCE: Well, Mr. Bullough, since neither Suzanne or May wants to read, go ahead.

BUFORD: Ah will! (*He tears into his huge manuscript, going through its many sections, searching for something*)

SUZANNE: He's like a man changing a tire.

BUFORD: Hit's just where to begin, you see.

MAY: How about the beginning, dear Mr. Bullough?

SUZANNE: Or the end.

(*Buford finds the portion of his manuscript he wants to read*)

BUFORD: Here! Ah got hit.

(*Now he plugs his phonograph into a wall socket. From the box he takes a record in a faded dust jacket. He puts the record on the phonograph and puts the dust jacket on the table face down*)

SUZANNE: Music yet. What are you going to play for us, Bullough? "Hound Dog?" "Detour"? "The Great Speckled Bird"?

(*Pause. Buford stares at his manuscript. He takes a deep breath, drinks quickly from his soda can, wipes his forehead with his kerchief. Then he begins to read.*

(*From the moment he does, Constance, who has been managing all this as best she can, comes at once to life. It is as if she wakes from a sleep, and her senses and perceptions are all suddenly very much alive. Buford reads in a very heavy Southern accent, but the language he creates in his manuscript is quite different from the halting speech of the Southern country man that he is*)

BUFORD: (*Reading aloud, at breakneck speed*) "On her bed, beneath the candleflame headboard that guarded her descent into bitterness and where, perhaps, madness overtook her, he lay dreaming, drunk and naked, with a woman named Edna Craig Somebody blundering around in the bathroom, picked up at the Paramount Paradise . . . "

SUZANNE: Just a minute.

BUFORD: ". . . Roadhouse four miles out of Ridersberg . . ."

SUZANNE: Just a minute! (*Buford stops reading and looks wildly about*)

BUFORD: Whut?

SUZANNE: The title. You forgot the title.

BUFORD: Huh?

SUZANNE: Title! Name of the thing. What it is called, for God's sake!

BUFORD: Oh. The whole thing is just a man's name. But this part is called "F.M."

SUZANNE: "F.M." what? I don't understand.

BUFORD: Just "F.M."

MAY: You mean *F* period, *M* period?

BUFORD: Yes, ma'am.

MAY: Then I don't understand, either. How can you call something by some initials, and we don't even know if it is a somebody or a something or what it is?

SUZANNE: I mean, is it Frequency Modulation, or Fred MacMurray, or what?

BUFORD: Oh, it means something, but that has to come out in the thing itself, you see.

CONSTANCE: Mr. Bullough, you don't have to have your titles yet. Titles are funny. They come before, during, and after a book. Let's say "F.M." for the moment means Fiction Material. How's that?

BUFORD: That's fine! Fiction Material!

SUZANNE: Or Freak Mouth.

CONSTANCE: Go ahead, then.

BUFORD: Ah'll commence again.

SUZANNE: "Commence again." Then he reads a sentence half a page long. This fellow doesn't add up.

BUFORD: (*Reading aloud, more slowly*) "On her bed, beneath the candleflame headboard that guarded her descent into bitterness and where, perhaps, madness overtook her, he lay dreaming, drunk and naked, with a woman named Edna Craig Somebody blundering around in the bathroom, picked up at the Paramount Paradise Roadhouse four miles out of Ridersberg, and brought to his mother's small house with shrieks and giggles . . ."

MAY: Mother? Did he say mother?

SUZANNE: I don't know.

(*Buford makes a change in his manuscript with a big felt marker*)

BUFORD: ". . . with whoops and giggles, while the good neighbors on their porches shook their heads in their chairs and rocked their disapproval—not a day in the ground, they said, not even twelve hours—and he tried now to focus . . ." (*Buford makes another change, quickly, feverishly, almost without stopping*) ". . . he tried to spend his whirling powers upon the thin body, the delicate, thorny foxfire woman he had buried that morning, tried to summon her back to him, with all her smiles and rings, her hands on her own breasts, and all her Chinese puzzles, if not to answer his questions framed apart from her for ten years, at least to speak to him who had not heard her voice for ten years, and listening all that time to Edna Craig Somebody, the large and friendly creature in the bathroom.

" 'How do you turn this light off in here?' said Edna Craig.

" 'By the wall cabinet.'

" 'Oh, yeah.' "

(*May and Suzanne look at each other and hold up their hands in dismay*)

"There was a pause while she found the light, turned it off, and blundered out . . ." (*Change with the marker*) ". . . came out of the bathroom into the hall.

" 'Hey! This here old thing a radio?'

" 'Yes.'

" 'Can I play it?'

" 'Why not?'

" 'Let's have some music then. What the hell.'

" 'Go ahead.'

" 'You want me to?'

" 'I said yes.'

"Drunk, naked, and dreaming, he lay in her bed, under the candleflame headboard. Mama? Mama?

"Which flowers grew where . . ."

SUZANNE: Wait a minute.

BUFORD: ". . . he could never remember . . ."

SUZANNE: Wait a minute!

BUFORD: ". . . and certainly . . ."

SUZANNE: WAIT A MINUTE!

BUFORD: Huh? Whut?

SUZANNE: I don't understand one word of this.

BUFORD: Whut if ah just keep on going? Maybe you will.

SUZANNE: May, do you know what this man is saying?

MAY: Not exactly. There's a man who's brought a woman somewhere . . .

SUZANNE: And put her in the bathroom, of course. I understand that. But whose bed is it, whose town is it, who is he and what is he doing?

MAY: I certainly don't know.

CONSTANCE: (*Quietly*) It is his mother's house. He has buried her that morning. Now, to her bed, he has brought a woman from a roadhouse. Is that right, Mr. Bullough?

BUFORD: Yes, ma'am.

SUZANNE: Ugh. That is the most sordid premise for a story in the history of fiction.

BUFORD: Yes, ma'am. Ah got to go ahead with this. Once ah commence reading, hit's awful to stop.

SUZANNE: "Commence" again. Did you really write all that purple prose, Bullough? You don't talk that way. You talk like a hick.

BUFORD: I know it. Hit's whut ah am. But hit's different when ah write. I reckon that's why ah do it.

CONSTANCE: Go on, Mr. Bullough. (*To May and Suzanne*) Take notes and let him read.

BUFORD: Lemme see now. (*He finds his place again. May and Suzanne ready their notepads. Buford plunges in once more, at his terrific, breakneck pace*) "Which flowers grew where, he could never remember, and certainly along that road, that hill, those cowpaths . . ."

SUZANNE: (*Writing note*) Cowpaths.

BUFORD: (*Reading aloud*) ". . . and between these birches, he cannot remember them all, all the biology bookful of flowers that in his lifetime before he left her passed from his tiny mother's waspish hands to his." (*Pause*) "Mama? Mama?"

SUZANNE: (*Writing note*) Mama, mama.

BUFORD: (*Reading aloud*) "He twists about in her bed and now reaches up to touch the candleflame headboard and suddenly she is there with him, she speaks to him as he lies naked and dreaming of her, moving toward him through a forest of gigantic flowers, and he sees again their pictures in the books and in the articles she cut out for him, and he sees them lying at their feet during the walks they took through the soft Southern air of his childhood. They walk together past the flowers she points out to him, white baneberry, whose stalks redden with age, whose china-white fruit is poisonous and gleams in the shade, and she says to him, *Oh, my darling, my heart is full of love for you, here, it's in here, touch my breast here* . . ."

MAY: Touch what?

SUZANNE: My God.

BUFORD: (*Reading aloud*) ". . . while they walk, over blood-root poppy, pink as dawn, when crushed giving a scarlet liquid, useful, she tells him, as war paint, dye, and it can even change the color of a man's eye, and she says, *Kiss me, my son, my only child, my darling boy,* passing lank green swaths of wild yam and meadowrue, where they stop and he kisses his mother, bereft forever of the passion she seeks in him. They embrace, surrounded by nodding suns of black-eyed Susans, yellow sweet clover, turkscap lilies and four-leaf loosestrife, Solomonplume, orange with stems that zig-zag and berries green and red all at once."

MAY: (*First note, indignant*) They don't zig-zag.

BUFORD: (*Reading aloud*) "And then the laughter, sweet and soft at first, and her eyes not yet wild, her voice not yet hard or cold, *Well, darling, come along, if you don't understand how much your mother loves you, you just don't, it's all right, come along.* Her stride picks up, over scarlet fireweed, bull thistle and thimbleberry, and he is desperate to follow her."

MAY: (*Note*) Some of those are not even real flowers.

BUFORD: (*Reading aloud*) "Her laughter becomes shrill now and hard, her step begins to rush along the path above the little town, her prison, over crowpoison and Allegheny goats-beard, whose brownish blossoms become quickly infested with insects. She turns to look back at him, and her stare goes through him now like a needle into cloth." (*Buford looks at the phonograph*) Got this music to play right here. It goes with it real good. (*He takes the record out of the faded jacket and puts it on the little phonograph. Suzanne picks up the jacket*)

SUZANNE: Where did he get this? (*She passes it to Constance, who looks at the faded jacket thoughtfully*)

MAY: It isn't right to make up flowers any way you want to. Flowers are more important than that. They don't mean anything but themselves. I don't like this.

CONSTANCE: (*Looking at the jacket*) Edward Elgar.

(*The music plays. It is the beginning of the second movement of Elgar's "Piano Quintet in A Minor." Buford reads aloud again, but more slowly now*)

BUFORD: (*Reading aloud*) "From the ground, picking them up laughing, she makes for him dreaming as once she did in life, out of three leaves from a fig tree, some cellophane from her purse—laced wih pine straw and a rooster's comb of common daises and with flowers cascading down its back—a bridal crown. She holds it out, laughing at him, the eyes dangerous now, as she tries to put it on his head, saying, *You look like me, son, and I was beautiful, son, beautiful as the day we share in this place of flowers, with our bond singing in our blood. No one, no one, no one can ever alter that, for you look just like me, child, and I was beautiful, child, here, wear this as I did to beget you, so you will always always love me, and the two of us shall be forever one. Let me see, in your face, the bride I was, let me kiss myself upon your lips, angels the two of us, on earth, in gardens of delight.*

(*May jumps up, exploding*)

MAY: I will not have it!! I will not have it!! Shut off that awful music or I will break the damn record!

BUFORD: Please! Ah can't stop now!

MAY: Yes, you can! You pervert! (*She takes the arm off the record, stopping the music*) You listen to me, Mr. Bullough. I am a gentle woman. I am not the kind to get mad. But you make me want to blow you up with dynamite. I want to kill you!

CONSTANCE: Sit down, May. Why do you want to kill Mr. Bullough?

SUZANNE: Constance, when you can't even handle a writing course, why start group therapy?

CONSTANCE: Because I feel like it, Suzanne. Let's have it, May.

MAY: I want to kill him because of the flowers. This degraded, obscene writing takes the beauty of flowers and makes them part of some disgusting incest between a crazy mother and an infantile son, and if that's what people want to write about, all right, but leave God's clean, sweet, gentle flowers out of it! They don't deserve to be in hell, where this madman obviously is, but here on earth with the real and the true and the good!

SUZANNE: Way to go, May. I couldn't have said that better myself.

MAY: Thank you, Suzanne.

SUZANNE: I don't think he should read one word more of this. Constance?

CONSTANCE: (*To Buford*) Read!

(*Buford plunges on*)

BUFORD: (*Reading aloud*) " 'Hey!' the woman yelled from the hall. 'You still there?'

" 'Yes, Edna Craig.'

" 'I can't get no good music on this goddamned radio. Just a lot of fiddles.'

" 'That's short wave. You get Europe with it.'

" 'But not 'WRD in Ridersberg, huh? What the hell?'

" 'Forget it. Come to bed.'

" 'Oh. All right.'

"And she did, to his mother's bed, to lie with him beneath the carved candleflame headboard, where, against linen-slipped feather pillows which clung in the damp Ridersville night delightfully to the skin, he took off her cheap clothes, slowly, while eyes closed, Edna Craig Somebody moaned, breathed heavily, as sudden in lust as in roadhouse friendship, churning through the bed with her large hips until she saw him holding himself back, and staring at her. She folded her hands over the creased flesh at her throat, as if about to pat her hair, set herself somehow right, uncertain of him.

" 'Honey, come on. Do it. What's wrong?'

" 'Nothing.'

" 'Yes, there is. Is it me?'

" 'No. Honest.'

" 'Then is it you?'

" 'I have trouble sometimes.'

" 'Listen, so do I. Who don't? My old man and me bang together some nights like boxcars and nothing happens. Hush. Don't fret. Put your head here on Mama's tits and get some rest.' "

MAY: Oh!

SUZANNE: Oh, vomit! Vomit!

BUFORD: (*Reading aloud*) "He woke from sleeping against her, refreshed, as if both their bodies had undergone a sea-change, and when he reached for her now, it was with purpose. She opened herself to receive him. In mutual relief, and a taking of chance-grafted flesh, they moved each into the other until they were struck, held, they molded again into sleep."

MAY: The end! I hope!

SUZANNE: Is that really the conclusion, finally, of this nauseating exhibition of anti-female pornography?

BUFORD: No! Course not! He has to wake up and see his Mama again!

SUZANNE: I knew it!

MAY: I just don't think I can stand that, really, I can't. This course is not for me!

SUZANNE: It's worse than it was last year! I was a fool to take it.

MAY: So was I. And I mean to complain to the dean of this college. My trust has been betrayed.

SUZANNE: We'll both complain. (*To Constance*) Which won't do you any good here, I'll tell you that.

CONSTANCE: Go complain. Be my guest.

SUZANNE: What did you say?

MAY: Well, really!

CONSTANCE: (*To Buford*) Buford. Buford.

BUFORD: Whut?

CONSTANCE: The title. "F.M." It doesn't mean "Fiction Material," does it?

(*May and Suzanne stare at Constance*)

BUFORD: No, ma'am.

CONSTANCE: And it doesn't mean "Frequency Modulation," does it?

BUFORD: No, ma'am.

CONSTANCE: It means "Fucking Mother," doesn't it?

(*May and Suzanne stare at Buford*)

BUFORD: Yes, ma'am, hit does.

CONSTANCE: Wonderful!!

MAY: Oh, my God!

SUZANNE: That does it!

MAY: Let me out of here! This is altogether intolerable and downright repulsive!

SUZANNE: And you're finished with this course, Constance! Finished! Come on, May!

(*Exeunt May and Suzanne*)

BUFORD: 'Bye. (*To Constance*) Ah'm sorry to have bothered you. Ah never meant to get you in trouble.

(*Constance walks slowly to Buford. She takes a chair, sets it at the table beside his, about four feet away*)

CONSTANCE: Give me the bottle.

(*Buford hands her the bottle of bourbon. Constance starts to drink. Then she puts the needle back on the phonograph record and sits beside Buford. Music*)

Read on, Buford. Read on.

(*She listens, and only when he begins to read does she take another long, slow drink from the bottle. The same music plays again*)

BUFORD: (*Reading aloud*) "When he woke, the harsh morning sun was a glare against his mother's bedroom window. He was alone in the bed. He reached above him, and touched the carved flutings of the candleflame headboard, which represented, he now remembered, the Garden of Eden. Rosewood, he recalled. Bought in Tennessee, by his grandfather, and he himself born beneath it. And there, above his ear, his mother called to him once more, in a voice clear, and with laughter quiet, as if it was only a complicated joke they shared together.

And he saw her again, in freedom, shorn of all her burdens,
his mother within a burning garden of wood, and to the woman
whose hands had broken him, but in whose smiles was his
hope, and from whose pain came his understanding, he said,
Goodbye."

(*Music. Pause. Looking ahead. Constance reaches out her hand,
and Buford, looking ahead, takes it*)

The End

Jerome McDonough
JUVIE

Jerome McDonough

Texas playwright Jerome McDonough is the author of nineteen published plays that have been performed throughout the United States and Canada and in Hong Kong and West Germany. He makes his debut in this series with *Juvie*, a jolting ensemble piece on the devastating effects of juvenile delinquency. The work of this prolific playwright first caught my attention in 1974, when Mr. McDonough's one-act *The Old Oak Encounter* appeared along with my own award-winning play *The Knight-Mare's Nest* in the collection *A Pocketful of Wry*, edited by I.E. Clark.

In a streak of good fortune, five of Mr. McDonough's first plays were accepted for publication within a little more than a year. Widely available for production through several play publishers, titles now include *Stages; It's Sad, So Sad When an Elf Goes Bad; Eden; O Little Town; Requiem; Asylum; Fables; Plots; The Nearest Star; Filiation; The Least of These; The Betrothed; Transceiver; Dirge; A Short Stretch at the Galluses;* and *The Noble's Reward.* His most recent release, published in the fall of 1983, is the one act-play *Roomers.*

Two of Mr. McDonough's plays were winners in the Texas Educational Theatre Association Playwriting Contest: *Eden* (1979) and *Asylum* (1977). *Asylum* was also named fifth on the International Thespian Society's 1980 list of Most Produced Short Plays.

With a B.S. in Speech/Theatre and an M.A. in Creative Writing from West Texas State University, Mr. McDonough is a dedicated teacher and director who shares his expertise with students at Caprock High School in the Amarillo Independent School District. He has also conducted creative writing workshops at Amarillo College. Mr. McDonough resides in Amarillo with his wife Raenell and son Brian.

Conceived in a style popular with high school and college performers, *Juvie* uses ensemble and multiple role-playing techniques to achieve its stunning impact. Although the play has a documentary flavor in its presentation of juvenile offenders, the characters in *Juvie* are entirely fictitious. With devout religious convictions Mr. McDonough dedicates *Juvie* "to the Lord, who has kept the words coming for so many years and whose whispers will, I hope, continue."

Characters:

The Inmate Ensemble
   JEAN
   SUNNY
   SKIP
   CAREY
   ANDREW
   ANN
   PINKY
   JANE
GUARD 1
GUARD 2
VOICE (*Over loudspeaker*)
   [NOTE: *Other named characters in the script are all played by members of the Inmate Ensemble.*]

Time:

The Present

Place:

Juvenile Detention holding cells. The building is called "Juvie" by its inmates.

At rise, the stage is virtually bare. Dark wood planks or 1-inch dowels define the perimeters of two jail cells, one for boys and one for girls. These boards lie flat on the floor, and the two areas are divided in rough proportion to the number of each sex in the cast. Many roles may be played by either sex, so the size is flexible. The characters themselves define their incarceration by their movement; physical walls do not necessarily do so.

   Two guards will alternate bringing the inmates into the jail as the charges against each young person are read. Once the action of the play begins, the characters will be "locked up" during reality sections but may wander freely throughout the area when portraying another person or when involved in recollections. Each recollection ends, however, with all inmates locked up again.

As the cells fill with inmates, each establishes his or her own territory or his or her inability to establish it. Each inmate knows only who he or she is—there is no way to know who the others are—even the stories the others tell may be fabrications. This insecurity/instability should color each performer and performance. The feelings of each character within the whole must be constantly on each character's mind. There are two chairs in each of the two cells. There may also be a few pallets around, but they are probably not inviting. Power struggles for the two chairs may form secondary physical/emotional plots.

VOICE: *(As Guard 1 brings on Jean and locks her up)* Armstrong, Jean, female, 15. Apprehended in process of burglary of a habitation. Complaint pending, assault. Probation violation. Two prior convictions. Parent notification attempt unsuccessful. *(Jean will have progressive drug withdrawal symptoms as the play progresses. Cell door is shut [mimed] by Guard 1 as Guard 2 brings Sunny on. Reading of charges should be practically continuous)* Collins, Margaret, also known as Sunny, female, 16. Investigation of aggravated assault and unlawful flight to avoid prosecution. Action pending verified information, Woodson P. D. *(She is locked in. The action of bringing on each character and locking him or her in the cell is the same for each offender.)* Sanderson, Jeffrey, also known as Skip, male, 16. Driving under the influence, second offense; driving without a license, resisting arrest. Probation violation. Parent notification attempt unsuccessful. Miller, Carey, female, 16. Leaving the scene of an accident, hit and run. Parents notified. Marler, Andrew, male, 15. Communicating gambling information, specifically delivery of bookmaking and numbers receipts. Five previous arrests, varying charges—all dismissed on basis of incompetency. Remanded to Department of Human Resources, five times. Guardian notified. Ballew, Ann Elizabeth, female, 14. Theft over $20 and under $200, specifically shoplifting. Parents notified. Simpson, Charlotte, also known as Pinky, alias Charlotte Singleton and C. J. Simpkins, female, 16. Delivery of a controlled substance, possession of a controlled substance, carrying a prohibited weapon, unlawful flight to avoid prosecution, resisting arrest. Probation violation. Five prior convictions. Parents refused to appear. Probation officer notified. *(Pinky will have some drug withdrawal symptoms, even though de-*

nying them) Doe, Jane, Arrest Number 773, female, approximate age 13. Investigation of runaway, resisting arrest. Refuses to give name, address, parent's name or location. Department of Human Resources notified. Parents unknown.

(*Silence as the inmates regard each other carefully. Some shifting of locations may occur as value judgments are made. The guards reappear at the periphery of the stage. They will walk the perimeter of the performance space, and even the audience area itself, during the play, abandoning this activity only when needed within the action of the play. They carry nightsticks or shotguns. Pinky rises and surveys the crowd in the holding cells. She acts disappointed)*

PINKY: My, my. Is this Saturday night or not? Where are the regulars? (*Sees Andrew Marler and crosses to near the bars separating the boys' cell from the girls' cell*) Ah, here's a familiar face—Andy the Vege.

ANDREW: Don't you call me that.

PINKY: Andy the Vege, why don't you want me to call you Andy the Vege?

ANDREW: Don't. I know you. Don't call me that.

PINKY: What shall I call you?

ANDREW: Why do you call me that?

PINKY: What's two and two?

ANDREW: Four.

PINKY: Four and four?

ANDREW: . . . Eight.

PINKY: Eight and eight?

ANDREW: . . . Why do you call me that?

PINKY: What they got you for, Andy the Vege? White-collar crime? Counterspy intelligence ring? What, Andy the Vege?

ANDREW: Don't you call me that. I don't know why they got me. But I've got to get out. I've got to deliver the bags.

PINKY: Plastic bags?

ANDREW: No. Brown bags. With papers in them. If I don't deliver them, they'll fire me. I don't want to get fired. I have trouble getting jobs.

PINKY: No!

ANDREW: I've got to buy presents. I can't get fired.

PINKY: Maybe you can get a job in a salad, Andy the Vege.

ANDREW: Don't you call me that.

JEAN: (*Interrupting Pinky's next barb*) Back off from him.

PINKY: (*Turning to Jean*) What's it to you?

JEAN: You've got him enough.

PINKY: So who are you—Blondie the Vege?

JEAN: Jean. And I like being left alone.

PINKY: I'll bet that's how the guys spend their weekends.

JEAN: You've got a mouth that needs shutting.

PINKY: Come zip it, sister. (*They start for each other. Guard calls out*)

GUARD: Knock it off in there.

PINKY: What, no square dancing? (*Quietly, to Jean*) We'll settle this later.

JEAN: When you get out, bring your Medicare card. (*Jean turns away and Pinky abandons the effort and settles to a chair*)

SKIP: Too bad. I thought we'd see a cat fight. (*To Andrew*) Want to see a cat fight, Vege?

ANDREW: Don't you call me that. (*To Pinky*) See what you did?

PINKY: Can you ever forgive me?

ANDREW: I don't like that name.

JEAN: (*To Skip*) Why can't everybody leave him alone?

CAREY: Yes, leave him alone.

SKIP: Aren't mothers getting younger these days! You want to rock him to sleep? I'll find a rock for you.

JEAN: (*To Skip*) What've you got to be so mighty about? (*During the following [and the rest of the recollections] the lights may remain the same or some device to set the solo performer apart may be used. In this and all other solo sequences, the character portrays himself or herself in the recollection and is not confined by the imaginary cell walls. The other inmates [the "Inmate Ensemble] take roles as indicated*)

SKIP: I shouldn't be in here. So I was a little drunk, so I've got balloon breath, so what? If booze rots my guts, they're mine to rot.

JEAN: I'm for that.

SKIP: Anyway, I'm not the menace on the streets. Do you know who is? Old people. (*Skip picks up a chair and brings it down to the apron. Another male inmate also takes a chair and places it next to him, assuming the role of Sammy. These two will mime Skip's story as narrated by him*) I was out on the Interstate on Monday. Rush hour, bumper-to-bumper but we were movin' OK, sixty, sixty-five. Then it's like somebody put up a wall. Two old geezers are pokin' along in the center and right lane, maybe fifty miles an hour. Happy hour was sliding away and

I was sitting there, practically parked. The left lane was full of people going ninety, but this long clear stretch was comin' up on the right, so I just whipped it over on to the shoulder, two wheels on the grass and two on the pavement, and I opened her up. I hit seventy, eighty and passed those fools. I started to pull back on, but then I saw this light pole a couple of hundred feet in front of me. Sammy was ridin' with me that day and he's always been a real old lady about my driving, so I figured here was my chance. I headed straight for that pole. I thought Sam was going to climb out through the vent window.

SAMMY: Get back on the road, man! (*Pinky laughs*)

SKIP: I was maybe ten feet from the pole when I cut back on to the highway. Couldn't have missed it by a foot. Sammy just fell over.

JEAN: Great joke. Almost kill yourself and your friend.

SKIP: (*As Skip and the other inmate return the chairs to the cell*) Never even came close. I can tell how far something's in front of the car, no matter how fast I'm going. And I can judge even better after a few drinks. Really. Better. (*Lights up fully if not already so*)

JEAN: Stinking thinking.

SKIP: What?

JEAN: My brother was an alcoholic. They sent him to A.A. after his third fall. They call that stinking thinking.

SKIP: Who you calling an alcoholic?

JEAN: Drunks rationalize everything.

SKIP: It's OK. I'm coming off my little buzz every second, but how about you? You think I don't see the signs coming on? The moves, the eyes darting around? I'm getting better every second, but how about you? (*Indicating Pinky*) How about her? Maybe some of the others, too. I haven't made a comprehensive junkie count.

JEAN: Shut up!

SKIP: Sure. I'm getting better every second. How about you?

(*Everything quiets. The cells are silent. Carey rises and comes slowly to the edge of the cell area and looks out. The rest of the cast will animate Carey's story as indicated*)

CAREY: I wonder if there's some primitive place left in the world, a place with trees and beaches and warm weather all year and lots of children to play among it all. (*During speech, cast moves to up center and forms two circles, one inside the other, both facing inward. In slow motion, the circles start to move in opposite directions, symbolizing some universal children's game*) They could run on the sand and chase each other in the surf like dolphins.

CHILD'S VOICE: (*From within the circles*) Aunt Carey, you're sitting with us tonight, aren't you? You promised.

CAREY: Of course. I'll be there. (*Back to the island portrait fantasy*) I wouldn't need much. Just a quiet place near the beach so I could watch the children. (*Circle game stops, and the two circles start to move their still-joined hands and arms in slow motion suggestion of the ocean's waves*) And if one got too far into the surf, I could swim out and bring him back. Or if the weather turned bad, I could shout to them so they'd run and cuddle in their huts with their families until the storm had passed. (*During this last, the waves cease and the circles move together, arms raised and joined, suggesting the pointed thatched roof of a hut. Freeze*)

CHILD'S VOICE: Don't go, Carey. Stay tonight, too.

CAREY: I'll keep you Friday again. You pick the books we'll read. (*Back to the island*) I wouldn't need much. I'd stay there forever. Or until machines started coming in. Machines are the evil in us. We look for something to kill—like I killed.

MOTHER'S VOICE: He isn't dead, Carey. Don't think about it.

CAREY: What else can I think about? (*The hut breaks up, and several people take sides for touch football. Others watch from upstage. The quarterback takes the ball, fades back, and throws to a boy, who runs toward the apron. Carey mimes driving. On cue, a "car" hits the boy. Carey mimes panicked driving in place. The rest rush to the boy and watch him helplessly for balance of speech. Freeze*) Every night for the rest of my life I'll see that blonde head and that striped shirt. I'll see it for the split second before I crushed it under the machine, before I tried to drive so far and so fast that it didn't ever happen. And I'll see the red and the water from the Mother's eyes and the wheeling bed and the doors swinging closed, redder and more horrible than if I'd really seen it. Then I'll see it again and I'll open my eyes and try not to scream because my throat already hurts so much, but I'll scream anyway. And it won't dry even one drop of the red and I'll try to keep my eyes open but they'll sink again and I'll see it all over.

CHILD'S VOICE: Aunt Carey? . . . Aunt Carey? . . .

CAREY: I—hope I don't—have many nights.
(*The scene breaks, and the inmates return to the cell. Carey stands at the downstage edge of the cell, her hand slightly before her, as if half-reaching for something*)

GUARD: Hands inside the bars, girl.

PINKY: What's she gonna do, bend 'em?

GUARD: You know the rules, Pinky.

PINKY: Yeah, I know 'em.

GUARD: (*Toward Jane Doe, who has taken up residence in a far corner*) You, in the corner. You ready to talk? (*No response from Jane*) You're just makin' it tough on yourself. (*No response*) OK. (*Guard moves back to patrol. Skip turns toward Jane*)

SKIP: Keep it up, kid. Don't say anything and they can't hang anything on you.

JEAN: Or they can stick you with everything.

SUNNY: You don't have to *do* anything. You just have to be around when something happens.

SKIP: Oh, yeah. (*Mimicking*) "Really, officer, I was just standing there and these seven guys jumped in front of my machine gun."

SUNNY: You don't have to do anything. (*Indicating guard*) Can he hear me?

JEAN: They don't listen.

PINKY: Nobody believes anybody in here, anyway. You can't find your lunch meat for all the bologna.

SUNNY: We'd been smoking—a bunch of us—just sitting around listening to some music, and it got to where everything was funny. We smoked some more, and it got funnier and funnier. Then it just dropped. I was so bored I could have eaten the walls to get out of there. So Hank says:

HANK: (*Played by Skip*) Let's go get some beer. (*Car cue— Sunny and Skip set up chairs down center to suggest car*)

SUNNY: I didn't want any, but it was better than staying. We pulled up at the Pak-Mart (*Andy becomes the Pak-Mart clerk. Other action follows narration*), and the guy that works there was playing some video game, and he didn't even look up when we came in, just kept moving his shoulders the way guys do when they're destroying the universe with those things. (*Andy mimes the video game, facing off, near the right proscenium pillar*) We pulled two six-packs out of the cooler, and Hank started bugging the guy to wait on us, but he kept saying:

CLERK: Just a second, just a second.

SUNNY: Like he was going for the Guinness Book or something. Well, Hank was pretty far gone, and he kicked the plug out. The guy came unglued. He threw Hank up against the wall and started beating on him. The next thing I knew, Hank had a knife—it was in his pocket or he grabbed it off the rack, and he shoved it right in that guy's face. The guy was screaming and shaking Hank, but he couldn't see. Hank grabbed a can and hit the guy on the head. He dropped. He wasn't moving. Hank just stood there, moving his head from side to side, just moving his head. Then he threw the can down and grabbed me and pushed me in the car. He sideswiped a car that was pulling into the lot and I could see it was some kids from the party. Hank saw them, too, and he started twitching like he was having a fit.

HANK: They'll know who did it.

SUNNY: (*Playing the role*) "I didn't do anything."

HANK: You're with me, aren't you? We've got to get out of here.

SUNNY: (*Narrating again*) I didn't know what to do. I was afraid to cross him. (*Beat*) We stayed on back roads to avoid the Interstate.

HANK: Once we make it to the city, we'll just fade into the crowd.

SUNNY: We got into the city about sunrise, and Hank got even crazier. His eyes kept darting everywhere, and he started twitching again. He saw a cop parked by the curb, and he just went nuts. He took off about eighty miles an hour. That cop wasn't even looking at him, but when he took off, that cop called in the rest of the cops in the world. We were running lights and taking corners at fifty miles an hour, and I fell down on the floorboard and I kept screaming, "Hank, stop! Please stop!" But he wouldn't. He sheared off a lamp post and took a right down an alley. He thought he could make it between a truck and the wall, then at the last second he panicked and tried to stop. The car skidded sideways into the truck, Hank's side first. I saw red in front of my eyes. I guess I passed out. When I woke up, Hank was bent over the wheel with blood coming out of the corner of his eye. (*Pause*) Hank's going to be all right, they told me. But I don't know. I don't know.

(*Pause. Then the scene breaks and all return to cells as a guard enters*)

GUARD: Ann Ballew.

ANN: (*Rising*) Am I getting out?

GUARD: (*Unlocking bars*) Your lawyer.

ANN: Lawyer? I don't need a lawyer. It's going to be fixed. (*This last remark is met with amused skepticism by the experienced inmates*)

GUARD: This way. (*He leads her toward down left, where the lawyer, Beth Sims [one of the Inmate Ensemble], waits. There are two chairs down left*)

SIMS: I'm Elizabeth Sims. Your father contacted me.

ANN: I don't need a lawyer. It's all going to be fixed.

SIMS: It's not that simple. Stores are prosecuting now as a matter of policy.

ANN: They don't put this in the newspapers, do they?

SIMS: No.

ANN: If it got back to the school, I don't know what I'd do. I couldn't face that.

SIMS: Tell me what happened.

ANN: I pleaded with Mother for those clothes, but she wouldn't listen. So there wasn't any other way. (*An Inmate Ensemble member becomes a clerk and another a customer in the store. Clerk will show Customer items during the clothes-changing sequence. Action follows narration*) We have a charge account at the store, so I figured if I got caught they'd just put it on that and not make any fuss. I took two outfits in the dressing room. I put my own clothes on over one and laid the other one on the counter while the clerk was busy. But she followed me and when she caught up, she could see the other stuff under my shirt. Then they called the police. Just called the police even after I told them who I was! Isn't there some way to fix it? Surely Daddy can do something.

SIMS: We'll do the best we can and emphasize first offense.

ANN: Can I go home now?

SIMS: (*Shaking her head*) The processing isn't finished. After they set bail, we can get you out.

ANN: When will that be?

SIMS: It's crowded downstairs. It could take most of the night. (*Calling*) Guard? (*Back to Ann*) Don't discuss the case with anybody. We'll get you out as soon as we can. (*Guard takes Ann back. As she approaches, Pinky speaks*)

PINKY: Well, are they gonna give you the chair, or are

you hoping for lethal injection? (*Pinky finds great humor in Ann's terror*)

JEAN: Why is everybody your personal target?

PINKY: Because everybody deserves it. Look around here. Juvenile Detention. Aren't you all the pick of the crop, though!

SKIP: And you're not locked up?

PINKY: Junior, inside—just like outside—there is an order of things. You've got your higher forms (*Indicating herself*) and you've got your crawling things that eat their way through the dirt. (*Indicating everybody else*)

JEAN: You are scum.

PINKY: I am former scum—scum.

(*Pinky will drift through the cell areas and the downstage areas. Inmates will interact with her, portraying the various drug addicts and other characters in her recollection. Action follows narration*)

PINKY: The streets are full of earth eaters, and I see that they get taken every day. It's everybody else's turn. I've had mine. I was on the receiving end, hanging out with losers, scratching for a connection of some fourth-rate stuff so laced up with powdered sugar you're more likely to get diabetes than anything else. Then I took a look around. I'd been down here for two-bit theft and extortion and burglary and I'd done some time, and there was nothin' but more of the same facin' me. I figured if I was going to take a fall, it might as well be worth it. So I moved into management. Then all those empty eye sockets could come to me—on my terms. Whatever I wanted, they came through with it. And me rakin' off the best, no charge. If one'd cross me or undercut me with somebody else, he might not get his for a while or I'd cut it way down and make him think he'd slipped deeper. You ought to see 'em panic when they come back and say it wasn't enough. So maybe somebody catches you at it, cuttin' the stuff, what're they gonna do, call a cop? If they kick, you just back off and say, "Hey, mistakes happen. Here's some better—on the house." And you slip him maybe three times the strength he's had or some stuff with a little more strychnine in it than usual. You won't have that problem again. (*Junkie shoots up, overdoses, and dies horribly, center*) The word hits fast when somebody comes up gagging. Maybe business slacks off for a day or two, but then the pains start again, and those smilin' jerks are knockin' on your door again just like you were their guardian angel and a candy store all rolled into one. (*She sells to the Junkies*)

JEAN: Once a junkie . . .

PINKY: (*Coming back into the cell*) Nah, I don't do hard stuff any more. Maybe once in a while. Rarely. No sweatin' for me. No sweatin'. They can keep me a week, man, I'll be all right. Two weeks—no sweat. (*To Jean*) How are you feelin'—scum? (*Pinky's statement has silenced the cells. Those who were not asleep try to do so. The night is progressing, and fatigue mixed with fear is telling on the inmates. The cells are silent. A guard drifts past*)

GUARD: Hey, in the corner. Got anything to say yet? (*No response from Jane Doe*) OK. (*Guard walks on*)

(*Jane Doe, speaking in soliloquy, unheard by the others, comes forward to speak to the audience. Two Inmate Ensemble members and one of the guards will act out her story as action follows narration. No sound or actual contact in the mimed section*)

JANE: They want me to talk. Well, they can hang it out until it rots. I've done my talking. I've done my listening, too. (*One inmate becomes her mother, another her father*) I've heard enough footsteps in the night, my old lady sneaking in the back door, the old man sneaking out the front. (*Interior scenes played toward center, exterior toward right*) Who were they sneaking from? Neither of them could have cared less. I've heard the bottles falling and the blows falling. (*Mother slaps Father*) I've heard the screaming and the cursing. I've heard the knife come out of the drawer and the footsteps running into the yard. (*Father, with knife, pursues Mother into yard*) I've heard the neighbors yelling and the sirens pulling up to the house. I've heard the lies to cover up the horror. (*Mother and Father re-enter house. Policeman exits*) I've heard the cops pull away and heard the fists again. (*Father slaps Mother very hard. Freeze*) So I don't listen any more. And I don't talk. (*Pause*) By now, there's nothing to say.

(*Slowly she returns to her position. Other actors return to cell. Jane sinks to her position on the floor again. Pinky rises and crosses to Jane Doe*)

PINKY: Hey, loud mouth. (*No response. Pinky gives Jane a shove with her foot. Jane turns and looks at her*) You got a tongue? (*Jane does not respond*) You figure if you keep quiet long enough, they'll just wrap you up and drop you on Mr. and Mrs. America's doorstep, and the first thing you know you're on the cover of Miss Teen Queen magazine, huh? Well, if they don't know where to put you, they just put you any place—any

place that's exactly like home except for the bars on the windows and the locks on the doors and your new circle of friends.
(*Other girl inmates rise and form two groups. One group sits down center in a small circle suggesting lounging in the detention home courtyard. The other group, perhaps only two girls, is at the down left proscenium pillar. One girl in this group sits, leaning against the pillar. She is the Leader and the other girl is her Lieutenant*)

JEAN: (*To Pinky*) Don't you ever quit?
PINKY: I'm expanding this girl's education.
JEAN: You belong in a swamp.
PINKY: You belong under one.
SKIP: (*Rising, briefly, from his sleep*) Two points.
PINKY: (*Back to Jane*) I've been to several of those homes and, sister, you are ripe. (*Jane moves downstage and between the two groups. She looks around until the Leader beckons to her*) There are always some girls who've been there a long time and you're going to look like just what they had in mind. (*Leader beckons to Jane, who crosses to her*)
JEAN: Stop it.
PINKY: Shut up. (*Back to Jane*) Because these girls don't like to get their own cigarettes or make their own beds or wash their own clothes—or anything. They'd rather have somebody do it for them. (*During this sequence, Jane will be asked in mime to go bum a cigarette for the Leader. She will cross to the other group and request the cigarette from a girl, who will wave her away. She will point, indicating it is for the Leader, and the girl will grudgingly give Jane a cigarette. Jane takes the cigarette back to the Leader and lights it for her*) Of course you can say no, but it's amazing how many friends they have and how persuasive they can be. There's your choice—a slave or have your guts on a plate maybe twice a day. So you become her personal property and she'll take care of you so long as you take care of her— and anybody else she decides to have you take care of. (*About this point, the cigarette has been lighted and the Lieutenant shoves Jane, sending her away. This angers the Leader, who shoves the Lieutenant and beckons Jane to come back. The Leader then gestures the Lieutenant away, throwing her from power. She gestures Jane into the Lieutenant's place. As the sequence ends, the former Lieutenant has tried to join the center group but has been shunted and is alone between stage left and center. Pinky continues talking without interruption*) But you'll be perfectly safe—unless one day she needs some lipstick or a blouse somebody else has, and then

she might negotiate a trade and you are it. So you've got a new big sister, and the process goes on until you're a big sister yourself—if you live that long. (*The yard sequence breaks up, and Jane is returning to her corner*) Yeah, girl, keep your mouth shut. And remember to embroider a sign for your cell—"There's No Place Like Home."

(*The cells are quiet. Andrew stirs a bit and calls quietly over into the girls' cell*)

ANDREW: Girl?

SUNNY: Me?

ANDREW: No. (*Pointing to Jean*) Her. Her.

SUNNY: (*Poking Jean and calling*) Jean . . . (*When Jean looks up, Sunny points to Andrew*)

JEAN: (*To Andrew*) What?

ANDREW: Thank you.

JEAN: For what?

ANDREW: For, you know, when she was calling me that name.

JEAN: It's OK.

ANDREW: When someone does something for you, you're supposed to say, "Thank you." I learned that.

JEAN: Yeah.

ANDREW: . . . Thank you.

JEAN: You're welcome.

(*Pause. Andrew doesn't want this conversation to end*)

ANDREW: I wish they'd let me out of here. I have to deliver the bags or I'll get fired. It's hard for me to find jobs.

JEAN: Me, too.

ANDREW: Yeah?

JEAN: Yeah.

ANDREW: (*Pause*) Do you know what you're in here for?

JEAN: Yeah.

ANDREW: I wish I knew.

JEAN: (*Rising, looking out front*) Burglary of a habitation.

ANDREW: What?

JEAN: They got me for burglary of a habitation—a house.

ANDREW: Oh . . . You didn't . . . hurt anybody or kill anybody, did you?

JEAN: I . . . they got me for burglary of a habitation. (*Jean moves to down left and begins acting out her scene, gradually moving to right. The closet she speaks of will be center, facing right. The Old Man will enter from right and move into the "bedroom" from the upstage side*) The front door was open. Weird, isn't it? They're almost always open. Or there's a key under the doormat—or in the mailbox. You could tell it was an old guy's place—old books and pipes around, everything dusty. He lived alone, it looked like. But I wasn't worried about him. I had to get a couple of hundreds' worth to the fence, or I couldn't make my connection and I needed it. His TV was too big, and it was black and white, anyway, and those people never have stereos. There wasn't much in the back, either, but I knew that people that age always keep some money stashed some-where in the place. The Depression or something made them that way. I was digging through his shoes—the money's there a lot of the time—when I heard the front door open. I was stuck. He'd be blocking the hall, so I crouched down in the closet.

OLD MAN: Who's there?

JEAN: I quit breathing. I heard him coming into the bed-room.

OLD MAN: Who's there? (*He crosses to the closet, center*)

JEAN: I heard him touch the doorknob on the closet, and I slammed against the door. (*She pushes forward, but the Old Man steps back out of the way and she falls, right*) When I started to get up, he was holding a gun on me.

OLD MAN: (*Peering*) You're a girl! (*Pause*) What do you want?

JEAN: "I just wanted to get warm." He wasn't having it.

OLD MAN: Get up from there. (*Action follows dialogue*)

JEAN: I saw a cane leaning in the corner. I grabbed it and smashed his hand with it and snatched the gun up. (*Looking at gun*) A lighter! He'd been covering me with a cigarette lighter. (*Back to Old Man*) "OK, where is it? I know it's here someplace."

OLD MAN: Why are you doing this?

JEAN: "Give me the money, and I'll get out of here." (*She circles him on this line, moving toward center, getting to the center side of him*) Then he really set me back.

OLD MAN: You want it for drugs, don't you? You can't have it, not for that.

JEAN: (*Shoving the cane in his face*) "Where is it?"

OLD MAN: If you're hungry, I'll get you some food. If you need something, I'll try to help you. But not for that.

JEAN: "Where is it?"

OLD MAN: (*Indicating cane*) You're going to have to use that. I'm not giving you any money.

JEAN: I was really strung by that time, and I started swinging that cane at him. He never said anything, never yelled or anything. (*Action follows dialogue*) I could see that he was really hurt, but I didn't stop. It was like he was the only thing between me and the king high of all time. I hit him again and the cops were on me. (*Guard grabs her. Two more inmates enter, carrying two "cell bars" [thick dowel rods do well for this purpose]. When the time comes, the Old Man will be placed on these two bars and balanced so that they function as a stretcher*) The ambulance guys were fixing him up and the cops were trying to get his statement—and he wouldn't give one. They kept talking about how I'd beaten him up and how I was a junkie and they could maybe lock me up for good, and he still wouldn't give a statement. Then he did the weirdest thing of all. They were taking him out, and the cops were still trying to get him to sign but he just looked at me and said . . .

OLD MAN: No. She doesn't know what she's doing. (*Old Man is carried out*)

JEAN: Not like I was crazy, but like he forgave me because I really didn't know what I was doing. The first time in my life anybody ever cared one thing about me one way or the other and who is it, a guy I just beat up. (*Pause*) Maybe I *could* straighten out. Make a living or something. Maybe. I don't know. (*Pause*) I hope that old guy's all right. I want to see him—later—when I know what I'm doing. (*Her withdrawal symptoms get worse. She is silent*)

(*The cells are silent. The inmates who played the Old Man and the Ambulance Attendants return and take their places in the cells. The Guard enters*)

GUARD: They're ready to process these people. (*As each inmate is named, he or she rises and stands in line by the door to the cell*) Sanderson, Collins, Simpson, Ballew, Miller, and Doe. (*Doors are opened, and girls move out left, boys out right*) Somebody'll be by from D.H.R. for you, Andy.

JEAN: What about me?

GUARD: (*To other Guard*) Take 'em on. (*After all are gone, to Jean*) They're not ready for you yet.

JEAN: Why not?

GUARD: Another charge is pending.

JEAN: What other charge? He wouldn't sign the complaint.

GUARD: You may be processed on the adult side.

JEAN: Adult side?

GUARD: (*Pause*) The old man died, Jean. The autopsy will determine the charge.

(*Guard exits. Jean is stunned. She knows that the charge will be capital murder, since the killing took place during the commission of a felony. She moves to the chair, her face blank. There is silence for several counts. Andrew rises and stands, looking out past the audience, as if he can see all that he tells. No one acts out his story. Jean probably does not hear. Her fear and her withdrawal are taking all her attention*)

ANDREW: When I'm not in jail—I'm really not in jail very much—they always put me with nice people. But then the police come get me and I never know what it's about. Somebody told me one time that it's wrong to hurt people or to kill people and that you get put in jail for that and maybe even get killed yourself for doing it. But I didn't hurt anybody or kill anybody. I told them I didn't and they kept asking me why I said that and I said because it was true and then a nice policeman would come in and say, "Oh, that's Andy." And I told him that I didn't hurt anybody or kill anybody and he'd say, "I know, Andy, I know." I was glad he was there. I'd stay in jail for a day or maybe two days and then they'd take me to meet some new nice people. I don't know what happens to the nice people I was with before. Maybe they move away while I'm in jail. I had some special people a long time ago, real special for some reason—I can't remember why—and they moved away, too. Just one day I woke up and they were gone and I didn't know where. I cried, I think, and I stayed there for a long time waiting for them to come back but they didn't—and I got real hungry. I remember that. I started looking for something to eat out behind the place where we lived and there were a few things. And I found a cat that I liked a lot. And then a lady came and talked to me and then I started to meet the nice people, the first ones. They said I couldn't take the cat with me and I was kind of sad about that, but the people were nice and I was with them a long, long time and I didn't go to jail or anything. But then one day I did—and when I got out, I guess they'd moved. (*Pause*) I get kind of scared in jail. People aren't nice in there sometimes and they do things to me that make me hurt and I ask them to stop but they won't. And I can't make them stop because there's maybe two or three of them and I'm strong but I can't stop no two or three of them, and sometimes they have a knife and I'm scared of it. And what if that policeman isn't there sometime when they bring me in and I tell them I didn't kill anybody or hurt anybody and they don't believe me. They might kill me then. But I'll meet the nice people soon. Maybe tomorrow. And they won't move this time. And I won't get in jail again. And I'll go back where I lived and find that cat and bring him back with me. Everything'll be all right then. Everything'll be all right.

(*Guard re-enters and releases Andrew to meet the Social Worker off right. Jean is onstage alone. The inmates file back on and stand far downstage, facing the audience, line-up style. The Voice will read the verdict as each inmate steps forward in character. Following sentencing, each character steps back in line. A definite opening in the line-up is left for Skip, who is not present*)

VOICE: Miller, Carey—Hit and Run, guilty. Two years juvenile detention, ten years probation. Collins, Margaret "Sunny"—Accessory to Aggravated Assault and Unlawful Flight to Avoid Prosecution, guilty. Six months juvenile detention suspended to three years probation. Sanderson, Jeffrey "Skip" . . . (*Pause as spotlight focuses on the empty space where Skip should be*) . . . charges dropped. Accused killed in one-vehicle accident while awaiting trial. Two passengers also killed. Ballew, Ann—Theft, shoplifting, guilty. Sentenced to one year of weekend work in local retirement home and two years probation. Simpson, Charlotte "Pinky"—Delivery of a Controlled Substance, guilty; Possession of a Controlled Substance, guilty; Carrying a Prohibited Weapon, guilty; Unlawful Flight to Avoid Prosecution, guilty; Resisting Arrest, guilty. Tried as an adult. Sentenced to five years at State Detention Facility and ten years adult probation. Marler, Andrew—Gambling Violation, charges dropped, remanded to Department of Human Resources. Doe, Jane, Arrest Number 773—remanded to Department of Human Resources pending further information. Housed at Simmons County Minimum Security Juvenile Detention Facility.

(*The Guards watch as the inmates file off again, then follow them off. Jean is left alone in the cell, silent, moving only slightly as a result of her withdrawal. After several counts, the Voice is heard again)*

Armstrong, Jean—charges pending—Capital Murder.

(Slowly, the front lights come down, leaving Jean in the shadows of the cell. Just as slowly, the stage lights come down. Blackout)

Curtain

Author's Production Notes

Juvie is an ensemble play. All the young people who are being detained in the Juvenile Detention Center form an "Inmate Ensemble." All the roles except the Guards may be played by ensemble members; thus, the cast may be as small as six. Or the cast size may be expanded to include extra inmates, whose only function will be to serve as actors in the "recollection" scenes.

Regardless of cast size, the play should not be a star vehicle. It is intended to present the realities of crime and its punishment in the plainest possible terms. Show biz is not the business of *Juvie*.

The play is written and loosely blocked for proscenium production, but an intimate space, such as an arena stage, might prove even more effective. A means of locking the audience up with the inmates of *Juvie*, at least symbolically, could underscore the horror of the situation better than more traditional approaches. Environmental production techniques are a definite possibility.

The play suggests an entire night in the holding cells. Therefore, as the play progresses, more and more people will fall off to sleep. By two-thirds of the way through the play, everyone except those directly participating in recollections will be sleeping. The discomfort of this arrangement will help underscore the general unpleasantness of the entire scene.

Another progression is the subtle change from the first moment in jail through learning more about the others in the cell and making certain assumptions about each character's own condition. This progression may be to greater anxiety, to plans of punishment evasion, to plea bargaining, to any of hundreds of other options, pleasant or unpleasant, which may occur to the character.

Another progression is from first moment to realization of future moments. Is release coming or is further detention to be expected?

Each character must evaluate his own progressions—and play them—and, above all, believe them.

Patrick Tovatt

BARTOK AS DOG

Patrick Tovatt

Patrick Tovatt's *Bartok as Dog* delighted both audiences and critics at the 1982 Actors Theatre of Louisville's SHORTS Festival. Dudley Saunders, reviewer for *The Louisville Times,* commented: ". . . *[Bartok as Dog,]* which explores the hardhearted hiring practices of some employers, is an amusing tale about a young man who just wants a non-demanding meal ticket job so he can dabble in his hobby. But the world is outraged by and suspicious of such lack of ambition. It is a clever play and introduces us to one of the festival's more appealing characters." The successful production was repeated in the Actors Theatre of Louisville's 1983 Humana Festival of New American Plays.

Mr. Tovatt was born at home in December of 1940 in Garrett Ridge, Colorado, the first of three children of Anthony and Patricia Tovatt. His childhood was spent in Gunnison and Boulder, Colorado, and he later attended junior high and high school in Muncie, Indiana. He then attended Harvard University, Antioch College, and the London School of Film Technique before entering the theatre in 1965.

Mr. Tovatt's play *Criminal Dogs* was produced at the Actors Theatre of Louisville as an Apprentice Showcase in 1978, and his musical *Gun for the Roses* was seen during the 1981 season's SHORTS Festival. Two other plays, *Middle Class White* and *Romance,* were produced by the playwrights' workshop (which he formed with fellow writer Miguel Pinero) at the Los Angeles Actors Theatre. His other works include original radio dramas and a documentary film for the California Department of Education, *Mini Corps,* about the bilingual education of children of migrant workers.

Also an experienced actor, Mr. Tovatt has played in companies at Cincinnati's Playhouse in the Park and Baltimore's Center Stage and appeared in the first San Francisco season of the American Conservatory Theatre. At Actors Theatre of Louisville he performed more than twenty roles over a period of several years, including the roles of Ray in the 1979 production of *Lone Star* and Harp in the premiere of *Gold Dust.*

A director as well, Mr. Tovatt was the Founding Producing Director of the Virginia Stage Company. In the winter of 1982 he staged the national companies of the Broadway musical *Pump Boys and Dinettes.*

When not actually in a theatre or on a set, Mr. Tovatt lives with radio producer Meredith Ludwig, several cows, nine geese, and two dogs in Logan County, Kentucky.

Cast of Characters:

FITZROY, *a cool, tough, middle-aged lie detector veteran who knows how to get a good, active response on the machine. He gives his corporate clients a lot of lies for the buck.*

BARRY PARSONS, *a nice guy of thirty-five. Barry has been a lot of places, has done a lot of things and has participated in the spirit of the times. He is looking for a job in an attempt to "re-enter the mainstream."*

LOIS, *smart, attractive, and disciplined, at twenty-eight she is on her way. A "rising star" in the large corporate headquarters where she works.*

MRS. MCCORMACK, *an imperturbable black businesswoman of fifty or more. She has a keen eye and strong convictions.*

Scene One:

A bare office: functional, containing an L-shaped table, and two chairs. In the chair at the foot of the L is a man, crisply dressed in a managerial three-piece suit. He is connected to a polygraph machine. His eyes are closed. Behind the machine sits an older man, equally crisply dressed. This is Fitzroy. He is administering this polygraph examination to Parsons. Silence. Fitzroy rises, walks stiffly to the door, and opens it. He gingerly stretches his back. He turns back, impassive, precise, businesslike.

FITZROY: I've been at this since eight. It was getting stuffy, didn't you think?

PARSONS: Yes. Thank you. I've been concentrating and wasn't really aware . . . the air feels good. (*Pause*) One tends to lose perspective in this situation . . . I think.

(Fitzroy looks at his machine. He waits precisely fifteen seconds following Parsons' last word before he speaks)

FITZROY: What was your gross income for 1981?

PARSONS: (*Sucking air, holding his breath, then exhaling, trying to formulate a truthful, but not prejudicial, response*) Aaaah . . . Almost . . . five thousand dollars . . . (*Pause*) Closer to . . . four thousand dollars, I suppose. I worked on a private . . . project . . . aaah . . . a personal project in the daytime and worked part-time nights.

(*Fitzroy does not reply. He waits fifteen seconds*)

FITZROY: Try to keep your responses brief, please. (*Fitzroy waits fifteen seconds*) Have you ever been excessively overweight?

PARSONS: Absolutely not.

FITZROY: Have you ever been arrested?

PARSONS: Well . . . the whole episode was kind of silly, but I didn't think so at the time. I mean, I didn't know at the time it would turn out to be so . . . trivial. I was alarmed . . . my parents were alarmed.

FITZROY: Have you ever been arrested for drugs?

PARSONS: Aaah, that is the arrest I mentioned before. It was nothing serious, nothing that didn't happen to millions of kids.

(*Fitzroy waits, staring at the machine*)

FITZROY: Are you a habitual user of drugs?

PARSONS: No . . .

FITZROY: Are you homosexual?

PARSONS: No . . .

(*Fitzroy watches Parsons closely. He rises and moves to an angle behind Parsons*)

FITZROY: If you had a relative, an uncle for example, working for this firm, and you observed him taking cash from the register, would you report this to your supervisor?

PARSONS: (*Sucking air, exhaling, seeking a concise response that will deal with some of the moral complexity of the question*) I . . . suppose it would be my . . . responsibility. Certainly . . . I don't condone stealing . . . if that's what you mean . . . (*Fifteen-second pause*)

FITZROY: What is your religion?

PARSONS: I was raised Methodist.

(*Fifteen-second pause*)

FITZROY: Are you a practicing Christian?

PARSONS: Aaah . . . I hope so . . . what do you mean?

FITZROY: Do you actively practice your religion?

PARSONS: Not at present. But I hope I live . . . aah . . . in a . . . decent, upright way . . .

FITZROY: Have you ever purchased and used pornography?

PARSONS: What?

FITZROY: Have you ever purchased and used pornography?

PARSONS: You mean . . .

FITZROY: I mean have you procured materials for the satisfaction of a prurient interest in explicit deviant sex?

PARSONS: No.

(*Fifteen-second pause*)

FITZROY: Have you ever purchased and used pornography?

PARSONS: I just said no . . .

FITZROY: Thank you for your cooperation, Mr. Parsons. The voluntary polygraph phase of your personnel evaluation is completed. If you'll remain seated for a few moments, Miss Henderson will be in to disconnect you. I request that you don't smoke, as I have a number of candidates yet to examine, and some may be sensitive to cigarette smoke.

PARSONS: I don't smoke.

FITZROY: Give your completed 122 form to Miss Henderson and have a pleasant afternoon.

PARSONS: This is the 122? (*Holding up paper*)

FITZROY: That's the 122. You won't be processed unless we have it.

PARSONS: Does this . . . Is this a waiver of some kind . . . I mean, does this mean the results of my test will be sent to other prospective employers?

FITZROY: Just as it states on the form. If they request it. Good day.

PARSONS: Goodbye. (*Fitzroy exits. A pause as Parsons rereads the form. Then he mutters as the lights fade to black*) Holy shit . . .

Blackout

Scene Two:

A sofa, a canvas sling chair, and a coffee table. A component stereo system in a rolling cabinet. The fourth movement of Bartok's "Concerto for Orchestra" is on the turntable, rather loud. Parsons is hunched in the sling chair, listening intently, an almost empty beer bottle in his hand. Parsons finishes the beer, sets the bottle on the floor, and leans back. A key turns in the lock, the door opens, and Lois, an attractive young woman in business clothes, enters with a briefcase and a bag of groceries.

LOIS: Hi!

PARSONS: Hi, sweetheart. Need any help?

LOIS: I can manage. (*She exits to the kitchen. Then, offstage:*) What a day! Ackerman called another one of his famous Friday staff meetings for three, and then droned on without an agenda till 5:20. Finally his wife called with some urgent life-or-death message, and Maureen rang her through to the conference room . . . Ackerman was very annoyed . . . I think she invents these little crises just to get us off the hook. I was falling asleep in my chair. I can't imagine what my notes must be like . . .

PARSONS: I can't hear a word you're saying.

LOIS: (*Entering*) Why don't you turn down that music so we can talk, like normal people? You want another beer?

PARSONS: Please.

LOIS: (*Picking up the empty*) How'd the interview go?

PARSONS: Some sage once said, "the best job is the kind you'd otherwise do for nothing."

LOIS: Yes, but that's unlikely. How'd the interview go?

PARSONS: Well, I think. This is my favorite piece of music, I think.

LOIS: (*Exiting to the kitchen*) Is it short?

PARSONS: Too short.

LOIS: (*Offstage*) Were there a lot of other people interviewing?

PARSONS: How the devil would I know?

LOIS: (*Offstage*) Well, you were there, weren't you? Did you see many applicants?

PARSONS: I had this eerie feeling there were tens of thousands of them in the walls, MBAs with typeset résumés in identical gray wool suits, single file, like ants going to sugar . . .

LOIS: (*Entering with a beer and a glass of wine. She hands Parsons the beer and sits on the couch. She raises her glass*) Sköl!

PARSONS: Thanks. Sköl! (*He sits, listening. The fourth movement ends*)

LOIS: (*As the fifth movement begins*) Can we turn it down now? Even a little, to a manageable level?

PARSONS: We can turn it off. (*He rises and goes to the turntable. He lifts the tone arm but does not turn off the turntable*) I've heard this movement several times already. Self-hypnosis and daydreaming . . . (*He puts the stylus down on the record and holds the disc*) It's very short. One of my very favorites. (*He lets the*

disc go. The fourth movement begins) Intermezzo Interotto. A
great soundtrack album from a famous unmade movie.
(*Pause. Listening*)
Suspense.
Possibly in a forest.
A period movie about kings and small wars?
Or a modern romance in some industrial city in Belgium
with sports cars and lots of early morning. Yes? Early morning . . . anyway . . . a city waking up and rubbing its eyes as
taxicabs filled with black-market kingpins, counterspies, and
soldiers cruise among the crowds of foreign correspond-
ents . . . But not too heavy. No heavy blood unless we also
see a weeping nurse. *Blood?* What am I worried about? This
movie is in black and white! There is a chaplain and a
foreign nurse romance, a correspondent and a nurse, a
soldier-nurse, a doctor-nurse, and even a nurse-nurse
story . . . aaah . . . undeniably, the *lover's theme!*
    I mean, is this movie romance music? I mean meeting
during the war in a battered chapel filled with wounded
comrades kind of music? You know . . . old fashioned makes
you cry, you're so happy it worked out, happy sorta music.
(*Pause*)
But it ain't all schmaltz . . .
A shivering old dog in the rain, waiting for his wounded
companion . . .
Smiles through tears . . .
lingering lips and passionate cigarette smoke.
Do they know how tough it's gonna get? Not yet.
The wounded comrades haven't started to die . . . Not yet . . .
The old dog hasn't gone into mourning . . . yet.
(*Pause. Listening*)
Or what about . . . Cary Grant and Audrey Hepburn?
or . . . Doris Day and Rock Hudson?
After a bunch of crazy rich people antics, including a prat-
fall into a swimming pool in a tuxedo . . . the cock-eyed
world comes up roses for . . . *Doris* and *Rock!*
A whirlwind tour of the hot spots and watering holes on
the Côte D'Azur . . . a cruise among the Greek is-
lands . . . Doris and Rock (*Pause*), no hot thighs in this ver-
sion . . . just highballs and long looks through a soft-focus
lens . . .
Oh, yes . . . the war . . .

(Pause. Listening)
The now-forgotten wounded comrade, lying in the cold, old, bombed-out chapel, mutters . . . bitter at the sweetness, he mutters: How like life . . . aaah . . . How like life . . . in life, bitter is bitter . . . but in the romantic movie . . . bitter is box office.
(Pause. Listening. The fourth movement ends. He turns off the turntable and flops on the couch beside Lois. They sit quietly for a moment. Their glances meet, and they kiss briefly, sweetly)
I'm sure it is widely regarded by those who *know* as middle-brow Muzak.

LOIS: It ends kind of abruptly, don't you think?

PARSONS: Aaaah. I suppose, but I like to think it's Bela resisting manufacturing an arbitrary climax. It's the end of the fourth movement, not the end of the piece . . . I like it a lot. That's why I sat here all afternoon sucking beer and playing it over and over again. I think he heard it for the first time on the radio, lying in the hospital.

LOIS: Bartok?

PARSONS: I think he died not long after. You remember him as merely a famous dead composer, but Bartok was also a dog . . .

LOIS: I really always thought of him as a sacred cow . . .

PARSONS: Definitely, from one point of view, but we mustn't hold that against him.

LOIS: I don't.

(Parsons puts his arm around Lois. She settles into his shoulder)

PARSONS: You got any cigarettes?

LOIS: In my briefcase.

(Parsons rises, goes to her case, takes out cigarettes)

PARSONS: Menthol light 100s . . . ?

LOIS: I'm afraid so. Did they tell you when you'd know about this job?

PARSONS: Ten days. *(He lights cigarette)* Did I ever tell you about my old dog?

LOIS: Bartok?

PARSONS: He had one lop ear . . . scar from a quarrel over a white shepherd bitch . . . an almost white muzzle and serious eyes . . . and arthritis . . . Spanish was his native tongue . . .

LOIS: Why ten days?

PARSONS: Have to evaluate the lie detector test.

LOIS: Good Lord! You took a lie detector test to be a night clerk in a Minit-Mart? (*She laughs*)

PARSONS: You think it was funny? I tried to think it was funny myself, but couldn't. Mr. Fitzroy . . . he gave me, and I mean *gave* me the test. Mr. Fitzroy did *not* think it was funny.

LOIS: Not funny . . . it just strikes me as . . . unnecessary . . .

PARSONS: You, of course, would never be subjected to such an indignity. Rising young stars are not polygraphed because they might find out something they don't want to know . . .

LOIS: Oh, my darling, if somebody needed to know . . . they'd dissect all of us rising young stars without an anesthetic.

PARSONS: No, I mean they reserve the everyday, routine, degrading experience like the lie detector for every applicant for the night *manager* job, by the way, not night clerk . . . whereas anybody in a position to steal any *real* money would never be harassed. Such bad form, until after the fact . . . after some accountant stumbles over it in a computer . . .

LOIS: Barry, don't start one of your endless they, them, they, they bad guy dissertations, OK?

PARSONS: I promise. But just give me your sober, nice people, human opinion of . . . not as a management tool, mind you . . . that's the correct jargon, right, tool? Or instrument? Or am I the instrument? Certainly the tool . . . your nice young woman view . . .

LOIS: Of the lie detector?

PARSONS: Of giving everybody who comes in the office . . . a good, thorough going over.

LOIS: Well . . . I never really considered it. It sounds ridiculous, but . . . and in the first place . . . is it reliable?

PARSONS: Who gives a damn? Reliable . . .

LOIS: Well you should, for one!

PARSONS: That's not the question.

LOIS: I think it's terrible, all right? An invasion of privacy, but I can understand perfectly well why someone would consider it in a high-shrinkage business . . .

PARSONS: You mean you can't get past the influence of your job enough to respond as a human being and not a . . . not a . . .

LOIS: Bullshit!   PARSONS: . . . cockroach.

LOIS: More beer?

PARSONS: I'll get it.

LOIS: (*Holding up glass*) Would you mind?

PARSONS: Not at all.

LOIS: I said . . . and I refuse to believe this represents any deep moral degeneration in me . . . I said, that I could *understand* how a management could grasp at such a . . . a straw when they are being stolen blind by employees.

PARSONS: You're missing the point, my dearest . . .

LOIS: I am *not* missing the point . . . *You* are immune to any rational, non-hysterical response . . . for someone who wants, in his own words, to *join the mainstream* . . . your attitude positively stinks!

PARSONS: (*As he exits to kitchen*) That's because I'm angry, haven't I gotten that across yet? This afternoon I realized I was working under a mistaken assumption. I assumed that if I really wanted a job . . . I'd get a job. I somehow got this old without understanding . . . without understanding that what one absorbs, unarticulated as a child, principles like . . . if you really want a job, you'll get a job. You've heard that wisdom. Yeah? Popular gospel: "You *really, really* want a job, are honest, willing to work hard . . . regular, punctual, sober and loyal . . . pleasant, neatly groomed, show initiative" . . . all of which I am, to one degree or another. I'm the best candidate for some of these jobs. I *know* I am, from the point of view of wanting and *needing* to work, and I don't mean just as a way to get money, goddamn it, I mean a fucking job! I can do any of those jobs well, any of them . . . I guess I'm angry, you know what I mean, at myself as well . . . you know?

LOIS: Only too well, my darling, and even I, who am very fond of you, would not hire you in your present state of mind.

PARSONS: (*Entering with beer and full wine glass*) Fitzroy knew, too, boy. He *was* the lie detector. Cold, little electrons pulsing through his circuits. Two gray TV camera eyes in his clean machine. Gray suit. We looked just alike. We had a little chit-chat while Miss Henderson put the blood pressure–type thing on my arm and looped this chain around my waist . . . oh, yes, and these two little wired-up rings on my fingers. Ours was a double-ring ceremony. Then she placed my bare arm on two sponges and told me to close my eyes and keep 'em closed. The better to see my inner secrets, I suppose.

LOIS: Sounds like the electric chair . . .

PARSONS: I managed to fight the urge to plead diarrhea, get out, and never come back. I figured I couldn't afford to sacrifice the suitcoat. All the while I am acutely aware that in the TV cop dramas, sweat, pulse, heavy breathing, these are all registering on the machine while my heart races, and the sweat pops out all over me, runs down over my eyelids, drips off my nose. I know Fitzroy is watching me, zooming in with his TV eyes. Then, inexplicably, I start to repeat my mantra. I haven't really thought of it in years, but here I am, wired into the grid, trying to get my mantra out of synch with my heart . . . Miss Henderson closes the door . . . Fitzroy warns me to keep my eyes closed . . . "Are you comfortable, Mr. Parsons?" Why, "yes," I say. A first and particularly obvious lie. "This is a new experience. Kind of exciting," I say. You hear that positive attitude, Lois? "Barry, that is your first name, is it not?" "Yes." Ah, perfect truth. Nothing changes. My heart races, I'm soaked . . . then I had a very anxious thought . . . I showered for ten minutes, this morning. I used your extra-strength deodorant, twice . . . and I'm wondering . . . is this a real situation where my protection might not last? Is he noting down "stinks under stress"? It's the smell of fear, I thought and he's an attack dog . . . "Are your parents living, Mr. Parsons?" What happened to my first name? "Yes." All wool and a yard wide. I'm a little more relaxed. Then I become conscious of this long pause. Long pause. A minute, maybe. Long. At first, I thought, he couldn't think of the next question . . . "Do you engage in frequent extramarital affairs?" "No," I say, "I'm not married." Isn't that on my application? Single. Male . . . What's it to ya? "Have you ever stolen anything in your life?" Now ask yourself that one. That's a real blunt question under the circumstances. "No . . . nothing of any consequence . . ." feeling my whole pathetic, guilty being straining to confess. *Yes,* I took six copies of a newspaper last week and only paid for one . . . *Yes,* I used to rip off cans of caviar in an all-night supermarket in LA. *Yes,* I took those hood ornaments off those antique bodies in that junkyard in Cincinnati, and *yes,* somebody stole them from me. I have been associated with *rings* of thieves. But confess to you, Fitzroy, you tool, you pry bar, you stoolie, you ferret machine . . . Where was I . . . oh, yes. "Do you read detective novels?" was a good one. At first I was just nonplussed. Does he think I'm going to stand behind the counter reading all night . . . then, of course, fascination with crime, figuring out how to pocket a Snickers by reading Mickey Spillane. This is a mechanized personality profile. Then I'm wondering, how much weight does this carry up in Personnel at Fastway Food, Inc.? Who are you, Fitzroy? Can you read me without the machine? Can you spot me trying to ease in out of the fringe . . . picking up the shuffle and the bow and scrape . . . sucking up the lingo, trying to sound clubby and conspiratorial . . . snubbing old friends . . . the clowns . . . who, me . . . ? those fellows . . . ? certainly not . . . can you see through my new gray chrysalis trying like mad to make the metamorphosis into killer capitalist . . . that's your spot, isn't it, Fitzroy, to expose me, to reduce me, to get me out there naked with all my specters . . . in chains . . . failure . . . dissatisfaction . . . 1968 . . . all crowded around me so that you can see, clearly . . . I don't belong in your nice tidy, honest, local Minit-Mart because I'm weird, so I've gotta be untrustworthy, and I'm sweating because I'm afraid . . . afraid even to lie . . . to lie to save my ass! Intimidated by that simple-minded device like some paleolithic Injun meeting the magic of the white man . . .

LOIS: (*Making the "T" gesture with her hands*) Time out! More wine.

PARSONS: What are you trying to do, get loaded?

LOIS: Yes. Darling, you had a hard day. I'm celebrating your hard day. That's what you do in business, didn't you know that? "Oh, what a *day* . . . How about a drink?"

PARSONS: (*Quietly*) Uh, huh.

LOIS: Can I have some more wine? Please. Darling?

PARSONS: (*After a pause*) Sure. (*He takes her glass and goes into the kitchen*)

LOIS: Barry?

PARSONS: (*Off, softly*) Yeah?

LOIS: I was trying to . . .

PARSONS: (*Off*) What?

LOIS: Well, you get down on yourself, and I just want to get you to say, hey, you know, *It's fucked,* so what . . .

PARSONS: (*Coming to the kitchen door*) Is that what you say, Lois?

LOIS: Sometimes.

PARSONS: (*Exiting to kitchen*) Yeah, I'll bet.

LOIS: No doubt about it. No doubt, in this economic climate, getting a job is beastly work. I might not get my job again if I were looking now . . . but if you expect them to hire you, and you have to expect it or they won't . . . someone, especially you, because, let's face it, who needs an art therapist with a degree in outdoor education from a Commie college . . . right now, in the business world? Especially with your background, you have to have a bulletproof positive outlook. (*Pause*) Does that make sense? (*Pause*) Barry?

PARSONS: (*Emerging quietly with the beer and the wine. He gives her the wine. He sits in the sling chair, looking away*) Uh, huh.

LOIS: Don't pout. Are you angry with me now, because if you are . . . (*Pause*) . . . all I'm saying is, you'd better be prepared for more of this inhuman treatment. Business is at a loss, darling, in the whole hiring process. Nobody trusts the character judgments of personnel anymore because they've gotten burned . . . the seat of the pants is out because management can't objectify the seat of the pants. It's numbers and rigid criteria . . . so much of this, so much of that. If they hire jerks with no common sense, no charm, they live with it.

PARSONS: Assuming they'd know the difference.

LOIS: At least they can defend it. Look at this profile, they can say, fits the job description, which was, after all, written by somebody else . . .

PARSONS: Uh huh . . .

LOIS: Sköl?

PARSONS: Sköl.

LOIS: Why do you make it so hard on yourself? Why don't you look for *any* good job, instead of narrowing it to well-paid *night* jobs . . .

PARSONS: I can't take my photographs at night.

LOIS: In the early morning, at noon, in the evening . . .

PARSONS: You said: Set clear objectives, formulate a strategy for achieving them, stick to your plan. Your very words.

LOIS: I'm suggesting it might be wise to re-examine your strategy . . .

PARSONS: Because it isn't working? What happened to the stick-to-it-iveness we value so highly?

LOIS: What are you going to do tomorrow?

PARSONS: There's gonna be a tomorrow? Oh yes, you business critters believe in such things. Strange religion. And another thing . . . I totally underestimated Execumerican as a dialect. I'm trying to talk business talk, and today I began to hear myself reach for those . . . trendy phrases and not quite get 'em. Your dialect is very ethnic in a totally WASP way . . . But tomorrow? . . . should it happen, will find me showering for ten minutes, coating my pits with your Mitchum's extra strength, shaving very carefully . . . maybe twice, putting on my last clean shirt, donning this oh-so-right-for-success suit you generously fronted me, and taking the bus out to Mill Run Pike. There I will manfully compete for a job at Morris Interstate Transfer. I will pray they do not rely on a lie detector to make the choice in this matter.

LOIS: You're going to smile, and you're *not* going to read the news before you go. You need all the help you can get staying . . . I mean *getting* positive.

PARSONS: I won't even look out the windows of the bus. Might see something depressing, like real life.

LOIS: Are you getting another beer?

PARSONS: Most assuredly.

LOIS: Will you fill this? (*Holding out her wine glass*)

PARSONS: Yeah, you betcha, babe.

LOIS: Barry . . .

PARSONS: (*Exiting, stopping at kitchen door*) Hmm?

LOIS: I love you.

PARSONS: (*Exiting*) Must be a flaw in your character.

Blackout

Scene Three:

A bare office. A desk with a chair and a second hard chair in front. An energetic, gray-haired woman is seated at the desk. Parsons, looking slightly seedier and definitely less self-assured, is sitting in the hard chair. Mrs. McCormack is reading Parsons' application. Parsons is smoking.

PARSONS: The résumé is up to date. If there's any additional information you might require, I can have it out here in a jiffy . . .

MCCORMACK: I don't think it's necessary. Very interesting

background, Mr. Parsons. I'm a little puzzled by your application for the night security position.

PARSONS: I'd prefer to work nights. Ah, I work on some personal projects that require daylight. Photography projects.

MCCORMACK: You're a photographer?

PARSONS: I am when I have the money to buy materials. Most people don't realize it, I think, but photography is an expensive form.

MCCORMACK: Oh, yes. Our family has spent a fortune on vacation snapshots alone. But of course we wouldn't trade them for anything. We always couldn't wait to get the prints back from the drugstore. Now that our kids are grown, my husband has a Polaroid . . .

PARSONS: Yes, well, I've been making photographs for a good while. I've had some in shows. Mostly on the West Coast.

MCCORMACK: But you're not applying for a photographer job, Mr. Parsons.

PARSONS: No, but good experience is good experience. I feel . . .

MCCORMACK: I suppose. But I'm afraid that's neither here nor there. You are, and I'm sure this is not news to you, you are overqualified for anything we have available.

PARSONS: But that really has nothing to do with my ability to do the job . . . I mean, at this particular time, who isn't overqualified? There are Ph.D.'s driving cabs.

MCCORMACK: And applying for this job.

PARSONS: I suppose it would be useless to tell you that I work very hard and I'm always on time if I have to be . . .

MCCORMACK: Where is that indicated here? This employment history is . . . and I'm sure you put the best possible face on it . . . is spotty . . . to be kind.

PARSONS: Well . . . I've lived lots of places.

MCCORMACK: We're one hundred and four years in this city, seventy-eight years in this building in a profitable business. Experience is our only guide, of which we have plenty. Mr. Parsons, I look for one or two key things in job applicants . . . I'll be hiring someone who shows they are ready and capable of assuming the responsibility demanded of our night security force. Nowhere in this résumé do I find . . . not in your presentation of yourself, I might add . . . Have you ever maintained a long, stable home relationship? Have you ever been married? With this galavanting all over the country ... Give me, for instance, the length of your longest, wholesome, stable association, at the home level ... ?

PARSONS: Aaaah ... Two years ... yeah ... two years. Very nice two years.

MCCORMACK: How many times? Looks to me as if you've never been *anywhere* more than two years.

PARSONS: That's pretty nearly true. But, you know ... I know you're looking for evidence of dependability, etc., in my record and . . I really feel the best evidence in these matters never reaches a résumé ... for example, I maintained a very nice, stable, home-level relationship with a terrific dog throughout this traipsing around the country. Fifteen years of it ... And ... I simply feel ... stability is indicated by lots of other factors ... Aaah ... his name was Bartok. You probably think a dog is trivial, but the way it's been going, in the world I mean, aaah, any fifteen-year relationship counts as far as I'm concerned.

MCCORMACK: You've been looking for a job for a good while, now, haven't you?

PARSONS: Off and on, a long time. By my standards, anyway. (*Pause*) Why do you think I'm sitting here? I'm trying to break this vicious damn circle and make *that* commitment ...

MCCORMACK: I'm *sick* and *tired* of being called a vicious damned circle! You're finally facing the consequences of a haphazard, self-indulgent life and because the nut's a little tough to crack, you blame some vicious system! Well, I'm part of this circle. I'm proud of it, and I can tell you how it goes in *my* part of the world. You're not gonna get this job ... not because you didn't ask nicely enough. You had a very good veneer there, for about five minutes ... your materials are presentable enough. I suspect your girlfriend or somebody who has a job showed you how to organize them. You're healthy, you say you're smart, I'll even take your word for it. It's the *content,* the message here, that causes the difficulty ... This is a dismal history of self-indulgence and sloth. You can get away with this for a while ... but this ... you're 35 years old. Are you paying a life insurance plan? Silly question. Give me a good reason why any business would give you the opportunity, yet again, to walk away from responsibility *once again,* as soon as you've gotten the wherewithal to finance another damned adventure. And don't think for one damned minute I'm insensitive to your paranoia about discipline and routine . . . I've been doing this job, in this office, for twenty-three consecutive years, so I damn well know the price and the benefits of discipline and routine. You think I'm a drudge, but I don't care, because I'm not sponging and I'm not fighting self-disgust, and don't tell me you're not, because I can smell it.

(*Pause. McCormack shuffles papers*)

PARSONS: You know, this may be one of those situations . . . where . . .

MCCORMACK: And I *know* right down to the bedrock bottom of my mean, stony old soul, that there's *not a thing* I can do for you.

PARSONS: I was thinking, maybe I oughta go . . .

MCCORMACK: You shoulda thought of all this *years* ago . . .

PARSONS: Mrs. McPherson . . .

MCCORMACK: Mrs. McCormack. Now I'm going out to get a cup of coffee.

PARSONS: (*He starts to laugh*) OK.

MCCORMACK: I want you gone before I get back . . . I suggest you go somewhere and quietly reflect on your situation.

PARSONS: (*He is laughing steadily now*) OK.

MCCORMACK: There are those who set a steady course and those who wander aimlessly . . . If I hired you, I'd be sabotaging my company, and I wouldn't do that for *anybody!* There's nothing worth stealing in that desk. (*She goes*)

PARSONS: (*Laughing steadily, unnerved. Tired*) OK. (*Laughter*) OK. (*Laughter*) OK.

Blackout

Scene Four:

The apartment as in Scene Two. Parsons is sitting in the sling chair listening to the familiar fourth movement of the Bartok. Six empty beer bottles and a crushed empty pack of cigarettes litter the floor beside the chair. The key turns in the lock, and Lois enters. She stands inside the door looking at Parsons.

PARSONS: Hi.

LOIS: Hi.

PARSONS: Late meeting?

LOIS: Something like that. (*She goes to the empty beer bottles, picks up several, and heads for the kitchen*)

PARSONS: Hey, I can get those ...

LOIS: I know.

PARSONS: Hey, I was going to clean up this mess.

LOIS: (*Re-entering and shutting off the turntable*) I know.

PARSONS: Now, don't start on me, Lois ... I've had an extremely foul day, and I'm not in the mood ... not in condition for it ...

LOIS: The kitchen is a filthy shambles.

PARSONS: I had the leftovers for lunch. Out of cash, you know ... no options. Come on, sweetie ... you've been slaving over a hot desk all day, but don't take it out on me ... I'm kinda fragile ...

LOIS: Actually, no hot desk. One of those "a job so good you'd do it for nothing" days.

PARSONS: Good. Good ... had a rather easy, very pleasant day sorta day myself ... once, many years ago ...

LOIS: Are all the cigarettes gone?

PARSONS: Ah, yeah, didn't you stop by the market? Because I certainly didn't ...

LOIS: I'm going out in a few minutes.

PARSONS: Oh, well, that explains no sack of groceries. Ah, business, the expense account and the busy young executives.

LOIS: I only have a few minutes. I have to shower and dress so ... ah ... we don't have long to discuss this ...

PARSONS: Listen, while you're in the shower I'm going to run out for some beer. If you've got a couple of bucks, I've got the change ... ?

LOIS: Barry ...

PARSONS: Lois. You don't have to say anything ... I know ... me being totally broke is becoming a complete drag. But, babe, I've got to keep *something* going to remind myself that I'm still human, you know, and ... and my choice is the luxury of a cold beer when I want it.

LOIS: I've got a dinner date this evening, Barry.

PARSONS: I know. I'll finish the peanut butter or something. But I'd like to wash it down with cold beer ...

LOIS: You're not hearing me. I've got a date.

PARSONS: Ah. A date-date. Not business?

LOIS: Not business.

PARSONS: *Ah.* Well . . . I'm . . . I'm . . . *this* is what we don't have much time to discuss. Slow, Barry, old skate. I thought this night was different, but I knew not *how* different . . . right?

LOIS: Are you drunk?

PARSONS: Probably . . .

LOIS: Our situation has changed, Barry . . . you said you wanted the luxury of a cold beer to remind yourself that you were still human? Last week, in the middle of a horrendous morning that included Maureen being canned by Ackerman over a petty mixup in appointment times and you calling with that . . . admittedly devastating experience of the job that you were promised that somebody else gave to the boss's nephew . . . I had a brief meeting with the lawyer who's taking over as chief counsel for my department.

PARSONS: Spare me the blow-by-blow, ah . . . if that's the operative term in the executive suite. (*Lois slaps him, hard. They stand face to face for a long moment. Then, very quietly:*) A wounding joke, Lois.

LOIS: (*Quietly*) I know.

(*They stand silently looking at each other. Pause*)

LOIS: You're jumping ahead of my story.

PARSONS: So he asked you to lunch.

LOIS: Yes.

PARSONS: For today?

LOIS: Are you going to cross-examine me?

PARSONS: So he's bright, no doubt, aggressive, . . . a promotion, this new job?

LOIS: Yes.

PARSONS: All right. And you're going to get promoted, too, right?

LOIS: Yes. (*Pause*) I took the afternoon off . . .

PARSONS: With him?

LOIS: Give me credit, Barry. I went to the chiropractor. And then drove out to see Judy at her shop. It's beautiful.

PARSONS: I don't know Judy.

LOIS: I was letting something sink in, Barry. I've been watching you practice guilt and self-loathing for months, and believe me, if I felt it, I'd be good at it . . . but . . . I'm definitely needing something to remind me that I'm still human and . . . I'm not getting it. Are you . . . I mean, other than beer? Don't answer that, because basically, I'm gonna do this because I have to—because I'm getting sad, Barry. I don't want to *provide* for a while . . . I want it to flow toward me . . . I'm selfish, of course, but I never claimed not to be selfish. Why do you think I'm such a good manager . . . I recognize self-interest instantly . . . and I confess, I gravitate toward it. This is totally beside the point.

PARSONS: Are you drunk?

LOIS: No. Possibly. I had wine at Judy's. The point I was making is *this:* We share a fairly adult debate about important issues; let's not let this one descend into regrets or recriminations, because you must agree, the way things were going something was bound to happen . . . and it has.

PARSONS: Well, well, let's not descend into uncomfortable vituperation, especially when one has to shower and dress for a dinner date. Can I ask a question?

LOIS: What?

PARSONS: Do you have any money?

LOIS: In my purse. Leave me thirty dollars.

PARSONS: And, it's going to be very difficult for me to be out by the time you get back . . .

LOIS: Don't be unreasonable. We'll handle this . . . I can't worry about it now, in any case . . .

PARSONS: I'll *try* to be gone by the time you get back, but it's *doubtful* . . .

LOIS: Barry . . . suit yourself. (*She gives him a quick kiss*) But don't do anything you'll regret. (*She exits into the bedroom*)

PARSONS: OK. Let's see. (*Parsons goes to her purse, takes out a wad of folded bills, counts, then takes four dollars. He puts back the bills and closes the purse. A shower goes on in the bathroom*) I took *four* dollars. I'm going to get a pack of cigarettes and a newspaper! As well! (*No answer*) But first I'm going to listen to *just* a little bit . . . (*He finds the right part of the fourth movement, turns it up full blast for the duration of the long, loud, melodic string passage. Then he turns it down*) Now, I'm going to go out. (*Raising his voice*) and get some *cold* beer so I can come back and sit back . . . (*Shouting*) and say . . . (*Screaming*) Hey, you know, it's fucked . . . so what? (*Pause, the shouting*) Lois!

(*The shower goes off. Lois appears in the door with bathrobe and towel*)

LOIS: (*Turning off the turntable*) You're not going to act stupid, are you? No screaming, promise.

PARSONS: I was trying to bring you abreast of events over

the shower. Now that you're standing right here, no need to shout. Where does all this leave me . . . in your view?

LOIS: Precisely where you find yourself, Barry. It doesn't matter what *my* view is, does it? (*Pause*) This is awkward and incredibly uncomfortable, Barry, because I don't know what to say . . . I mean, this is a major change in our lives and . . . I have to get dressed. That's just the way it works out. (*She exits abruptly into the bedroom*)

PARSONS: (*He stands, restarts the turntable, low, and bends down, peering about. He begins a coaxing sound, as if trying to rouse a dog to follow*) Come on, old pal . . . come on, old dog. Come on, Bartok, shake it out and let's shamble. (*He is whistling and snapping his fingers*) Thataboy! Come on, ready for the street, old fella? Yeah, gooooood dog . . . (*He pats the imaginary dog on the head, glances at the closed bedroom door, and begins to speak louder as he moves with the "dog" to the door*) Let's get a good stretch out! Good for us . . . Good for old dogs! Brisk run to the corner store . . . been a while since *you've* been *out*, hey, big fella . . . need a good stiff walk on the outside . . . Come on, Bartok! Come on . . .

(*He closes the door. Bartok's "Concerto for Orchestra" swells*)

Blackout

Corinne Jacker
IN PLACE

Corinne Jacker

Once again, Corinne Jacker displays her dramatist's instinct for selecting disquieted characters at critical moments in their lives. Set in Las Vegas, *In Place* brings together a former professor of literature attempting to break into blackjack dealing, an almost liberated woman on the verge of divorce, and an independent boarding house proprietress whose pragmatism assists her boarders in surviving the threats of the ominous clouds overshadowing both their city and their lives. *In Place* joins Miss Jacker's two other works in the *Best Short Plays* series—*Bits and Pieces* in the 1977 edition and *The Chinese Food Syndrome* in the 1979 volume.

A winner of a double Obie award for *Harry Outside* and *Bits and Pieces*, the author was educated at Stanford University, where she received her B.S., and at Northwestern University, where she earned her M.A. In 1954 she was named a Lovedale Scholar, and in 1955 she was honored as a University Scholar.

Her other published and produced plays include *Travellers; Night Thoughts; Seditious Acts; The Scientific Method; Breakfast, Lunch, and Dinner;* and *Among Friends.* Her play *My Life* was performed by the Circle Repertory Company in New York in 1977. *After the Season* was presented at the Academy Festival Theatre in Chicago during the summer of 1978 with Irene Worth as star; it was later produced by the Phoenix Theatre in 1979.

Additionally, Miss Jacker has published the following books: *The Biological Revolution; The Black Flag of Anarchy: Antistatism in the United States; A Little History of Cocoa; Window on the Unknown: A History of the Microscope;* and *Man, Memory, and Machines: An Introduction to Cybernetics.*

Miss Jacker also has written extensively for television. Her *John Adams, President* was acclaimed as one of the most dramatic episodes in *The Adams Chronicles* series, and she was presented with an Emmy citation for her participation in the *Benjamin Franklin* series. Her TV play *The Jilting of Granny Weatherall* appeared on the NET American Short Story Series in 1980. In 1981–82 she served as head writer for the NBC daytime series *Another World.*

Recipient of numerous playwriting awards, Miss Jacker was given a Rockefeller Grant in 1979–80 and was selected for the O'Neill Playwrights Conference in 1971 and 1974. She also served as dramaturge in the Conference in 1976 and 1979.

Most recently, her full-length play *Domestic Issues* was produced at the Yale Repertory Winterfest in 1981 and in New York at the Circle Repertory Company. She is currently working on two new scripts commissioned for public television and a movie-of-the-week for CBS television.

Characters:

DAISY STODDARD
JERRY MAZLISH
LOUISE ELLIOT

Scene:

This largish living room has been turned into the public room of Daisy Stoddard's boarding house. It would be more logical to say that Daisy rents out rooms—two of them, to be exact. But she wants to be regarded as a proprietor, a sort of beginning entrepreneur who is about ready to capitalize on her initiative and turn this small, slightly run-down place into a hotel on the main strip in Vegas. The furnishings are acceptable, but not special, not put-together. She bought a "suite" a few years ago and has personalized the room with photos, knickknacks, ash trays—that sort of thing. But whatever else, her two boarders do get a place to sit down, a TV to watch, and a breakfast. Daisy is preparing for breakfast right now, setting the table, pouring out orange juice, etc. Jerry Mazlish has his electronic computer game–player rigged up to the TV screen and is busy at it. He has a blackjack game in and has been at it for an hour or so.

DAISY: You know how you get a feeling of romance—a sniff of aftershave lotion does it for me—I have that feeling right now.

JERRY: Not while I'm working, Daisy.

DAISY: Somewhere in a casino downtown, right at this very minute, there's a machine, and it is saying, "Come on, play me, come on, the jackpot's ready to go." It's ten, maybe twenty quarters down the line. And it's beckoning to me, saying, "Come on, lover, come on, get into a cab and come on down here, I'm waiting, all hot and juicy. Come on, lover." And I would, I'd run to my red-hot machine and drop my lucky quarter and get my fingers around that handle and just squeeze it down. The quarters would pour out, a silver stream of them, right into my handbag. Overflow it. I'm down on the floor, scooping up all the treasure. The big win of the day. But I can't go. Because I don't know which casino it is, just that it's there. My lucky day. Days like this only come up once, maybe twice in a lifetime. And I am standing at this Formica-topped table pouring orange juice for a blackjack nut and a soon-to-be divorcee.

JERRY: (*Throws the controls down in disgust*) I went bust again. How can the house go bust? It's against statistical probabilities. Next thing you know the ground will open under my feet and swallow me up.

DAISY: The trouble with you, Jerry . . . No. I guess it isn't trouble. Not really.

JERRY: (*His mouth full of a piece of toast*) What would you do if the house drew a pair of jacks?

DAISY: Split and play both hands.

JERRY: Sure. That's what I did. . . . What happened? I got a two and a three and then a pair of Kings. Wiped out.

DAISY: There are other professions in this world, Jerry. You're an intelligent man.

JERRY: What am I doing wrong? My hands are cursed.

DAISY: I've told you—it happens at birth. Like some people are born with a caul around their heads and they're lucky. Some babies come out of the mother and they're washed clean and that stuff is put in their eyes and when they open them, they have the look—the look of the winner. You don't have that look, Jerry.

JERRY: I ought to be able to do it. Figure out what's right and what's wrong. What do statistical probabilities matter. Instinct, right? I just have to find the right instinct.

DAISY: You can't learn an instinct.

JERRY: If I play five more hands, it could all fall into place.

DAISY: Besides, The Sands doesn't need any more dealers. People are standing in line all the way to Utah to be considered for dealing at The Sands.

JERRY: I had a personal interview, didn't I?

DAISY: I'm not denying that, am I?

JERRY: You could have more confidence in me. That might turn the tide.

DAISY: Well, you're wonderful in bed.

JERRY: That doesn't give me confidence when I'm dealing the cards.

DAISY: You're the best I ever experienced in bed. (*Jerry begins dealing out another hand*) I'm not exaggerating. It's no compliment. You're terrific.

JERRY: OK.

DAISY: You are the only good thing I ever got out of this town. (*Louise Elliot comes in and heads for the breakfast table*) I wake up every morning and I say to myself—I hate this town. I hate it! I'm in the wrong place. It does nothing for me.

LOUISE: It's better than Cincinnati.

DAISY: Is it really?

LOUISE: Have you ever been to Cincinnati? And it's better than Columbus, and it is certainly better than Whitewater, Wisconsin. I know. I've been to all those places—and Chilcothe, Idaho; Duluth—some people like Duluth, but I don't. (*She stops abruptly, picks up her glass of orange juice, drains it to the bottom in one series of gulps. She slams it down on the table. Daisy fills it again from a pitcher on the sideboard.*)

DAISY: What time are you leaving?

LOUISE: About an hour. It should be plenty of time—

DAISY: I meant tomorrow.

JERRY: (*To Louise*) You want a ride? I've got an appointment at the Sands this morning—

LOUISE: No. I ordered a taxi.

JERRY: You can cancel it.

LOUISE: No. Thank you.

JERRY: You're welcome. (*He comes to the table, drinks his juice, and nibbles on a piece of toast while standing*)

DAISY: That's how you get flat feet—eating standing up.

LOUISE: I ordered a cab because for once in my life I want to go somewhere in class. I am tired of buses. If I had been alive during the French Revolution, they would have used up all the tumbrils on the nobility, and I would have walked.

DAISY: You aren't the first woman to sit at this table and talk about having her head cut off.

JERRY: A taxi's a nice idea.

LOUISE: It's tricks, finding ways to get me there.

DAISY: Jerry, if you don't sit down, I am going to knock you down.

(*Jerry does sit*)

LOUISE: I'm so afraid of going. I looked out the window upstairs when I first got up. It's not the usual sort of day. There's a heavy cloud, just sitting at the edge of the city, dark gray, but low, so you can still see above it. And the sky above it is gray, too, but that shiny kind that looks like elves have been up all night painting the firmament. Pearl gray, and hard. . . . I'm not a young woman. It's not as if I could just go back home and get a job at some rich lawyer's office as receptionist. You know what there is left for someone like me? I could run the box office at a movie house, or sell sweaters and cardigans at L. S. Ayres.

DAISY: That heavy cloud you were talking about—the one that is just below the pearl gray shit. People say it never used to exist. It came when they did all that testing, atom bombs going off five and six times a week. There is also a rumor, which may or may not be accurate, that the testing changed all the odds at the tables, everywhere in L.V., that it jogged the cherries loose in the slots and they came back in a different order. Every once in a while you'll see an old-timer go up to somebody who's just lost a bundle at the craps table, and he'll say that if the guy had only been there before the A-bomb, he'd 've won a bundle.

LOUISE: What do they do if you cancel out?

DAISY: My theory is that we breathe this contaminated air, and we are the ones who've changed. We don't play the games the same way.

LOUISE: What would my lawyer do if I called in sick?

DAISY: Did you travel more than a thousand miles not to get a divorce?

JERRY: You could have German measles, or the mumps— no judge wants to give a divorce to a contagious person.

LOUISE: I don't want to go there.

DAISY: Drink your orange juice.

LOUISE: I can't stay away. I've been planning this day for years, four years, five years. It is meant to be the climax of every waking hour of my time. And all I wanted to do this morning when the alarm went off was to lie in bed and pull the blankets over my head and tremble.

DAISY: Have a piece of oatmeal toast.

LOUISE: I don't look it right now, but inside me, deep inside, I am shivering, quaking.

JERRY: Ninety days and nights on Devil's Island, right? It sounds so short, three-months residency requirement. Anyone can live ninety days in Las Vegas. That's what they say out there, the other side of the world. It isn't true. The clouds pass over our heads, they sap our energy. We stay and we stay, and we forget what we came for.

DAISY: Not everyone is like you.

JERRY: She is. Aren't you?

LOUISE: What are you like? I've only known the two of you for ninety-one days. I knew my husband, the doctor, for 3,787 days—only counting the married ones. And I didn't know him at all.

JERRY: Don't cry.

LOUISE: I just don't know whether I really want a divorce.

JERRY: *"Il pleure dans mon coeurs*
  Comme il pleut sur la ville,
  Quelle est cette langueur
  Qui penetre mon coeur?"

DAISY: Don't start that, Jerry.

JERRY: (*Translates for Louise*)
  "It weeps in my heart
  As it rains on the town,
  What is this langour
  That cuts through my heart?"

DAISY: Do you know what he does? In bed, after I think we've had a particularly exquisite orgasm and I am lying there . . .

JERRY: Replete is the appropriate word.

DAISY: He sits up and lights one of his old-fashioned unfiltered coffin nails and turns to me, making sure that he has the words in the right order, and says something like that, what he just said to you.

JERRY: Not like that at all:
  "Les femmes, les enfants ont le même tresor
  De feuilles vertes de printemps et de lait pur
  Et de duree
  Dans leurs yeux purs."
(*He begins to translate. Daisy talks right over the translation*)
  "Women and children have the same treasure
  Of green leaves of spring and pure milk
  And time
  In their pure eyes."

DAISY: (*Over the translation*) OK, it's a happier poem, but it's the same thing. Something French, some wonderful turn of phrase. What does it matter to me? If he gave me a "Wow!" or "That really gets to me," I'd have something I could really understand.

JERRY: (*Bitterly*) Wow! That really gets to me, kid! (*He gets up and goes back to his electronic setup*) I have to get to work. I'm not ready for the interview yet.

DAISY: We've been lovers for fifty-seven days now. He hasn't run out of it yet.

JERRY: When I was back east, Daisy, teaching "Existential Parameters in the Novels of Herman Melville," you might have been able to get to me. Not now. (*To Louise*) I decided last month, forty-two days ago, that I was failing here because I had too much in my head. Failing in life, unable to move. Have you ever had the feeling that life was this sticky paper and you were a fly caught on it, unable to move, just condemned to being in one place till you starved to death?

DAISY: No.

JERRY: So I decided to just empty out this storage tank up here behind my eyes. Unwind the RNA, unreel all the stuff. Quotations in the original German from Rilke: "*Wie soll ich meine Seele halten, dass sie nicht an deine ruhrt?*"

DAISY: Have another piece of toast, Jerry.

JERRY: "How shall I withhold my soul so that it does not touch yours?"

DAISY: That's how it's been. Quotations, lines of poetry, sometimes whole sonnets come out, exhaled like gas. Stuff that's been in him, messing up his whole system for years. When you walked in here, Jerry, and I realized you were an intellectual, I thought it was going to be incredible. That you were what I'd been waiting for. That you would fill me up to the gills with poetry and get me down to the machines.

LOUISE: If I don't leave soon, I'll be late. They'll call my name, and then they'll call it again. My lawyer will look at his watch. The judge will tap his fingers on his—whatever they call it, podium maybe. And the court reporter will check the cloud to see how close it is. They'll call my name once more. No response. Case postponed indefinitely.

DAISY: I haven't gotten down to the slot machines in months. There's one at the gas station on the corner. I drive in, tell them to fill it up, open my purse. I don't have any quarters.

JERRY: You don't understand. I'm trying to get rid of it. Empty myself out. What am I supposed to do with all those years accumulated? You want me to find a garbage truck, saw the top of my head off, and just do a handstand on the rim of that trough they dump the cans into?

DAISY: A divorce wasn't enough for him. He had to stay. He had to find his vocation. His great ambition. He wants to be a blackjack dealer at the casino in The Sands. Midlife crisis.

JERRY: Gauguin wanted to paint.

DAISY: (*To Louise*) You have a return plane ticket?

LOUISE: Tomorrow. Divorce today. Back to Cincinnati tomorrow.

DAISY: Swear to me you are going to leave.

LOUISE: Why would I stay?

DAISY: That's what I said. That's what he said.

JERRY: You ever wonder about all the people you see walking around Las Vegas? They never play the machines. They just walk, or sit in the sun on the benches at the bus stops. *Detritus.*

DAISY: (*To Louise*) That means dead-leaf fertilizer.

JERRY: My theory is that when it all gets out of my head, I'll be able to deal blackjack; instead of losing every hand, I'll win.

(*Jerry begins spouting poetry, becoming more and more frenzied. Louise goes to the window to see the course of the cloud. She calls Daisy over to observe it with her, and they have a conversation. It is very important that they talk while Jerry becomes more and more frenzied, tearing pieces of paper, ripping the tablecloth away, generally turning the place into a shambles. If we make a choice, we should hear the women's conversation*)

LOUISE: Are you sure that cloud is harmless?

DAISY: It happens all the time. Haven't you seen it?

LOUISE: Not since I've been here. Shouldn't we do something about him?

DAISY: It doesn't do any good. He has the fit and he stops. It's like he's right. He'll come to the end of a reel and just shut off.

JERRY: "*Je peux rarement voir quelqu'un sans le battre.*" "I can seldom see anyone without beating him up." Henri Michaux.

"*Wiederum in Eure Kreise komm ich so auf gute Weise, während, verd ich Stein und Erz, nur ein Vogel seinen Sterz oder gar ein Mensch von Wert seinen Witz auf mich entleert.*"

JERRY: She doesn't understand. I'm not being melodramatic when I say this is the city of the walking dead. You shouldn't have come here. You'l get divorced, then get out. I figure if I find something to do—if I can get a job dealing, I'll be different. I'll be part of the town. But I must get short circuits, I send out vibes to the cards that makes them turn against me. So during the day I try to learn a whole new vocabulary, me and the TV and the cards. And at night I try. God knows what I try.

DAISY: He's never done it during the day before.

LOUISE: Maybe it's the cloud.

DAISY: Nobody really knows what that cloud is. They've even taken little bits of it in bottles. Nobody can analyze it.

JERRY: *"Et qui n'est, chaque fois, ni tout*
a fait le même
Ni tout a fait une autre, et m'aime
et me comprend."
(*Suddenly Jerry is singing, on his knee, imitating Jolson*)
"Mammy. How I love you, how I love you,
My dear old Mammy.
I'd give the world to see you once more
Standing on that Swanee shore."
(*He's back with the Verlaine*)
Car elle me comprend, et mon coeur, transparent
Pour elle seule, helas!"

DAISY: One of the meteorologists at Stanford claims it's a vapor created by the collision of matter and antimatter.

JERRY: I won't translate that. It's not translatable. Oh, God, my head's too full of the stuff. You ever go after roaches?— you know, in some apartment that's full of the little bastards, and you squirt in the Raid or the Treatment MX or the whatever, where you know they are, and right away, hundreds of them come out, pouring out of the woodwork out of holes you didn't know were there, dying right in front of you. It's like that in my head, see? (*Jerry has calmed down considerably. He sinks onto the sofa, now munching on an apple. Little by little he will fall asleep. Daisy sets about cleaning up the mess Jerry has made*)
"*Arma virumque cano. Troie qui primus ab oris . . . Omnia gallia divisa est in tres partes . . .*"

DAISY: He'll be fine when he wakes up. I've told him that it's not him. It's a short circuit. He somehow wired his computer blackjack thing to the atmosphere; he gets a jolt when the cloud comes over. Just a short circuit.

LOUISE: You should take him to a doctor. No. Don't. I wouldn't take him to my husband . . . If I don't leave in ten minutes, I won't get to court on time.

DAISY: Then leave. Right now.

LOUISE: The taxi never showed up.

DAISY: Lots of them don't like to go outside on days like this.

LOUISE: You know what he said to me? My husband, Dr. Henry Elliot, when I was getting the taxi to come here to get my quickie divorce? He was drinking a beer out of the bottle, Coors, all he'd drink. Ever. He took a big swig and he laughed and he said—no, he asked me—What would happen if I took the "I" out of Louise? And I said, What? And he said I'd turn into a louse. L-O-U-S-E.

DAISY: He's got a quick mind.

LOUISE: Quick and mean. God knows what he does to his patients.

DAISY: You never talk about yourself.

LOUISE: I'm not good at confrontations.

DAISY: I'm beginning to understand.

LOUISE: You understand why a man would stand there holding a bottle of beer in his left hand—he is left-handed—and laugh at his wife as she is leaving for a divorce, and the last word he says is that she'll turn into a louse if she loses her "I"?

DAISY: You better leave.

LOUISE: I can't. The cloud is almost over this house. I'm not going outside under that thing. Not even for a divorce.

DAISY: They don't take pollution as a reason for not turning up in court.

LOUISE: Henry was being vicious. That's how I see you. Just downright in his heart vicious. He hated me. He wanted to keep me there. So he insulted me. That's the way his mind works. So I started to cry, but I picked up my suitcase and I walked out on our new slate porch and down the stained-wood stairs to the cab, crying. I cried on the plane. I cried when I got the cab at the airport to come here. And then when you gave me that nice tall glass of apple juice, I stopped crying. I'm not crying now, am I?

DAISY: You don't have to worry. The courts are always behind. You've got another hour, maybe more.

LOUISE: I can trade the return ticket in. There must be plenty of places I could get to that aren't Cincinnati.

DAISY: You know what gets your courage going? Talking about the future. Jerry won't talk about anything past today—his test at The Sands is today. We'll talk about the future, and you'll be driven to the courts. Are you going to keep your married name?

LOUISE: And be Mrs. Louse Elliot?

DAISY: So what will your name be?

LOUISE: Ms. Louse Rabashevsky.

DAISY: Your name is Louise.

LOUISE: Not after I get the divorce. He said it to me. He knows what he is talking about. He's the doctor in the family.

DAISY: I'm telling you what to do. You have to have to-morrow covered, not just empty, not a blank on your calendar. I didn't. Jerry didn't.

LOUISE: My husband uses me for practice. We went through Freudian analysis together, and Jungian, Reichian, Karen Horney variations, primal. For two months I was on Thorazine, walking around the house like a zombie. He was getting a room ready for shock therapy. If I'd stayed, it would have been a lobotomy in a year, or something worse.

DAISY: Did you ever love him?

LOUISE: Once. More than once. If you drew a line of my marriage it would be like that. (*She takes a paper and pencil, from Jerry's place, draws*) A straight line. It begins. And it ends.

DAISY: You stopped?

LOUISE: I stopped.

DAISY: Why?

LOUISE: It was September 16th. We set a record. The hottest September 16th since 1873. I feel like that cloud is right over my head.

DAISY: (*Looking out the window*) There's a taxi out there.

LOUISE: Is it here, over us?

DAISY: More to the right, about a block away.

JERRY: "Midway in our life's journey, I went astray from the straight road and woke to find myself alone in a dark wood."

DAISY: Whatever you do, after you get the divorce, don't

play a slot machine, just for luck. That's what you'll tell yourself. The divorce papers will be in your hand, and you'll feel hot, like you can't lose, and what's a quarter once you are a free woman, so you'll put one in, you won't win, you'll try another.

JERRY: "Margaret, are you grieving, over golden grove unleaving. You with your fresh thoughts . . ."

(The poetry comes out of Jerry in fits and spurts this time; he most resembles a car backfiring because of sand or dirt in the gas line. Each time he starts up, it looks like he will run smoothly, but he gives a spit, a sort of cough, and his motor dies. During this, Daisy will be talking, and again, it is she we should be able to hear)

DAISY: I hate those goddamned machines. They've stolen everything from me. I could have left this town a dozen times. But I wanted to leave with something. I have bad luck. I got my divorce. I played what money I had away. I said, that's it. I'm ready to leave. No money. New life. I got into my car, drove for a block, and it broke down. So I sold the car. And I was at the station, waiting for a bus. I had a quarter in my hand, to buy a Baby Ruth, but they were out. So I went next door, to one of those sleazy downtown places. I put the quarter in, watched those wheels go 'round. Bump, bump, bump, one lemon. Bump, bump, two lemons, bump, bump, bump, bump, one cherry, and I was hooked. A couple of months later, I won $3700 playing the dollar machine, and then, the same night, another $5000. I took it to the bank, got a loan,

JERRY: "The force that through the green fuse drives the flower, drives my green age . . ."

"Batter my heart, three-personed god . . ."

"Let us go then, you and I, through certain half-deserted streets, the muttering retreats of restaurants and dah-dah cheap hotels . . ."

"Two Chinamen, behind them a third,
Are carved in lapis lazuli,
Over them flies a long-legged bird
A symbol of longevity . . ."

This is my favorite poem! Do you realize that? I can't remember it, not all of it. Wait! Here it comes!

"One asks for mournful melodies;
Accomplished fingers begin to play,
Their eyes mid many wrin-

and got this place. I haven't-played the machines since. I'm afraid to.

kles, their eyes,
Their ancient glittering eyes
are gay."

JERRY: I can't remember any more. That's it. It's all gone. It was my favorite poem. Last stanza, last poem. I've done it. Nothing more stored up in the old noggin.

(*He gets a deck of cards, breaks the seal, takes the cards out, hands them to Louise, who shuffles and cuts them. He deals for a hand of blackjack*)

DAISY: I'll miss it. You sure you don't have any more? (*Jerry shakes his head "no"*) All emptied out? (*Jerry shakes his head "yes"*) That figures.

JERRY: (*To Louise*) Look at your hand. What have you got?

LOUISE: A nine and an eight.

JERRY: Seventeen. You freeze?

LOUISE: I'll freeze.

JERRY: (*Triumphantly throws his hand face up*) Ace and king. Blackjack. (*He deals again, turns his head up*) Blackjack!

DAISY: I suppose I could go into court with you, Louise. And then go out, very casually. Sneak up on it. Find myself an old, dilapidated, worn-out, tired slot, put my quarter in, pull the lever—I wouldn't even have to look . . .

(*Jerry has dealt again*)

JERRY: Six and eight—fourteen. I'll take another card.

DAISY: Slot machines are the junk of this town.

JERRY: Ten. Twenty-four. Wipe out!

DAISY: No real gambler will waste his money on them. It's just a question of luck.

JERRY: I thought for a minute—with my head clear . . .

DAISY: No skill, no system will get you a win on the slots. Jerk the lever hard, pull it slow, tilt the machine a little. Nothing matters. So it's a roomful of beginners, to get their feet wet, or crabby old women with plastic purses who don't have the guts to walk into the big room, meander over to a roulette table and put a chip on seventeen red, and then put two chips on red, odd, and then cover their corners.

JERRY: (*He has been calculating*) The house is down $25,000. That's in less than half an hour. That's $50,000 an hour.

DAISY: You ever see the guy start the wheel moving? It's scary if you've got any money riding on it at all. A woman like me, all he has to do is start that wheel moving, and I am ready to pee in my pants or have a stroke.

JERRY: (*He's done more figuring*) Two million a week, $104 million a year. Who is going to hire a dealer who loses $104 million a year?

LOUISE: What am I going to do if I don't get my divorce?

DAISY: Put another way, what are you going to do to-morrow when you get home to Cincinnati?

LOUISE: Well, if I came home without the divorce, I'd be a laughing stock in my neighborhood. That's for sure.

DAISY: You wouldn't have to tell anyone. Whose business is it? Who is going to come over to your house and ask to see the papers?

LOUISE: That's absurd. I have to get the divorce. Henry's counting on it. He says it makes him nervous when I change my mind all the time.

DAISY: Are you still in love with him?

LOUISE: I don't miss him.

DAISY: I don't miss my mother. I still love her.

LOUISE: If I don't get the divorce, I don't have to leave, do I?

JERRY: Why would you want to stay?

DAISY: This is the emptiest place I ever came to. (*The room darkens*) Don't move around too much, Louise. Not while it's right over our heads.

LOUISE: Is it all right to sit down?

DAISY: If you do it slowly. . . . That's why Jerry stayed on. He didn't think he'd be able to find a better place to empty his head out.

JERRY: Well, it's done. But I'm not doing any better with the cards.

DAISY: I'm going to miss those beautiful words. It is so sweet. Poetry and fucking just seem to go together.

JERRY: My wife used to fall asleep when I'd say a poem to her.

DAISY: She is a professor of mathematics.

JERRY: She has other problems, too. She's frigid.

LOUISE: If I don't get the divorce, and I go home, he'll try some new experiment on me. I know he will. The names he can give what I did—deep-seated neurotic displacement repressive syndrome.

DAISY: You don't have to go home. You can go someplace else. Anyplace.

LOUISE: My plane ticket's for Cincinnati . . . I could stay here.

DAISY: You don't want to do that.

LOUISE: It's very comfortable here.

DAISY: I only have two rooms to rent out. You'd be cutting half my income.

LOUISE: I could still pay rent.

DAISY: No. I couldn't take it. Only when a person's divorcing.

LOUISE: Jerry doesn't pay any rent?

JERRY: I'll get a job. Now that dealing's out I'll find something else. Bag boy at a supermarket, pin setter in a bowling alley.

LOUISE: Can't you go back to teaching?

JERRY: Not when I've forgotten it all. I'd have to learn it again. My ex-wife would be amused. Now I've got a head that doesn't have any words in it, and I still can't deal cards. You know what she did? She took Rubik's cube, the first time she held it in her hand, one, two, three—ten moves and she had it solved. Then she tossed it to me. Told me to try it. I tried. For two hours. I bought the book that's supposed to show you how to do it. I tried some more. I let my seminars go, working over the damn thing. Three, four in the morning. One day, she turned off the alarm clock and sat up in bed, looking at me, and asked, What's the good of all that poetry you teach if you can't solve Rubik's cube?

LOUISE: What did you say?

JERRY: It was a good question. I'm still working the answer out. That's why I wanted to learn about blackjack. Defeat her at her own game. She worked out a strategy, a mathematical equation for blackjack, how to win. She sent two students to Atlantic City to try it out. They came back millionaires. She won't test it, of course, destroys her scientific objectivity.

LOUISE: You could try it here.

JERRY: You think she'd trust me? A man who couldn't even solve Rubik's cube?

DAISY: It's getting a little brighter. The cloud must be moving.

JERRY: So I've got a dream. She'll come down here on vacation some time, and she'll be ready to try her system. She'll come to my table and see me and laugh because her system is mathematically correct. I'll deal her a hand. She'll freeze at eighteen. I have twenty-one. House wins. I deal another, she has twenty-one, but I have an ace, king. Blackjack. House wins. She collapses on the floor, becomes catatonic with rage, never develops another equation. Mazlish's revenge!

DAISY: She deserves it!

JERRY: But she won't get it. Don't forget, I'm $104 million down. I have no talent for dealing blackjack.

LOUISE: You could be something else. They use a lot of stand-up comics here.

JERRY: Where's the revenge in that?

LOUISE: If I'm getting the divorce, I'd better leave.

DAISY: You're fine on time. They never conduct court business when the cloud is this heavy. The papers always have a story—men and women who just went outside, and they come back, clothes all covered with some heavy black ash. Sometimes they get sick. The hair falls out of their heads. Occasionally they die. Nobody who stayed inside with the windows closed has ever died or lost his hair.

LOUISE: I don't want a divorce. I don't have to get one. We can be separated. I can go to any hotel in town and get a job—hat check girl, cigarette girl. My legs aren't perfect, but they're good enough. If Henry Elliot wants a divorce, he can give up his practice for a couple of months and come and get it himself. Why should I do all the work? . . . He wouldn't come. He wouldn't do me that favor.

DAISY: The cloud's gone. You notice the quality of light? That's what happens when it moves on. The sky turns that perfect color, like the ocean's upside down over our heads. All the dust cleaned out, vacuumed away . . . Jerry, there's no point in sitting there playing with the cards if you aren't going to be a dealer.

JERRY: This is probably the worst day in my life.

LOUISE: You could go and take the test anyway.

JERRY: I'm going to take a shower. Throw all that stuff away, will you, Daisy?

(*Jerry leaves. Daisy clears away the blackjack game, disconnects it from the TV, and gets the cards*)

LOUISE: What's going to happen to him?

DAISY: He'll manage. He'll feel better all emptied out. But I'll miss it. Some nights we used to keep on for hours, sex and poetry, sex and poetry. The man was inexhaustible. There's no point in your thinking you can stay here. You don't seem like the sort.

LOUISE: You can do it.

DAISY: I'm not afraid of the clouds. You are.

LOUISE: I'm afraid of the emptiness.

DAISY: That's what I mean.

LOUISE: I'll wake up and look at the calendar. There'll be all these blank spaces that have to be filled in, and I won't know what to put there. The ballpoint pen will run out of ink and I'll rip the calendar off the wall, but it'll still be there. The squares with the empty spaces will have gone through the calendar and will be on the wall. And there won't be any way of get rid of them. Like when I gained twenty pounds and stopped looking in the mirror. It wasn't any help. I still knew I was fat. I'll still know when I get up that it's a new day and there has to be something to do. Weeks and weeks of thinking up things to put in those blank squares! Sometimes being married is better than that, no matter who you're married to. Or being divorced. I just have to get on with it. Whatever . . .

DAISY: Well, you see, if you stay around here, you won't be able to fill that calendar in. We don't have them in Las Vegas.

LOUISE: That taxi's still out there.

DAISY: You're lucky. He probably decided to stay put until things cleared up.

LOUISE: (She pulls the window up, yells out of it) I'll be right there.

DAISY: Then your room will be available tomorrow?

LOUISE: I guess so.

DAISY: You getting the divorce?

LOUISE: Or going back to Cincinnati. They seem like the same thing.

DAISY: Tell the lawyer you want the maiden name back. Rabashevsky's a beautiful name.

LOUISE: Thanks.

DAISY: Bring a bottle of wine when you come back. So we can celebrate. Oh, would you take this? (She fishes out a mimeographed paper) Put it up on that bulletin board they have in front of the courthouse. Someone's sure to want a room and see the sign.

LOUISE: You want to come along, like you said? I'd stake you to a quarter machine.

DAISY: Maybe some other time. I'll have to clean your room out.

(*The taxi horn honks*)

LOUISE: I could help with that.

DAISY: No. That lucky machine I was talking about already paid off. I can feel it. Have to wait for the next moment of inspiration.

(*The taxi horn honks again*)

LOUISE: I'll be back for lunch.

(*Louise leaves. Daisy pours two more glasses of orange juice. It empties the pitcher. Jerry comes down as she finishes*)

JERRY: (*Noticing Louise's absence*) So she went to get divorced.

DAISY: Have a glass of orange juice. It's good for depression.

JERRY: We'll miss her.

DAISY: No we won't. Next month you won't remember her name.

JERRY: All happy divorces are alike?

DAISY: I could be in Ashtabula right now. I could be back there on a beautiful day like this, growing soy beans, happily married.

JERRY: Daisy, what's going to become of you?

DAISY: All I wanted was just once to win the big jackpot. Just to say I accomplished something. But I'm never going to get it. The one today was mine. It had my name on it. There might be another one, a thousand years from now, when there's some other Daisy Stoddard playing the machines. But that won't do me much good, will it?

JERRY: You know what hit me, just now when I was upstairs in the shower? You know what I am? What purpose I serve? I'm the oddball statistic, the number that skews the results. I was born, and the good fairy stood over my crib and something clicked, the order came down from somewhere. They needed the exception to prove the rule. And I was there. And when you were born, I bet the same thing happened. The two of us, we're the evidence. My wife used to draw these bell-shaped curves, normal curves they're called, and they have these little, squinched up places at each end, you can hardly see them, but they have to be there to give the curve its shape. So that's our purpose in life.

DAISY: You're not leaving?

JERRY: Why should I? Everybody who lives in Las Vegas isn't a blackjack dealer. Something's bound to turn up. Odds are.

DAISY: I better get the place cleaned up. Louise'll be back any time, and she'll want to celebrate. You want to do the shopping?

JERRY: You think there'll be any more clouds?

DAISY: Not today. Not for a while. Not if everything stays normal.

The End

Harry Kondoleon

SELF TORTURE AND STRENUOUS EXERCISE

Harry Kondoleon

Harry Kondoleon is a 1981 graduate of the Yale School of Drama, where he twice won the Molly Kazan Playwriting Award for best original script—for *The Côte D'Azur Triangle,* produced in 1980 at the Actors Studio and for *The Brides,* produced the same year at the Lenox Arts Center and published in *Wordplays 2.* Another play written at Yale, *Rococo,* was produced for the Yale Repertory Theatre's first Winterfest of new American plays in January 1981.

While Mr. Kondoleon was still a graduate student at Yale, he sent the editor of this anthology several of his short plays for consideration. Recognizing a unique theatrical voice, I immediately selected *Self Torture and Strenuous Exercise,* an antagonizingly ludicrous account of an egotistical writer, his suicidal wife, and their closest friends, who batter each other's egos with the vigor of primal therapy. Months later I had the privilege of seeing the play hilariously produced by the Double Image Theatre in New York. Reviewing this presentation (coupled with Kondoleon's *The Fairy Garden*), New York *Daily News* theatre critic Don Nelson wrote: "To say both are funny understates the case. Kondoleon has written comedies of considerable sophistication without being precious. The effect is a style that might have emerged had Noel Coward written for the Theatre of the Absurd . . . Kondoleon is a welcome new jouster to the theatrical lists. We could use more of his sharp sallies." And *New York Post* Marilyn Stasio observed: ". . . Harry Kondoleon has already developed a clever, captious style that is as bright as it is original."

In 1977 Mr. Kondoleon received a fellowship from the International Institute of Education to study the Balinese theatre, and in 1982 his teleplay *Clara Toil* was selected for the O'Neill Playwrights Conference. In March of 1983 the Manhattan Theatre Club offered his *Slacks and Tops,* which, according to Frank Rich, theatre reviewer for the *New York Times,* "snakes through the theatre like an air-raid siren." Two months later Playwrights Horizons produced his full-length play *Christmas on Mars.* Mr. Kondoleon's achievements were honored by the Obie award for Most Promising Playwright.

Self Torture and Strenuous Exercise appears here in print for the first time.

Characters:

ALVIN
BETHANY
CARL
ADEL

Time:

Fall. Late.

Setting:

The dining room of Alvin and Bethany. There is a round table with a white tablecloth and the remnants of a late-night supper. There are dirty plates, half-filled glasses, unfolded napkins, unlit candles, and a centerpiece of flowers. As much occurs on the floor, a raked stage would be an asset.

Carl, Alvin, and Bethany are seated at the table.

CARL: Alvin, I'm in love with another woman.

ALVIN: Good! Good for you Carl. I'm glad. When Adel died, I can't tell you the psychic exhaustion I suffered worrying who you'd find to take her place. I didn't want to cook. Tell him, Beth. I just stood at my cutting board, surrounded by raw vegetables, and thought, Why go on? I wanted a sign from above. I wanted God to say, "Al, go on." Death is so depleting. I know you loved Adel, but did you know I did? I loved her. I don't mean I was sleeping with her—I loved her as a spiritual sister, are you following me? Then I thought how everything goes back to the mixing bowl. How we cannot expect to be given any clues to God's great recipe. Follow? And then I picked up my knife, ready to cut again, and thought, Adel is back in God's kitchen: There is no call for mourning.

CARL: Alvin, I've told you one hundred times, Adel *attempted* suicide. She was *not* successful. She is still *alive* and the two of us have *separated*. Do you understand? Adel lives. Adel lives, and I am in love with another woman.

ALVIN: And I'm glad! I'm happy. I look down at our dirty

plates, some bones and fat left over, some pits from fruit, I look down at these plates and I say, "God bless us!" Do you know what I'm getting at, Carl?

BETHANY: I feel dizzy. I need to lie down. I'm going to lie down. (*She lies down on the floor, mummy-like.*)

CARL: I'm in love with your wife!

ALVIN: I look at these dirty plates, and I think, "God! aren't *we* the dirty plates?" Aren't we the plates who have been taken off the shelf, heaped with little portions of prepared nourishment, eaten off of, finally laid on the table, dirty and waiting to be taken back into the kitchen to be cleaned and what?—used again! and again! The life cycle! Revival! Hope! Divine Design!

CARL: Alvin, I'm in love with your wife, Beth. *I love her.*

ALVIN: But of course you love her! It's the most natural thing in the world. What could be more natural? You love her and you love me, and she loves you and she loves me, and I love you both. And before Adel died, we all loved her.

CARL: Adel is alive. I love Beth. I love her and want her. I want to go away with her.

ALVIN: I'm not surprised! With Adel gone—though in your grief you temporarily block her burial—you look to new female companionship. What could be more natural? It goes without saying. You see Bethany as surrogate female companionship, am I right? And look—Beth in her beauty and acceptance has sought to duplicate the position of dead Adel. *Look* what she's doing for you Carl. Now how can you say we don't love you?

BETHANY: The floor is turning under me. Just me. Your floor is still. My floor is moving.

ALVIN: Bethany, would you like another glass of wine? A mint?

CARL: Alvin, I wish you'd just sit still for one minute and try to get all this information straight. (A) I'm in love with Beth and Beth's in love with me, (B) Beth and I have been sleeping together for several *years*—long before I left Adel, and (C) Beth and I want to go away together, live and love together. Is it all clear now? You understand?

ALVIN: You love Beth and Beth loves you, you've slept with Beth and Beth's slept with you, you want to go away with Beth and Beth wants to go away with you. I understand.

BETHANY: Make something matter. Somebody make something matter.

CARL: Beth, get up off the floor and we'll go away together. Alvin understands.

BETHANY: I can't.

CARL: Alvin understands. He says he understands.

ALVIN: What's there not to understand?

BETHANY: I can't.

CARL: Beth!

BETHANY: I can't. I can't get up.

CARL: Let me help you.

BETHANY: No!

CARL: Beth! What are you saying? Are you saying you don't want to go away with me? After all this time? After years?

BETHANY: I can't get up. I'm stuck.

CARL: Get up!

ALVIN: Can I get you a pillow? A blanket, Beth? There's an autumn chill that seeps right in through the floor—not having a basement, the dampness of the earth becomes a problem for us.

CARL: *Beth, get up!* Our plans, think of our plans! The down payments on the cottage, your return to poetry, my new novel!

ALVIN: Down payments? Poetry? A new novel?

CARL: Beth! What's wrong with you? Alvin, did you give her something? Did you put something in her wine? Or food?

ALVIN: A new novel, Carl? I'm so glad. I thought perhaps with the tragedy of Adel you'd get blocked. You're turning a new leaf?

CARL: Why is she acting so peculiar—did you add something to the food?

ALVIN: Carl, I put lots of things in the food. I was at the range all day, mixing things in bowls, adding this and that—all intuitively.

CARL: What is going on here?

ALVIN: This afternoon I was out picking the last string beans from the vines. These were late beans—did you think them coarse?

CARL: Beth, what are you doing? Are you turning this into a joke? Adel tried to *kill* herself when she found out about us, and you're turning the whole thing into a joke! Bethany!

ALVIN: I stood there among these late vines—late beans—and thought, My God! the glory of nature! I mean, I was picking beans that later that same day we would be consuming. Chewing and eating the same beans that hours previously hung at the mercy of a changing season. You follow? I think the vines thanked me, taking in their children before the autumn chill. I felt blessed, special. When Beth and I moved into this house, I debated the idea of a city garden. All that extra work, I thought. I hadn't forseen the spiritual feedback. And now *you* have a new leaf, Carl. Tell us about it.

BETHANY: (*Still recumbent*) You're a stingy writer, Carl. You have one barely articulated point of view projected on too many thinly disguised characters.

CARL: Bethany!

BETHANY: *The Motel of the Heart?* With all those characters? They were really one character, they all had one problem, one point of view.

CARL: What are you saying?

ALVIN: Beth's an insightful critic.

BETHANY: The character of Georgette? You meant to base her on me. But it wasn't me, Carl. It was you. When Georgette says she doesn't know how to love, that she flies from one set of arms to the next in the desperate hope of finding the right pair, it is you speaking, Carl, your search for the right pair. I lie here, and I say nothing matters. I shout, Somebody make something matter! And in your next book, Carl, you'll call me Renata or Thalia, and I'll be standing in a train station; my lover will appear and I, dropping my handbag, my overnight bag, my little wax bag of grapes, will fall into my lover's arms and say—moan—Bring me back to life, resurrect me in your house of love.

CARL: What is all this about? Is this a joke, a joke on me?

ALVIN: Don't interrupt.

BETHANY: I can't tell you the death I feel when I see myself disguised in your books, Carl. When I see you playing me.

CARL: Don't say this! Don't say this! You're torturing me. I love you. I'd never do anything to hurt you.

BETHANY: And Adel? Where is Adel now?

CARL: Adel is home!

ALVIN: Oh, the perversity of grief!

BETHANY: It's you, Carl, you standing in the train station with the bags, with the beaten thesaurus in the overnight bag.

CARL: You're not yourself!

BETHANY: Every writer comes to a point of breakthrough. When he sees the lies from the lies, the Georgettes from the Georgettes.

CARL: I love you!

ALVIN: You're not well, Carl. The emotional strain. The absence of Adel. Your new book. Too much. Don't you think I noticed how you more or less *pecked* at your food, Carl?

CARL: Bethany!

BETHANY: The floor is moving under me. I'm moving.

CARL: You're speaking nonsense deliberately—you're trying to drive me off—you're *testing* me. But I won't be tricked. I'm taking you away, and if you won't get up I'll *pick* you up.

ALVIN: (*Scraping a plate*) Carl, you're torturing yourself!

CARL: Beth, I'm going to pick you up and carry you away!

ALVIN: You can't pick her up.

BETHANY: A weak novelist.

(*Carl picks Bethany up and carries her like a bride*)

ALVIN: You're picking her up!

BETHANY: I'm being picked up. I'm in the air now, Alvin. There's nothing I can do. I'm being carried away. You'll know I didn't walk out on you.

CARL: (*Moving out toward the door*) We're going now.

(*Bethany and Carl exit*)

ALVIN: Wait! Wait! I can't believe this. What about the autumn vegetables? What about me? Beth! The pumpkins! Beth, the pumpkins aren't ready yet. Pumpkin pie, pumpkin pancakes, pumpkin seeds—Beth, where are you going? Carl! Beth! Come back! In the spring everything will be in bloom! (*Sits back at his place at the table, considers what has happened*) Well, that sure took me for a loop. Just whisked her off the floor. Guess who's left with the dishes? Times like this I think of my mother and my father. I reconsider them. I think of my mother, who said, "No matter how well you prepare a meal, no guest will ever fully appreciate it." And I think of my father who, the day after my mother died, thought with a sudden sense of profound despair as he dropped a frozen pouch into a pot of boiling water, "I loved that woman, I loved her!"

(*Enter Adel. Her hair and clothing are disheveled, her make-up smudged. Her wrists are thickly wrapped in white gauze*)

ADEL: Where is the fucker?!

ALVIN: An apparition! Dear God in heaven.

ADEL: What? Alvin, it's me, Adel. Where's Carl?

ALVIN: Adel! Adel! You're *alive!*

ADEL: Of course I'm alive! I'm here, aren't I?

ALVIN: I'm in shock, Adel.

ADEL: Where's Carl? Carl and Beth?

ALVIN: They went away, Adel. You didn't see them? Carl was holding Beth.

ADEL: Then that was them! I saw somebody with a bundle running down the street.

ALVIN: That was them.

ADEL: Is it too late to catch them?

ALVIN: Adel, you're really alive. I thought you were dead.

ADEL: That's because Carl wants me dead!

ALVIN: Carl said that you were alive.

ADEL: Carl wants to kill me, Alvin!

ALVIN: No.

ADEL: Yes!

ALVIN: Carl?

ADEL: Yes, Alvin. Carl wants everything in his path dead. He wants you dead too, Alvin. He's probably telling Beth right now that you're dead.

ALVIN: But I'm alive, Adel.

ADEL: I know, Alvin, but we're talking about *Carl.* Don't you know who Carl is?

ALVIN: I know Carl.

ADEL: I hate him! Look at me, Alvin: I'm a mess! And who's made me a mess?

ALVIN: Who?

ADEL: *Carl!* Don't you know what he's done to me? How he sucked me dry and then tried to bury the evidence? Do you know what I'm talking about, Alvin?

ALVIN: No, Adel, I really don't.

ADEL: I'm talking about seven years! Seven years with a bloodsucker! You don't think I have scars, Alvin? I have them! I've kept them from people—out of embarrassment and humiliation! I've had to keep my true self down to accommodate Carl.

ALVIN: Accommodate Carl?

ADEL: Who do you think wrote *The Motel of the Heart?* Carl? Carl can't even spell! I wrote *The Motel of the Heart* and he stole it! Right out of my head!

ALVIN: Adel, this is so baffling.

ADEL: What's baffling? (*Opening her locket, a kind of pillbox on a chain around her neck. She pops some Valium. This action does not interrupt the lines*) That Carl has used terrorist tactics to publish a novel? You don't know the real Carl, Alvin. You don't know how this sort of man operates! You have any extra Valium in the house?—I'm running low.

ALVIN: Adel, I don't have Valium, and I don't think badly of Carl. All people are good at heart, Adel. Even in times of severe strife you must not forget this. I do understand that you must feel a little cut off from things right now, but we can't blame our spouses for our shortcomings, Adel. I'm positive Carl wants to reconcile himself to you, that he still loves you deep in his heart and will share his royalties with you. Carl is very spur-of-the-moment. He and Beth will be back—they've only gone out for a short walk or something. A vacation is all Carl needs. Being a creative artist . . .

ADEL: Carl is *not* a creative artist! He's a destructive journalist! His novels are no more than a "misconstruance" of the affairs he himself perpetrates on the people around him. Because my love *blinded* me, I have been *duped* into transforming his vile logs into the kindling of fiction. Don't you see the evil? *I'm* the creative one. Alvin! I've been tricked—we've all been manipulated for Carl's personal gain! Don't you see how one by one Carl will attempt to wipe out those who *know*. Don't you see, Alvin, that unless we—the Anti-Carls—mass together we will face extinction! (*Picking up a platter with a cake on it. It has one slice missing*) Pretend this is us, Alvin, our kind . . . (*A quick sniff*) What is this, cheesecake?—Watch me. (*She raises her fist and brings it down violently onto the cake. The cake splatters*) *That's* what they want to do to us!

ALVIN: I don't think God would ever permit such a thing, Adel.

ADEL: God has nothing to do with this! You think God cares about bestseller lists and ripped-off wives? Alvin, I am telling you, they want to wipe us out!

ALVIN: They? *Who* are you talking about, Adel?

ADEL: Carl! You don't think he works alone, do you? Not at this point in his rise to recognition. He has *people!* Hired people! They follow me, Alvin. They know my every move! They followed me here on the bus!

ALVIN: You didn't take a taxi?

ADEL: I did! They took the bus. (*Fishing through her pockets and bag. The bag empties itself onto the floor*) Where'd I put my Valium? They must have known I was coming here! You didn't tell anyone, did you?

ALVIN: Adel, until a few minutes ago I thought you were dead.

(*Adel dives under the table to search through her things*)

ADEL: (*Her head bobbing up for a moment*) That's my point exactly! You don't know the hell I've been living these past weeks. Pure hell! (*She bobs down under again*) If I don't find my Valium in one minute, I'm going to die right here. Alvin! Come down and help me!

(*Alvin descends*)

ALVIN: Here it is, Adel! I found your Valium.

ADEL: That's my lipstick. Keep looking. (*Leaping up*) I found them! Help me collect this junk. Only two left. I need two. I had two in the taxi.

ALVIN: You need something to drink with that?

ADEL: No, I take 'em dry. I've gotten to the point where I can't depend on a ready water supply. (*They are both off the floor now. Adel is stuffing her things back into her bag. She remembers her locket*) Oh Jesus! I forgot my locket!

ALVIN: Save those for an emergency, Adel.

ADEL: This is an emergency. (*Noticing the leftovers*) What'd you serve? Is that lamb?

ALVIN: Oh Adel, I made . . .

ADEL: Listen to me, Alvin—I'm talking about my life! I came here to *kill* Carl! How much longer do you think I have, Alvin? How much longer before Carl gets me? Do you know he threatened to pull my stitches out? He did! I had to ward him off with the dogs—Prince and King. The next day he let them go. He said, "I'm going to release the dogs," as if it was Bastille Day or something. My only source of protection let out on the street to be run over. "Why don't you release yourself, Carl?" I said, "Go stand in front of a truck!"

ALVIN: Adel, you don't mean these things!

ADEL: Don't I? You know what I have in my pocket, Alvin? Guess!

ALVIN: Valium?

ADEL: A letter! A letter to Carl!

ALVIN: You've written Carl a letter?

ADEL: No! It's a letter from a literary society. It came today.

ALVIN: You didn't open it, Adel, did you?

ADEL: Of course I did! What are you thinking of?! I opened it, and I read it, and do you know what it says? (*Brandishing the letter*) *The Motel of the Heart* has won some national book award. There's an invitation to a ceremonial banquet!

ALVIN: A ceremonial banquet! How marvelous, Adel! A gift from God. I'm so happy for Carl—and for you, Adel. Surely Carl will take you to the banquet.

ADEL: Alvin, I think you've been sitting in the kitchen too long. You're not seeing anything clearly! Do you still not know that Carl was sleeping with—fucking with—your wife, Beth? Years he said! Years! Of deception! What do I care about banquets!

ALVIN: God, Adel, I would think . . .

ADEL: I'm talking about *Satan,* and you keep bringing up God! I'm telling you, Carl is the maker of all things evil on this planet—all betrayal, mockery, and injustice! (*Banging her elbows, since she cannot use her fists, on the table for emphasis. Some glasses may fall over*) Carl must be destroyed! Time is running out! He will take over the world!

ALVIN: Adel, I *insist* that you calm down. You're beginning to distort things.

ADEL: You mean relax? *Relax.* That's what my doctor says. "Relax, Adel," she says, "Relax and stop persecuting yourself with self-analysis. Just relax." (*Picking up a fork and demurely sampling some splattered cake*) Yuck! (*She flings the fork away*) That's too sweet!

ALVIN: Beth did the cake.

ADEL: (*Spitting it out*) Tastes like poison.

ALVIN: It is sweet.

ADEL: I don't blame Beth. Though I wrote and typed *The Motel of the Heart* and it was dedicated to her—I don't blame her.

ALVIN: Well that's good, Adel. The less blame and animosity you have, the better.

ADEL: (*Pushing the cake platter aside*) Alvin, I've been working on a *new* novel. Did you know?

ALVIN: No.

ADEL: Well I have. An exposé! An exposé novel on Carl.

ALVIN: Sounds absorbing, Adel.

ADEL: It is. I'm exerting the smallest effort to disguise Carl's identity. Soon the world will see this great minor writer as the forger and bloodsucker he really is!

ALVIN: You have the book with you?

ADEL: It's in my head. All I have to do is *type* it! I carry all my notes here near my bosom. (*She takes out a small packet of notes*)

ALVIN: It's so little, Adel.

ADEL: It's in code! And it's going to stay in code until I can find a safe place.

ALVIN: A safe place?

ADEL: Yes, Alvin!

ALVIN: Right before my mother died she said that. She took my hand and said, "Alvin, I'm going to a safe place."

ADEL: I need that place, Alvin! (*Adel leans over to take Alvin's hand and accidently knocks over a decanter of wine. It crashes to the floor. Adel jumps*) You see! The peril of every moment! Things seeking my destruction! Alvin, I must write my exposé before it's too late—let me move in here—now that Beth's gone, you have lots of room. I won't be any trouble. I'll type real quiet. I'll do the dishes. Say yes, Alvin—save my life!

ALVIN: All right, Adel, I listened to you, now have another Valium and listen to me. Carl is good at heart—yes, Adel! Listen to what I have to tell, Adel. Carl may have gone astray, but he is *not* a bad man. He and Beth have probably just gone out for a walk . . . (*Adel attempts an outburst. Alvin cuts her off*) . . . or maybe they just went away for the weekend—there is no sin in a short holiday.

ADEL: Short holiday?! They are fornicating right this minute on some front lawn!

ALVIN: Silence, Adel! Listen to me. Perhaps Carl went temporarily insane with the belief of your death.

ADEL: Alvin, he didn't believe I was dead—you did. He wants me dead, but he knows I'm not.

ALVIN: Adel, listen to me. I'm going to take my car out and bring back Bethany and Carl. Then we'll discuss this all together.

ADEL: How are you going to find them?

ALVIN: They couldn't have gotten very far. Carl was carrying Beth.

ADEL: You're going to bring Carl back? Don't tell him about the letter; let me.

ALVIN: OK, Adel, but you have to promise to calm down, OK?

ADEL: Relax. I know, "Relax, Adel." Alvin, before you go, could you get me something?

ALVIN: Adel, I told you we have no tranquilizers in the house.

ADEL: No. Hot water. Could you bring me a bowl of hot water and a washcloth? And soap.

ALVIN: You want to bathe? Why don't you use the bathroom, Adel?

ADEL: Don't ask.

ALVIN: I'll get it for you. (*Alvin exits*)

ADEL: (*To herself. Between lines she picks at leftover food with increasing speed and appetite*)
Carl thinks he's rid of me!
Perhaps Carl will come back.
I don't need Carl!
But I still love Carl!
I should sacrifice myself to a man who is unfaithful, manipulative, and self-centered?
But sometimes he's so gentle and understanding and strong.
You want to be choked by him?
No, but I like when Carl holds me.
(*Alvin enters quickly with a silver tray on which is a bowl of hot water, a washcloth, and a bar of soap. He places it on the table*)

ALVIN: Here you are, Adel. Try not to make a puddle. I'll be back as soon as I find them. Now, you're not depressed or anything, are you?

ADEL: No.

ALVIN: Good. See you in no time.

(*Alvin exits. Adel washes herself. After some moments Bethany enters, crawling on her hands and knees*)

BETHANY: Carl is a trap.

(*Adel, surprised, jumps and drops her bowl of water*)

ADEL: Beth, is that you?

BETHANY: Adel! Adel, you are here! Forgive! Forgive me, Adel!

ADEL: You're not with Carl?

BETHANY: Carl is a trap! I know that now. He stopped at a phone booth to call his agent and found out about some book award. He started leaping and clapping in the booth and then went on to make over a dozen calls, while he left me lying on the sidewalk. As I was lying there among the dead leaves, I realized what a conceited shithead Carl really is and, more important, how I have transgressed you, Adel.

ADEL: Me?

BETHANY: When I started to crawl home—I couldn't stand—Carl was still on the phone. He probably doesn't even know that I've left him. Adel, your shoes are all wet.

ADEL: I've been bathing.

BETHANY: Let me dry them! (*Bethany uses her hair to dry Adel's shoes*)

ADEL: Your hair! You don't have to do that, Beth.

BETHANY: I want to! I want forgiveness! Will you give it to me, Adel? Will you?

ADEL: Does Carl know I'm here?

BETHANY: (*Wringing her hair*) Carl is a trap!

ADEL: (*Avoiding Bethany's grip*) My whole life has become a trap, Beth! Everyday I wake up, and there's a trap. I don't mean just *traps*—I mean *real* traps. I mean, I can't get from my bed to the kitchen without things falling in my path—falling on my head! I try to be careful, I try to take things slowly, watch where I'm going, but—POW! I get it. Glasses fall from the shelves, plates slip from the drainboard, knives unhook from the walls. I touch the toaster and I get electric shock. I make a pot of coffee and it tastes like poison. The kitchen wants to kill me! It's not nine in the A.M. yet, and already I have death on the brain. Do you know what that's like, Beth? Everywhere I turn it's death! I can't get in my tub without thinking death—I think it's a coffin. Death, Beth! I take a shower and I think gas is going to come out. I'm taking sponge baths! Sponge baths over a basin! Why do you think I have my hair all pinned up like this? Because it's dirty! I can't bear to put my head under water!

BETHANY: Let me do something for you, Adel. Please let me! What can I do?

ADEL: You can—stop hugging my ankles!—you can . . . you can brush my hair.

BETHANY: Yes! I can do that! Let me!

ADEL: (*Removing a brush from her bag*) I can't stand it—my scalp's driving me crazy.

(*Bethany kneels behind Adel's chair and begins removing her hairpins and brushing her hair*)

BETHANY: Do you hate me, Adel?

ADEL: I wanted to die when Carl told me he was in love with you. I tried to end myself when he said you'd been ... sleeping together ... for so long. (*A knot in her hair*) Ouch!

BETHANY: I'm sorry, Adel! I'm sorry!

ADEL: Christ, am I itchy!

BETHANY: Forgive me!

ADEL: I thought you were my friend, Beth!

BETHANY: I am, Adel, I am! I don't know what I was thinking of at the time.

ADEL: For four years? Ouch!

BETHANY: I'm sorry.

ADEL: I don't know what it was, but I didn't feel safe anymore. I started suspecting everything. My doctor—she's an idiot—she said, "Adel, don't ever kill yourself without first making your bed and doing all the dishes in the sink." Well, I *never* did those things to begin with. So I fired the maid. Now my bed's an unmade mess and I haven't a clean plate in the house and I'm *still* alive!

BETHANY: Adel, I don't love Carl. I don't love him. I don't think I *ever* loved him. I think I only loved the way my body moved beneath his. I think I was loving myself. I never thought of Carl. I'm not thinking of him now.

ADEL: OK, now start styling it.

BETHANY: I never loved Carl. I only loved making love to him. I think I realized this when it no longer was a secret, when Carl told Alvin.

ADEL: Stop brushing and start styling!

BETHANY: You know, Adel, I've never had a orgasm with Alvin. Never. I don't even know if he knows it. Sometimes I think he's oblivious to everything. Living in a world of pots and pans.

ADEL: I asked Alvin if I could move in here because I can't stand living at home alone.

BETHANY: You don't want to move in here, Adel. You don't know what it's like to live with Alvin. Do you know what he does? He labels everything, puts little gummed stickers on everything with its name on it. As if he's going to forget everything in a minute.

ADEL: I hate living alone.

BETHANY: We have a girl come in on Fridays to vacuum—
Alvin *helps* her!

ADEL: (*Picking up the silver tray and holding it up like a mirror*)
Oh, Beth. I like what you're doing!

BETHANY: Alvin is a terrible lover. He gives silly little chip-
munk kisses.

ADEL: (*Holding up a hairpin*) Here's another pin.

BETHANY: (*Standing up*) You know what, Adel? We should
go away together, go away and leave everything.

ADEL: Go away with you?

BETHANY: Yes! What do you need Carl for? Carl was no
good for you anyway.

ADEL: No good for me?

BETHANY: He said you were completely unresponsive.

ADEL: Carl said this?

BETHANY: He said that you were squeamish.

ADEL: Carl told you this?

BETHANY: He said that he's always loved you, though.

ADEL: Carl said these things to you?

BETHANY: Carl is a trap! Let me massage your back. (*Bethany gets up on the table, kneels, and massages Adel's neck, back, and
shoulders*)

ADEL: Carl once told me that I was boring in bed. That's
what he says about Zoe in chapter twenty. I want him dead!

BETHANY: Where is your tension? Let me massage it.

ADEL: Carl used me!

BETHANY: Carl is a trap.

ADEL: Don't you think I know about traps, Beth? Seven
years, and I appear *briefly* in the last chapter of a book which
holds *no* interest past the middle—no matter *what* the national
book people say!

BETHANY: How does this feel? Let me undo these buttons
so I can really get in.

ADEL: I have something to learn about traps, Beth? A
man—and I'm talking about Carl—who in bed called me every
possible name—Claudia! Valerie! Laura! Gaby! Zoe! Marsha!
Barbara! Amy! Seven years, and never Adel! "Open your eyes,
Carl!" I'd shout, "Open your eyes and see *who you are fucking!*—I'm not a Zoe or an Amy, I'm an Adel!" Now you,
Beth—and I never blamed you—want to tell me about traps?
If my mother had lived to see my trap coming, she would
have killed herself and then me!

BETHANY: Is this working, Adel?

ADEL: You want to know who's *really* boring? Carl and his love novels! And I am *sick* of that love-shit. She loves him, he loves her, you love them, they love you—love-shit! (*Taking a gulp of what is left of a glass of wine. Wincing*) What year is this? It's so bitter!

BETHANY: I feel my poetry returning to me.

ADEL: That's good. Harder. Easy. Easy. Good. Real good. I'm coming back to life. "Forgive and relax," my doctor says. Advice at her rates I don't need. She can go to hell! I'm writing an exposé novel on *Carl*. You hear me, Beth? I will reveal each of his cruelties in detail—it'll have to be published in volumes.

BETHANY: Good, Adel!

ADEL: Want to collaborate?

BETHANY: I must return to poetry. Carl has stunted my muse. To write I must dip into my well of pain. How deep it is! Carl has no well and therefore must dip into ours. That's why he's always hanging over us. Although he doesn't seem to need us, he does. He sits waiting to dip in.

ADEL: I know the well of pain, Beth! I know it. I keep choking, and I don't know what to do. Every night is the same as the last. Spiders crawl up onto my bedspread and tell me I'm no good. They talk to me, Beth! They tell me I'm worthless and should go die. It's not a nightmare—it's my life.

BETHANY: Life is a torture chamber, Adel. I thought of that while crawling home. Ten men stopped me and offered to put me in a taxi, and I said no! Let me crawl home, maybe then I'll miss a few of the flying knives that come out each day to attack us.

ADEL: Those are the knives from my kitchen!

BETHANY: I'm returning to poetry, Adel. I'm turning my back on love. I'm turning to the cauldron of art. My muse is back!

> *Betrayal weighs on me like so much fake jewelry,*
> *Seized by a gloved hand,*
> *It falls like so many unstrung beads on a tiled floor . . .*

Look how the lines are coming to me, Adel!

> *Love is the rack I have been tied to,*
> *A machine of delicate tortures.*
> *My heart on fire seizes the whip*
> *I once cracked under . . .*

Adel, listen!
And pushes me, pushes me . . .
(*She stands on the table*)
Adel, the floor is turning! Do you feel it! Under our feet.
(*She loses her balance for a moment*)
The earth *twists* under our shoes, Adel!
I am the master of my . . .
(*Losing her balance again*)
Adel, hold me! The floor is turning! I can't stand up!
(*Adel gets on the table with Bethany. They support one another*)

ADEL: Beth, did you say that Carl has always loved me?
He said that? That he's always loved me?

BETHANY: (*Back to poetry*)
Betrayal! Betrayal! And vengeance:
The perfume of history.
The noxious scent of coupling . . .
Coupling what, Adel? Help me.
So many lovers falling away like rows of . . . rows of . . .

ADEL: Valium. Rows of Valium?

BETHANY:
Like so many rows of Valium,
The tiny tombstones of the spirit.

ADEL: I like that.

BETHANY:
What is love but torture?
The thumbscrews of the heart tightening,
Gripping the half-hopes . . .

ADEL: Carl thinks *he* can write!

BETHANY:
. . . and chokers of disappointment,
The brooch of promises,
That stick-pin of the breast
And the mismatched earrings of marriage:
The culprit on top of it.
What is love?

ADEL: Torture!

BETHANY:
Again: What is love?

BOTH:
Torture!

ADEL: (*A tiny voice*) But I still love Carl.

BETHANY:
 And men: What are men?
 Tell it, Adel!
ADEL:　Torture!
BETHANY:　Again!
BOTH:
 Torture!
ADEL:　(*A tiny voice*) But I still love Carl.
BETHANY:
 The weak men and the strong men!
 Together they are dust.
 So much dust soiling
 The apparel of women.
 So much filth emerging
 From the misguided wombs
 Of their unhappy mothers.
 What is life?
 What is life, Adel?!
BOTH:
 Torture!
(*Enter Carl*)
ADEL:　Carl!
BETHANY:　Vengeance!
CARL:　Beth, I'm sorry. I guess I made a lot of phone calls.
I got carried away by my award.
BETHANY:　DON'T EVEN TOUCH ME!
CARL:　I guess we're a finished chapter.
BETHANY:　(*Throwing a dish of chocolates at Carl*) Eat shit!
CARL:　The affair is over, that's obvious. Hello, Adel.
ADEL:　I came here to kill you, Carl.
CARL:　No, you didn't.
ADEL:　Yes, I did. Didn't I, Beth?
BETHANY:　Don't trust him—he's a rat with a necktie!
ADEL:　(*Uncertain of her path*) I'm going to kill you, Carl.
CARL:　You're not going to kill me or anyone else. You
couldn't even kill yourself, Adel.
ADEL:　He's trying to pull out my stitches! You see!
CARL:　Who took you to the hospital, Adel, and sat with
you for ten hours until they said you could go home? Who
signed the papers of responsibility, so you wouldn't have to
spend the night in the hospital?
ADEL:　My doctor.

CARL: No, Adel. Your doctor was the one who said she wanted to discontinue treatment because your progress was too slow.

ADEL: No!

CARL: I'm the one who persuaded her to keep you on.

ADEL: You did?

BETHANY: LIES!

CARL: Has Beth told you about the award?

ADEL: (*Taking out the letter*) I have the letter.

CARL: And you came here to deliver it to me. How sweet of you, Adel. And in two weeks, Adel, we'll be able to go to the award banquet, and you'll sit next to me. Maybe you'll be all healed by then. Then we could forget all this. Wouldn't that be nice?

ADEL: Home with you?

BETHANY: And be killed, Adel? Save yourself!

ADEL: I'm writing an exposé on you, Carl. An exposé for the world to read.

CARL: I'll help you with it.

ADEL: You won't be very popular after it's published, Carl. You'll be banned in libraries.

CARL: That's good.

BETHANY: The table's moving!

CARL: I have the dogs back. I've gotten Prince and King out of the kennel, and they want to see you.

ADEL: Prince and King are back?

BETHANY: Adel!

ADEL: Beth says you don't love me!

CARL: I do.

BETHANY: What are you saying, Adel?!

ADEL: Beth says you don't want me.

CARL: I do.

BETHANY: Stop it! Everything is getting twisted!

CARL: What's twisted, Beth? Explain it.

BETHANY: You think I'm Georgette. Georgette, chapters seven through eleven.

ADEL: Eight through eleven.

BETHANY: We're just characters in your goddamned plagiarized books! Adel—you're Zoe, Zoe in chapter twenty. Shoplifting lingerie in expensive stores. Adel, let us spit on him!

CARL: Bethany, apparently some demon has taken residence in you.

BETHANY: (*Throwing down a plate*) I won't be a character in a book!

CARL: Try to get some facts straight. (A) My books are fiction. (B) The critics have awarded my book . . .

ADEL: (*Interrupting*) I typed it, Carl.

CARL: . . . *The Motel of the Heart*—the *best* piece of fiction of the year, and (C) Any similarities to *life* are coincidental.

ADEL: A,B,C.

BETHANY: BULLSHIT! Crawling through the gutter while you were on the telephone, I realized something: I am not a victim in a novel, I'm a poet! (*Grabbing a flower from the centerpiece*) I WON'T WEAR LOST LOVE LIKE A COR-SAGE . . .

CARL: You're really gone, Beth, aren't you?

BETHANY: I'm a better writer than you are, Carl. We're all better than you are! You're a *bad* novelist, a *bad* man!

CARL: A poet! How long are you going to go on sending the same five poems to *The New Yorker*, Beth? You think they're amnesiacs?

BETHANY: (*Spitting out each word*) I HOPE YOUR BOOKS DON'T SELL!

CARL: Why don't you shut up?

BETHANY: You think you're God! A little miniature God—a fraud!

(*Enter Alvin*)

ALVIN: I had a visitation.

ADEL and CARL: Alvin!

ALVIN: I had a visitation. On Park Avenue. I saw God.

BETHANY: Alvin, I don't love you anymore. I don't know what love is. I hate love.

ALVIN: Beth, you're back.

CARL: Alvin, Adel and I are getting back together.

ADEL: What?

ALVIN: I saw God standing in a kind of kitchen.

ADEL: On Park Avenue?

ALVIN: It was indescribable. Sharp knives and forks, a huge cutting board, all kinds of vegetables.

CARL: Alvin, are you all right?

ALVIN: Everything's in season. There's no frozen food. It's like paradise.

ADEL: What did He say, Alvin? What did God say?

ALVIN: He didn't say anything.

ADEL: Nothing?

ALVIN: God doesn't say anything because He knows all the recipes by heart.

BETHANY: I'm dizzy. Dizzy and sick.

ADEL: You mean you didn't ask Him anything?

ALVIN: I didn't, Adel. I didn't ask Him anything. I was ashamed. I don't know why, but I was ashamed.

BETHANY: I feel the table moving. Slowly. In a circle.

CARL: She's back on that kick again.

ALVIN: Look at all the broken things.

ADEL: Carl, the apartment wants to kill me. I can't bathe. I can't eat. I can't go in the kitchen.

BETHANY: Let's go away, Adel—we'll eat out all the time— we don't need them!

ALVIN: Are you in love with Adel?

CARL: Let's go home, Adel, come on.

ADEL: Home with you?

CARL: Come on, Adel.

ALVIN: You know that I love you, Beth. I love you still.

BETHANY: (*Pushing things off the sides of the table*) Enough! I've had enough!

CARL: Come on, Adel, I have a taxi waiting outside.

ADEL: What should I do, Beth?

BETHANY: Adel, don't go.

ALVIN: I know now that things are not what they seemed.

BETHANY: They're even worse than that, Alvin, they stink!

CARL: (*Picking Adel up like a bride*) Adel's coming with me.

BETHANY: Adel!

ADEL: (*Pleading*) Beth, I don't want to be alone, I'm afraid. I don't want to be alone, forgive me. I don't want to be alone, I can't.

ALVIN: Something is happening to us. We are being punished.

BETHANY: The floor is moving!

CARL: That's because the earth is moving. It's turning on its axis. (*Moving out toward the door*) We're going now.

BETHANY: The floor is moving!

ALVIN: Oh God, say something. I'm so unhappy.

The End

Ken Jenkins
CHUG

Ken Jenkins

Ken Jenkins' *Chug*, like his *Rupert's Birthday* in *Best Short Plays 1983*, was first presented by Actors Theatre of Louisville in one of the annual SHORTS Festivals. This lively monologue, performed by the author in the 1981 Festival, was described by Jay Carr in *The Detroit News* as "... a shaggy frog story in the Mark Twain tradition. Jenkins was hilarious as he fatalistically escalated the scale of his mishaps as a big-time frog rancher, emptying six-packs and letting it dawn on us that what we thought was an avalanche of frozen chicken parts tumbling from his fridge was in fact frozen frogs' legs. Like some landlocked Flying Dutchman in his trailer in Indiana, he's doomed to eat his mistakes."

A Rockefeller Playwright-in-Residence at Actors Theatre of Louisville, Ken Jenkins also demonstrates his versatility as an actor and a director. Among the plays Mr. Jenkins has directed for Actors Theatre are Preston Jones' *The Oldest Living Graduate*, *The Glass Menagerie*, *The Lion in Winter*, and *Bus Stop*.

Mr. Jenkins has appeared as an actor with several other nationally recognized regional companies, including Long Wharf Theatre in New Haven, The Hartford Stage Company, The Alley Theatre in Houston, and Cincinnati Playhouse in the Park. He has played classical roles, such as Hamlet, Cyrano de Bergerac, and Petruchio, and has appeared in the contemporary roles of Brick in *Cat on a Hot Tin Roof*, Starbuck in *The Rainmaker*, and McMurphy in *One Flew Over the Cuckoo's Nest*.

Chug appears in print for the first time in this anthology.

Characters:

CHUG EVERS

Scene:

Somewhere in southern Indiana. August. The present. Interior of a small mobile home, plainly furnished: a table, two chairs, a refrigerator, an upright freezer, odds and ends. A small window over the sink. An eight-track tape recorder is playing a Strauss waltz, which is heard over outside speakers. Offstage we hear: "Freda! Freee-da!" Chug Evers enters. He carries two six-packs of beer in glass bottles. He sees that no one is in the room.

CHUG: Well, I'll be durned! (*He puts the beer on the table and crosses to the tape recorder*) It's too hot for waltzes!
(*He removes the tape and inserts a new one. He pushes the "play" button, and out comes "mellow Muzak." Crossing to the table, he picks up the beer and goes to the refrigerator. As he opens the refrigerator door, hundreds of plastic sandwich Baggies filled with . . . something . . . spill out onto the floor*)
I don't believe it. I don't believe it. Free-da! OK. OK. I can handle this. This is just a temporary situation. Just a temporary situation. (*He begins stuffing Baggies back into the refrigerator. It's a losing battle*) Durn! Freee-da! Where is she? OK. Now. OK. Now. There . . . I can handle this. (*He tries to stuff the Baggies back. They fall out again*) Shit! This is crazy. Maybe there's some room in the freezer.
(*He crosses to the freezer and opens the door. Hundreds more Baggies filled with the same thing fall on the floor*)
OK. OK. I can handle this. I can handle this. This is only a temporary situation. I can handle this. (*He begins putting the Baggies back into the freezer, methodically*) Just a temporary situation. Only temporary. This is not the worst thing that ever happened to me in my life. I can handle this.
(*He carefully closes the freezer door after managing to get all of the Baggies back in place. He begins working on the refrigerator Baggies once again*)
I can handle this. No problem. Child's play. Easy. Take your time, Chug. Don't panic. You can handle this. (*He pushes*

one pile off the top of the refrigerator onto the floor behind it) Easy
does it. One by one. (*He pitches several out the door*) OK. OK.
(*Looking for a place to put the last one, he quickly pops open the
butter tray, flicks the Baggie inside, closes it, and steps back*) Ta-da!
(*He carefully closes the door. Stepping back, he sees one more
Baggie on the floor. He picks it up and starts to open the refrigerator
door. Changes his mind. He crosses to the sink and tosses the Baggie
in a drainer*)
Dinner! (*He crosses to table. Twists the cap off a bottle of beer.
Chugs it. Burps*) I hate beer in cans. Makes it taste like metal.
(*He opens another beer and drinks about half of it*) This ain't real
beer, anyhow. Chemicals, mainly. Carbonation. It ain't good
for you. (*He finishes the second bottle. Opens a third*) Now . . . my
Uncle Brewster used to make *beer.* He made beer that was
thick . . . like soup. It had a *taste.* He'd say, "Here, boy, have
a chug of this! 'N' I'd say, "Chug it, hell! Gimme a spoon!"
'N' he'd laugh, "Go on, boy, chug!" So I would! Like chuggin'
molasses! Thick beer. Had a real taste. *Good* beer.

I used to win some money around in bars and pool halls
bettin' guys that they couldn't chug a quart of Uncle Brewster's
beer. Nobody could. I was the only one who could do it . . . 'sides
Uncle Brewster. Then he died. So I was the only one. But—
'course then there wasn't no more beer. Uncle Brewster left
me his recipe in his will . . . and all of his equipment. But, I
just don't seem to have the knack.

So . . . I drink this stuff. (*He regards the tape recorder*) I don't
think I can take any more of this.

(*He removes the "mellow Muzak" cartridge and inserts an "environments" tape. Bells. Tintinnabulation. Very Zen. He loads it
but does not push the "play" button. He picks up the remaining
beer and crosses to the refrigerator. Changes his mind as he reaches
for the handle. Puts beer on table. Sits*)
This is only a temporary situation.
What I need is some more freezer space.
This is just a temporary situation. (*He plays with pieces to a
jigsaw puzzle*)
Like this house trailer? "Mobile home"? Whatever? It's only
temporary. I been here three years . . . but it's only temporary.
Actually, we own a very nice home in Florida. Freda inherited
it from her parents. They got killed in a hurricane. Nice house.
Three bedrooms. We'd be livin' there now if the City Council
would've let us put the pits in down there. But—you know

what they say . . . you can't fight city hall. I believe it. So . . . we moved up here to Indiana three years ago. Temporarily. (*He crosses to the sink. Sits on stool*) See?

I was in this bar down in Louisville with a buddy of mine by the name of Drunken Rush. His name is really Duncan, but we all call him Drunken . . . 'cause he is. Anyway, we were settin' there in this bar . . . watchin' this . . . ah . . . lady fiddle player . . . ah . . . fiddle? . . . when in through the door walks this red-headed woman in a frilly yella' dress wearin' high-heeled shoes. 'N' she is accompanied by a totally bald-headed guy with a beard wearin' a white robe . . . covered with beads and rhinestones and pieces of broken mirror.

'N' these two walk straight over to me and Drunken and the red-head says, "I'm Freda."

'N' I says, "You're something else."

'N' she says, "My guru, Moo-Moo here, feels that you represent a great 'resonance' for me. Do you mind if we sit down?"

Well . . . what the hell. I been around some. I am *not* a child. What's the pitch, I'm thinkin'? Where's the gimme?

But, I says, "Please do. Drunken, meet Freda and her Guru, Moo-Moo. This is my buddy, Drunken Rush. How do. How do. My name is Chug. Actually, my name is Cardwell Hoover Ubell Garnett Evers . . . but, I'd appreciate it if you'd call me Chug.

'N' the Guru looks at me 'n' says, "Mooooooooooo."

'N' Freda looks at me 'n' says, "You're cute."

'N' Drunken, he looks at me 'n' says, "This is too crazy for me!"

'N' he went off to find a "hillbilly bar with some straight *people* in it."

So I looks at Freda 'n' says, "What's the catch?" 'N' she looks right back at me 'n' says, "How high is up?" And the Guru, he looks at both of us 'n' says, "Moo-oo-oo."

(*He crosses to tape deck*)

Anyway . . . that's how we met. In a bar. We resonated.

(*Punches "play." Tintinnabulation. "Environments." Bells*)

Resonated. Get it? Sonar? Sound? Vibrations. Very big into "vibrations," and "harmony," and "rhythm," and "resonance" was Freda. And me? I was very big into Freda. Now don't get me wrong. I liked her for other things than her body. There was her car, her credit cards, her private plane . . . nah . . . I'm just shittin' ya. I liked Freda because she made me *aware*. Yeah. She really made me aware of . . . my ears. She made me aware of my whole body, but . . . she really made me aware of "listening." She would say to me, "Listen, Chug. Really listen. Just stop. Stop twitchin' around 'n' makin' noise. Just stop. Stop thinkin'. Just listen.

(*He listens*)

And I would. I would do it.

(*He listens*)

I really got to like it.

(*He listens*)

You know . . . you listen to something for a long time, 'n' you start to feel like you understand it. You start thinkin' that you know the story behind what you hear. Like . . . you listen to ocean waves, 'n' you hear stories about fish, and ships, 'n' sailors, 'n' storms, 'n' deep, secret places. You listen to them glass wind chimes? . . . wind might come all the way from China. Or another galaxy. And music? Brahms. Bach. Beethoven.

'N' . . . Bullfrogs.

(*He crosses to the tape recorder and removes the "Environments" cartridge. He inserts a tape of* Stone Flute *by Herbie Mann but does not push the "play" button*)

Bullfrogs. (*He opens another beer*) See.

On the 4th of July . . . Independence Day . . . 1976 . . . Bicentennial. Myself, 'n' Freda, 'n' Moo-Moo were at a folk art festival and goat roast down in northern Mississippi. Lots of good people. Good vibes. Lots of resonance. Well . . . we ate some roasted . . . goat . . . drank a little wine . . . were kinda laid back into the scene. Homemade music and dandelion wine. Not too bad. Not too shabby.

Well . . . long about sunset some of us were layin' around on a grassy slope near a little pond. Tellin' lies. Smokin' native grasses. Watchin' dragonflies. When Moo-Moo started moooooin'. Real low. Mooooo . . . moooooooo. 'N' he kept it up . . . moooo . . . until he had everybody's attention. Mooooooo. Then he quit.

It was *quiet*. I mean it was real quiet. Then . . . we all heard the bullfrogs. They'd probably been singin' right along and we didn't notice. But, when we all shut up . . . we could hear 'em. And . . . we all got in to it. It was a real experience. We all sat there listenin' to the bullfrogs sing for an *hour* or more. Just listenin'.

'N' then Freda turns to me 'n' says, "Bullfrogs, Chug. It's bullfrogs."

'N' I says, "It sure is."

'N' she says, "This is the most resonant thing I've ever heard."

'N' I says, "Very resonant."

"Fantastic rhythm!"

"Harmonious."

"There is only one mind here . . . and it has many voices."

"You said it."

"Chug. Chug," she says, "Chug . . . we have a lot to learn."
Ain't it the truth?

(*He crosses to the sink*)

Next day? The 5th of July. Freda's parents were killed in a hurricane in northern Florida. Their house wasn't hurt . . . except for where a huge palm tree fell through the roof of the bedroom. That's how they were killed. In their sleep. Peacefully.

Still . . . that's a hell of a way to go, you know? Havin' a tree fall through your bedroom roof and mash your guts out? Well, we all gotta go sometime. At least they were at home.

(*He checks on "dinner"*)

Anyway, Freda went down there to take care of things, 'n' she found out that she had inherited the house and about twenty thousand dollars in life insurance money . . . after taxes. So, she called me and Moo-Moo 'n' said to come on down. Said she had an idea. So we did. And she did.

(*He sits at table*)

I think that her folks dyin' unexpectedly like that sorta unbalanced her mind some. You know? It happens sometimes. Temporarily.

Anyway, what she wanted to do . . . was to take her insurance money and buy a piece of property somewhere . . . with a pond on it . . . and spend the next year or so . . . listenin' to and studyin' the songs of bullfrogs. You see what I mean? Now, that's the kind of idea you get when your mind is not quite right. In a state of shock. Temporarily.

But, then . . . on the other hand . . . why the hell not?

So, we lived there in her parents' house while we looked

around for a place with a pond . . . but we couldn't find anything that we liked. So, I thought . . . why don't we just build us a pond? You know? Get a bulldozer over here and scoop us one out? So, we tried. But, the ground is too sandy down there. It's hard to get a pond to seal. Know what I mean? Hold water.

We messed around for several months and didn't have anything to show for it, 'n' one day Freda says to me, "Chug? Chug, we've been wastin' our time. We don't know any more about bullfrogs now than we did before. Right? What we need to do is to find out some facts about frogs. Right? About amphibians in general. Right?

'N' I says, "Right." I mean . . . why the hell not?

Well, we spent the whole winter of '76 in Florida *learnin'* about frogs. Amphibians. We read everything we could get our hands on. Government papers. Wildlife management surveys. Articles in obscure scientific journals. We wrote to research labs. We talked to people. All kinds of people. Fishermen. Scientists. Cajuns. Everybody.

'N' we found out two very interesting things. Number one: Nobody had ever successfully raised frogs in captivity. 'N' number two: There were people who would pay a fair amount of money to anyone who could deliver frogs to them on a regular basis. How much money? Would you believe ten dollars a frog? No foolin'. Ten dollars a frog. You figure it out.

(Crosses to tape deck. Punches "play." Stone Flute. Herbie Mann)

There was this old Cajun fella from Louisiana who trapped wild frogs and sold 'em to a research lab in Tampa for ten dollars a frog. I went with him several times. The guy that ran this lab said that they would pay ten dollars a frog to anybody who brought 'em in live and uninjured.

I said, "How many can you use?"

He said, "How many can you get?"

I said, "A thousand?"

He said, "Bring 'em on."

I thought, "Hot damn! Hah-ah-t damn! I have stumbled on to a pile of money! A green-gold, bullfrog-singin' *pile* of money! All I had to do was to figure out how to do it.

"Well," I thought, "I can handle that. Nothin' is *that* hard. Frogs can't be *that* hard to raise. I'll just figure out how to do it . . . 'n' then, by God . . . I'll do it." *That* is the American way. *That* is how the West was won.

(*Frogs begin singing quietly, mixing with the music*)
So, I read. Buddy, I read everything there was to read about amphibians.
(*He 'announces'*)
Amphibians.

Wait a minute. I want to tell you one thing. Frogs do *not* say "ribbett." No frog I have ever heard has said "ribbett." "Ribbett" is not something that frogs say. "Ribbett" is something that humans say. For some reason or other, humans think that it is funny when another human says, "ribbett." Hey! Do you know *why* bullfrogs *sing*? Wait a minute.
(*'Announcing' again*)
Amphibians.

"In zoology, a class of vertebrate animals whose young usually have gills and live in the water and later develop lungs. They include: (a) the frogs, or *'anura;'* (b) the toads, or *'salientia;'* and (c) the tailed salamanders, or *'caudata.'*" The *singing* amphibians are the frogs, or *'anura.'* (*He sits at table*) Did you know that the frogs, the *anurans*, have five digits on each limb? How does that grab you? Five fingers? Five toes? "Ribbett."

All right . . . now for the big question. Why do bullfrogs sing? Easy. Right? Everybody got it? The bullfrogs sing . . . because the lady frogs *like for 'em to!* Yeah. They *like* it. The lady frogs are attracted to the songs of their mates. The bullfrog sings, and the lady frogs come along to check him out, and in some species the bullfrog will grab at anything that moves within his reach. In some species the lady frog shops around until she hears the voice that really turns her on. Then she comes up behind the frog of her heart and whispers softly in his ear, "You're it, Baby."

But, whatever their "courtship mechanism," all frogs mate pretty much the same way. A *Joy of Sex* manual for frogs would only have one illustration. Or one set of illustrations.
(*"Waltz for My Son" from* Stone Flute *plays on the tape recorder*)
The bullfrog sits on the back of the lady frog and holds on with both arms. Real tight. Then . . . they go for a swim. Then . . . they swim around like this until the lady frog is ready to lay her eggs. And . . . when the lady frog is *ready* . . . she stretches out in a certain way . . . and her eggs pop out.

Now . . . *at the same time* . . . the bullfrog excretes his seminal fluid! At the *same time*. Got it? At the same time. They do it *together.* Every time. That's the way it's done. Every time. They come together. Every time.

No marriage counselors. No sex clinics. No shrinks. No guilt. No blood, sweat, and tears. He sings a little bit. She grooves on his sound. He hops on. They go for a swim. And . . . at exactly the right time . . . she stretches out . . . and . . . pop! "Together Again." Just like me and Freda. Nah . . . I'm kiddin' . . . Freda don't like the way I sing.

(*He crosses to tape deck. Removes tape*)

Yeah. They sing. They sing.

(*He opens another beer*)

There's a little frog called *Xenopus.* You take a urine sample from a female human that you think might be pregnant, and you squirt some of the human urine under the skin of the lady frog . . . and . . . if the female human is pregnant . . . the lady frog will drop her eggs almost at once. I wonder why?

(*He looks out the door*)

Dendrobates is a little tree frog who lives in South America. Natives down there make poison-tipped arrows from the secretions in his skin. Deadly. Like curare. I'll tell you one thing, buddy. *Nobody* sneaks up on ole *Dendrobates* and bites *his* ass! Nobody.

Anyway, what we found out was that we could maybe grow 'em in concrete pits . . . like wading pools. Breeding pools. Hatching pools. Tadpole pools. Junior pools. Adult pools. So, we decided to build some shallow concrete pits. But, the city council wouldn't let us do it. Zoning regulations . . . all that shit. So, we said, "Who the hell needs you?" We were not really enjoyin' bein' in Florida anymore, anyway. Freda was gettin' bad vibes from the house . . . and the neighbors. And I was gettin' tired of lookin' at the big palm tree outside my bedroom window. So . . . we decided we'd move.

(*He crosses to the sink. Takes flour, salt, and pepper, and a small paper bag to the table. Prepares to cook "dinner"*)

Moo-Moo faded out. He wandered off to the beach by himself and spent day and night inside a lean-to, mooin' at the fish. He quit eatin' and drinkin'. I think he evaporated. Anyway . . . we lost touch.

So, me and Freda moved back up to Kentucky. Three years ago we used the rest of Freda's insurance money to buy this place over here in Indiana. Real isolated. Lots of wild frogs around. Good place to have a frog farm, we figured. The first year we built four pits. Just got 'em done in time to put some adults in the breeding pits. American bullfrogs. *Rana temporaria. Rana temporaria. Temporaria.* Meaning that they're only frogs temporarily, I guess. What are they next, I wonder? "Ribbett."

Well . . . the bullfrogs sang . . . and the lady frogs did their thing. By May we had thousands of eggs in the breeding pits. Most of the eggs hatched.

By June we had maybe fifteen thousand tadpoles in a pit eight feet wide by sixty feet long. And when they started absorbing their tails and developing their lungs and becoming frogs for real, I transferred them to the juvenile pits. By the thousands.

By July we had at least six thousand frogs in the juvenile pits. Then . . . in August . . . along came a virus called *Aeromonas hydrophila.* Frogs get it in unfiltered water when they're under stress. Every frog on the place? Died. We had upwards of seven or eight thousand frogs—young and old. All of 'em. Died.

Stink? I reckon. We hired a guy to bulldoze us a big hole and push 'em all in it and cover 'em up. *Rana temporaria.* We almost quit. But, for some reason or other, we decided we'd give it another try. "How the West Was Won."

So, we borrowed some money. We built more pits so they wouldn't be so crowded and stressed. We installed filter systems in all of the pits. We put in fans to keep the air circulating. We even put up speakers outside so we could play music for 'em on hot afternoons when they didn't feel like singin'. We had a better system. No doubt about it. We sold about three hundred frogs that second year . . . to a lab up in Indianapolis. We didn't show a profit . . . but we were on our way.

That winter? Came a real hard freeze? Cracked every one of them pits wide open. Turned them concrete pits into gravel beds. Very expensive gravel beds. Obviously, it was time to quit. But, I guess I'm what you would call hard-headed. "How the West Was Won."

We tried it again. The third time. Borrowed more money. Rebuilt the pits. Put in filters. Put in fans. Put in *heaters.* Put in *oxygen pumps.* Put in *roofs* over the pits. Put in a new sound system. Bought new adult frogs. *Rana temporaria.* American bullfrogs. *Rana temporaria.* Ready to go! Third year's the charm!

And . . . this year? This year . . . we got frogs! We got frogs out the . . . wazoo!

There are maybe ten thousand frogs out there in eight pits eight feet wide by sixty feet long. I got letters here from ten different research labs that want as many live frogs as I can send 'em. So why am I sittin' here on my ass instead of shippin' frogs?

(*The frogs sing*)

Two weeks ago this coming Friday, two guys drove up here in an olive green, government-issued station wagon. They said that they had heard that we were runnin' a hatchery out here and that they wanted to take a look around. They said that they were "inspectors." From the Federal Department of Hatcheries. They "inspected." They were very impressed, to tell the truth. They had never heard of anybody doing anything like this. They were real interested in the frogs. They wanted to know what I was going to do with 'em. Who I was plannin' on sellin' 'em to. Lots of questions. So I play the big shot.

"Oh, I got contracts to ship 'em to several research labs in Florida and other places."

"Frozen?"

"Frozen? Hell, no! Alive! And kickin'! Dead frogs ain't no good to a research lab."

"You plannin' on shippin' *live* frogs? Out of state?"

"You got it."

"Son. You better go talk to the Interstate Commerce Department before you go shippin' live animals across the state line."

"The Interstate Commerce Department?"

"Yes, indeed. There are regulations governing Interstate Commerce, you know."

And they drove off.

Thanks a lot.

So I went to see the people at the Interstate Commerce Department. I saw several people until I found a guy who seemed to understand what I was talkin' about.

"What I need to know is whether or not I can haul live frogs across the state line."

"How many frogs are you talkin' about?"

" 'Bout ten thousand."

"Ten thousand? Ten thousand live frogs?"

"You got it."

So a bunch of 'em had a conference. Looked through various bound volumes. Jawboned for an hour or more. Finally, this real skinny guy comes over and gives me a look.

"Well, we all seem to be in agreement. You will definitely require a license to transport live frogs across the state line for the purposes of selling them."

"Fine. Where do I get it, and how much does it cost?"

"Well . . . that's just it. There ain't no such license."

"Then how do I get one?"

"You don't."

"I don't?"

"You'll have to file a special appeal to both the State and Federal government to create a new license."

"How long will that take?"

"Maybe a year."

Maybe a year. *Maybe* a year. *Maybe* more. Maybe . . . never. (*He shakes the paper bag containing the flour, seasoning, and meat.*)

I've sold some to labs here in Indiana. I tried to sell 'em to restaurants. They're the wrong kind. What I got is *Rana temporaria*. American Bullfrogs. What the restaurants want is *Rana esculenta*. *Rana temporaria* tastes just fine to me, but the restaurants only want *esculenta*. So. There you go. I got *temporaria*. *Lots of temporaria*. And I don't know what the hell I'm gonna do with all of 'em.

A cub scout troop in Terra Haute said they'd take some off my hands. Said they wanted to have a frog jumpin' contest.

I said, "Fine. How many can I ship ya?"

Little boy said, "Well, sir, we need *sixteen* frogs. And an alternate."

I thought about freeze-dryin' 'em and sealin' 'em up in clear plastic cubes and sellin' 'em as paperweights 'r knick-knacks. But I couldn't see any money in it.

Some high school boys took a bucketful of 'em over to the Stop 'N' Sock golf driving range to see how far they could knock 'em. The owners made 'em quit, though, after two grade school teachers got sick to their stomachs. I don't know. I can only eat so many frogs' legs.

(*Noticing that the second six-pack of beer is getting warm, he picks it up and heads for the refrigerator*)

Oh, well, what the hell . . . life is short.
(*He opens the refrigerator door. Many Baggies fall to the floor*)
This is just a temporary situation. I can handle this. "How
the West Was Won." Freeeee-da.

Blackout

DATE DUE